To Heal the World?

How the Jewish Left Corrupts Judaism and Endangers Israel

JONATHAN NEUMANN

ALL
POINTS
BOOKS

All Points Books is an imprint of St.Martin's Press.

www.allpointsbooks.com

Designed by Kelly S. Too

The Library of Congress Cataloging-in-Publication Data is available upon request.

ISBN 978-1-250-16087-4 (hardcover)
ISBN 978-1-250-16088-1 (ebook)

Our books may be purchased in bulk for promotional, educational, or business use. Please contact your local bookseller or the Macmillan Corporate and Premium Sales Department at 1-800-221-7945, extension 5442, or by email at MacmillanSpecialMarkets@macmillan.com.

First Edition: June 2018

10 9 8 7 6 5 4 3 2 1

To my parents

CONTENTS

INTRODUCTION

On the second night of Passover in April 2009, several White House staffers gathered in the Old Family Dining Room for Seder night, the Jewish ceremonial dinner that takes place on the first two evenings of the festival. It was not just the setting that made this night different from all other nights, but the host: President Barack Obama. Never before had a Seder taken place in the White House itself, and never in history had a sitting president attended, but from then on the Seder night was an annual fixture in the presidential calendar over both of Obama's terms.

Of all the many Jewish occasions that could have been adopted by the new president, why the Seder? Partly, it was sentimental: Obama had joined an impromptu Seder night on the campaign trail the year before and had pledged a repeat of the event: "Next year in the White House." And partly, it was tactical: upon coming into office his administration had quickly soured relations with Israel, and some positive headlines in the Jewish press might confound critics and reassure the wider Jewish community, which had voted overwhelmingly for Obama in the election.

But the Seder also had a much deeper appeal. Obama was no stranger to this ritual—he had attended a Seder every year for the previous decade and understood its significance in the liberal imagination. The themes he invoked when he opened the first presidential Seder—universalism and the struggle for liberation—are at the core of an ideology with which he was intimately familiar: *tikkun olam*. In numerous speeches, the president declared how this Hebrew concept—healing the world—had "enriched and guided my life." Now it would inspire his administration. From his nomination acceptance speech—which he described as "the moment our planet began to heal"—through the eight Passover Seders held during his tenure, this was the apotheosis of tikkun olam in America.

So what exactly is tikkun olam?

Essentially, tikkun olam is the Hebrew moniker for Jewish social justice, and the two terms are often used interchangeably (and will be in this book). As Jane Kanarek, a leader of the Conservative movement, usefully puts it, tikkun olam "is used throughout the Jewish world to summarize the efforts of Jewish social justice movements."[1] Given the superlative popularity of tikkun olam in the American Jewish community, David Saperstein, who has spent his life advocating for tikkun olam in the nation's capital on behalf of the Reform movement, is entirely justified in describing social justice as "serving as the most common organizing principle of Jewish identity."[2]

And what is social justice?

Social justice is a political philosophy that advocates the redistribution of income—and sometimes even wealth and other property—in order to achieve economic egalitarianism. It's often used synonymously with the terms "economic justice" or "distributive justice." In more recent decades, social justice has also come to include an agenda of permissive social policies that leave lifestyle questions to the discretion of the individual and promote gender diversity; an approach to foreign and defense policy that emphasizes multilateral diplomacy over military strength; a preference for comprehensive alternatives to the use of fossil fuels and nuclear energy for the sake of the environment; and other attitudes and policies associated predominantly with today's left-wing political parties.[3] (This assessment should not be controversial—your own experience ought to confirm it: just ask yourself what you think of when you hear the phrase "social justice," and which politicians you think are more likely to refer to it.) Over the past several years, campus radicals have tried to impose even more extreme conceptions of social justice on their universities through protests over safe spaces and microaggressions, and increasingly perceive social justice through the prism of intersectionality, which portrays society as the Manichean struggle for justice by powerless victims against oppressive power-holders.

For our purposes, the most important point to keep in mind is that social justice is a *political* ideology. It isn't concerned with just action toward one's fellow—which is achieved by a virtuous citizenry and upheld by courts of law. Nor is it focused on charity or volunteering at the grassroots level, which are occasionally referred to as "social action" or "direct service." While these localized efforts are sometimes subsumed within the category of social justice, ultimately social justice and its Jewish variant tikkun olam are about designing an economic and political system that guarantees certain economic and social outcomes. Social justice is about *political* change—therefore it inevitably takes the form of political activism. As the editors of *Righteous Indignation: A Jewish Call for Justice*, the bible of Jewish social justice, explain in their introduction to that volume:

> Volunteering in soup kitchens is certainly an act benefitting the social good, as is visiting the sick and elderly. But direct service alone is simply not enough. Such action addresses only immediate needs and not root causes. Further, there are justice issues that cannot be addressed at all—foreign policy issues, for example—without political advocacy.[4]

The distinction between charity and social justice is put into even higher relief in the essay by Jonah Dov Pesner, a leading campaigner in the Reform movement, who regrets that "too often in Jewish communal life, we confuse service-oriented work at soup kitchens . . . with the work of redemptive social justice." In fact, these sorts of projects can even distract us and "undermine our commitment to systemic change" (meaning fundamental and transformative change of our economic system and society).[5] So be in no doubt: social justice isn't about charity—it's about politics. And it's this political activism and its relationship to Judaism that interest us.

The most populous denominations, myriad independent organizations, and the leadership of American Jewry all espouse the politics of tikkun olam,[6] and it has become embedded in all aspects of American Judaism—including education and worship at all ages. For young children, the PJ Library books, including *Tikkun Olam Ted*, "help to open the family discourse up to difficult topics surrounding tikkun olam."[7] As these children grow up, they will encounter tikkun olam repeatedly in the curricula of their day schools and Sunday schools,[8] and also in their youth movement programming and summer camps.[9] They will be invited to act on this education by organizations such as the Religious Action Center, which offers high school students L'Taken Seminars "designed to expose students to a variety of public policy issues, explore the Jewish values surrounding these issues, and teach the skills of an effective advocate."[10] The Panim el Panim seminars, offered by Panim, and the Or Tzedek program of the Jewish Council on Urban Affairs, offer similar training.[11] For their efforts, particular teenagers' outstanding contributions to the cause of tikkun olam are recognized by the Helen Diller Family Foundation through their Diller Teen *Tikkun Olam* Awards, which "celebrate teens who have demonstrated remarkable leadership and are actively engaged in projects which embody the values of tikkun olam."[12]

At college, engaged Jewish students will likely participate in programming by Hillel International: The Foundation for Campus Jewish Life, which "helps students find balance in being distinctively Jewish and universally human by encouraging them to pursue . . . social justice [and] tikkun olam (repairing the world)."[13] Jewish students and young adult Jews might intern or work at any of the many organizations devoted to tikkun olam. Before doing so, they might receive training through Bend the Arc's Jeremiah Fellowship. Or they might go on JOIN for Justice's Jewish Organizing Fellowship. Or maybe the AMOS Fellowship at Uri L'Tzedek. Or perhaps they could enlist in Avodah Corps.[14] As young adults, they might live at, or participate in the activities of, a Moishe House, which houses a handful of Jewish community activists in cities across the United States so that they can host Jewish-themed events for their peers. One of the four priorities of such houses is to "repair the world."[15]

Finally, American Jewish adults will find themselves in the synagogue or temple hearing rabbinical sermons on tikkun olam, and may find their liturgy edited to emphasize the concept.[16] They might read one of the various periodicals committed to tikkun olam, such as *Tikkun* magazine and *Zeek*, or the many other journals to which writers in the field of tikkun olam contribute. Some adults might volunteer with campaigns such as the Jewish United Fund's Tikkun Olam Volunteers Network,[17] or join one of Tivnu's programs on the West Coast if they want "to do meaningful, physical tikkun olam."[18] And of course they could sit on their synagogue's own tikkun olam committee. Those who work as Jewish educators might be recognized by the Covenant Foundation as having "distinguished themselves in myriad realms, including . . . tikkun olam" and be honored with a Covenant Award.[19]

But no matter their involvement, American Jewish adults will be living in a community shaped by grants made by major Jewish philanthropic funds dedicated to tikkun olam, including the Jewish Federations of North America, which represents 148 Jewish federations, distributes more than $2 billion every year, and cites tikkun olam as the first of its three core values; the Charles and Lynn Schusterman Family Foundation, which values "a commitment to fulfill the imperative of tikkun olam (repairing the world)"; the Jacob and Hilda Blaustein Foundation, which grants money to several organizations dedicated to tikkun olam; the Rose Youth Foundation, which teaches children how to "practice the Jewish traditions of tikkun olam and *tzedakah* and . . . about responsible grant-making"; the Tikkun Olam Women's Foundation, which seeks to "honor our traditions of . . . tikkun olam"; Jewish Helping Hands, a grant-making organization that "invites the participation and support of all those interested in joining in *tikkun olam*"; and the Jewish Funders Network, whose members give $1 billion in grants every year and the first of whose "values" is tikkun olam.[20]

The political nature of social justice is borne out not only by the activism of the tikkun olam movement but also by its literature, epitomized by *Righteous Indignation*. The essays in this book—contributed by leaders of the tikkun olam movement and doyens of American Jewry—tackle the entire range of issues in American politics. There are chapters on economic issues such as economic justice and the labor movement; social issues such as abortion, stem-cell research, same-sex marriage, feminism, and transgenderism; constitutional and judicial issues such as gun rights and incarceration policy; immigration, healthcare, and education reform; foreign policy issues such as the War in Iraq, the crisis in Darfur, globalization, and the global AIDS crisis; ecological issues such as environmentalism, toxic waste, and renewable energy; domestic issues such as interfaith families, domestic violence, and disability; and Israel and antisemitism. Clearly, tikkun olam goes well beyond visiting the sick.

The agenda of Jewish social justice is all-encompassing, and naturally the approach is uniformly leftist. We're talking higher taxes, increased regulation of business, big labor, expanded entitlements, condemnation of any limitations on sexual expression, reduced military spending, greater reliance on international law and multilateral organizations, drastic overhauls to our economy and living standards in the name of ecology, and so on. The tools needed to repair the world are all liberal ones. This isn't charity—it's leftist politics. And it's all in the name of Judaism.

From Abraham to Amos, the Hebrew Bible instructs Jews in particular and mankind in general to repair our damaged planet, mend our broken economy, fix our unjust society, and perfect our world. Tikkun olam is a divine commandment—it is Judaism's first principle and most fundamental message. The Torah teaches that the greatest service a Jew can do before God and for humanity is to heal the world—to pursue social justice.

Or so everyone thinks. Tikkun olam may have seduced American Jewry and flattered the right gentiles in the White House, but the time has come to challenge its domination. The truth is that tikkun olam has no basis in Judaism. It was conceived by Jews who had rejected the faith of their fathers and midwifed by radicals who saw it as a pretext to appropriate Jewish texts and corrupt religious rituals—such as the Seder—to further political ends. Tikkun olam represents the bastardization of an ancient civilization and, for all the talk of liberation, the enslavement of Judaism to liberal politics. So complete has been the equation of Judaism with liberalism under the guise of tikkun olam that when, a few years back, a prominent politician was asked how he could be Jewish and yet also be conservative, he was flummoxed.

Social justice is a liberal political program, and the purpose of this book is to investigate and decry the association of that program with Judaism. For the avoidance of misunderstanding, it should be reiterated that social justice is a *political* ideology, and that is what is at issue. This book makes no suggestion that charity, good works, and grassroots welfare efforts targeted at Jews or gentiles—matters that are sometimes conflated with tikkun olam but that are in fact different—are in any way objectionable or undesirable. All Americans have the responsibility to care for their fellow citizens of other ethnic and religious backgrounds and nothing in this book should be interpreted to suggest otherwise.

This book sets out to slaughter the sacred cow of tikkun olam, at whose udder too many unlearned Jews have suckled. But notwithstanding the many defects of tikkun olam—for which the leaders of the Jewish social justice movement that promotes it are to be blamed—the many ordinary American Jews who want to heal the world are ultimately simply doing what feels in their hearts and seems in their eyes to be right. But the Bible demands that Jews not simply pursue what appeals to their hearts and draws their eyes, but that they stay loyal to the covenant between their people and its God and obey His commandments (Deut.15:39). And tikkun olam is no commandment.

Not only has tikkun olam enabled the misappropriation of Scripture, but its stridently universalistic aspirations undermine Jewish Peoplehood and in so doing give sanction to anti-Zionism and assimilation. This state of affairs is not sustainable. Tikkun olam is not the balm to heal the world but the disorder that afflicts American Judaism. If the treatment of tikkun olam in this book goes some way to ameliorating the condition of American Jewry, then it will have been worthwhile. And if there should be pushback, let it be, as the sages of the Talmud put it, a dispute for the sake of Heaven.

A Torah of Social Justice

On the evening of Wednesday, July 11, 1883, two hundred people gathered for dinner at a resort restaurant in Cincinnati to honor the delegates to the eighth annual meeting of the Reform Jewish congregations, as well as the four young men ordained as rabbis that day in what was the first graduating class of the Hebrew Union College, the new seminary of Reform Judaism. On the menu that night were shellfish and other varieties of seafood, which are proscribed by Jewish dietary laws. In addition, cheeses and dairy ice cream were served following meat courses—also a traditionally prohibited combination. Some of the more conservative guests walked out in protest, and the meal became known as the "non-kosher banquet" in American Jewish lore. The leading Reform figure of the day, Rabbi Isaac Mayer Wise, refused to condemn the fare served that night—and it became clear to all that he accepted the abrogation of traditional observances.[1] As the father of American Reform Judaism and accordingly one of the most influential rabbis in history, Wise is a principal protagonist in the story of the relationship of American Jews to social justice—and the non-kosher banquet was an important milestone in that relationship.

That story, though, starts back in Europe. Prior to the nineteenth century, European Jews had largely been confined to ghettos and excluded from public life. They clung to the faith of their fathers and the religious practices of their mothers, including strict observance of the kosher dietary laws, the Sabbath, and thrice-daily prayers recited in the direction of Jerusalem. Despised and persecuted by their gentile neighbors, these Jews' goal in life was simple: survival, in the hope that a better future awaited their progeny. Specifically, they prayed that that future would involve a restoration to the Land of Israel, from which the Jews had been exiled two millennia earlier, as part of a messianic redemption.

But then something major happened. In the late-eighteenth and early nineteenth centuries, the Jews in Western Europe were emancipated from the ghettos. In conjunction with the Enlightenment and rising nationalism on the continent, this new freedom offered Jews the opportunity to become fuller citizens in their host countries. Their responses over the following century varied. Traditionalist Jews either rejected modernity and retreated back into the ghettos or began to seek ways to sustain observance of Jewish law while living in gentile society. Other Jews preferred to assimilate or even convert, and many came also to join revolutionary socialist movements. Another group, particularly prevalent in Germany, did something else: it looked to remake Judaism in order to facilitate easier integration into local society.

Those in this latter category were faced with a double dilemma. First, now that Jews were apparently to suffer persecution no longer, their hitherto narrow focus on survival could be superseded by something nobler, but what? And, second, Jews were invited to become proper citizens, but at a price: they were required to abandon their collective Jewish identity and its nationalistic aspirations. You could not, it turned out, be a full child of Germany if you still identified with a distinct national community (the Jews) and prayed to return to its distant homeland (the Land of Israel). So if survival in the Diaspora in order to return to Zion could no longer be the dream, as it had been for centuries of Jewish exilic existence, what would replace it? These Jews' answer was to transform a global faith into a local patriotic religion: Berlin was the new Zion, Germany the new Promised Land, and the new role of the Jews—their new Torah, as it were—was to serve as a local model of the universalistic ethics of the great German philosopher Immanuel Kant. Thus Reform Judaism was born. And so was the Jews' interest in what would eventually become social justice.

This movement prized the ethical above all else: the rituals and beliefs of old had little place in this new Judaism. But although Reform was explicitly about changing Judaism and recasting it as a Kantian religion, in order to distinguish itself from secularism it still needed to root itself in the Hebrew Bible somehow—but do so in such a way that was fitting to its mission. Kant provided the ethical vision, but a generation later Julius Wellhausen delivered the exegetical rationale. Wellhausen was a Protestant theologian and academic who argued that the great contribution of ancient Israelite religion was the universal ethical message of its prophets. Judaism's law, particularism, and ritual—the very things to which the Jews had been clinging for two thousand years—confused, conflicted with, and even undermined that ethical message, and were therefore to be rejected.[2] Kant had concurred, infamously writing that Judaism—by which he meant its laws and rituals—should be euthanized. Believing that Reform Judaism would bring about this outcome, the great philosopher lent the Reformers his support. The idea that universalistic ethics represents the true "essence" of Judaism remains a prevalent misconception to this day—one inspired by gentile scholars who thought very little of Judaism.

Over in America, thanks to Jewish immigrants from Germany and its environs, Reform Judaism gradually made inroads and eventually became the dominant denomination, a status it still retains.[3] These immigrants introduced several innovations to Jewish practice, including shifting religious services from Saturdays to Sundays to coincide with the Christian Sabbath, relaxing the kosher dietary laws, and making greater use of English in prayers (partly because fewer and fewer of the laity understood Hebrew). The "Reverend Dr. Wise," as Isaac Mayer, a charismatic orator, became known to Jewish and non-Jewish audiences, was among the leaders of these Reformers. Born in Bohemia in 1819 as the eldest of thirteen children, he and his wife were spurred by local restrictions on Jews to move elsewhere and in 1846 he arrived in the United States. He introduced liturgical innovations to his synagogue to mirror the practices of American churches—choirs, an organ, replacement of bar mitzvahs with confirmation ceremonies, and mixed seating for men and women during prayers. The motivation of these American Reformers when they altered Jewish practice was, as with their German counterparts, in no small part to enable congregants to feel like full citizens of their countries.

American Jews wanted to be perceived as less alien by their Christian neighbors, whose religious praxis they were aping. Given the past experience of the Jews, even following Emancipation in Europe or in the freedom of the New World, their fear of rejection by their neighbors was strong—and not unreasonable.

As in Germany, these Reformist communities made theological commitments that prompted and justified the practical changes. Two theological concepts they found especially troublesome were Jewish chosenness and the exile from the Land of Israel. Both distinguished the Jews as a people distinct from other Americans (and indeed all gentiles), and therefore couldn't be reconciled with their drive to eliminate differences between themselves and their compatriots. Consequently, to varying degrees, Wise and his fellow Reformers, including the more radical David Einhorn, disavowed the concept of the Jews as a chosen people; repudiated the hope in a messianic restoration of the Jews to the Land of Israel and of the Davidic kingdom there; rejected contemporary political Zionism (which called on the Jews to return to the Land of Israel); eliminated any talk of a resumption of animal sacrifices at a rebuilt Temple in Jerusalem; abandoned the second days of festivals (which had differentiated the Diaspora from the Land of Israel, where festivals are kept for only one day); and also, inspired by a voguish German practice, bestowed the appellation of "temple" on Reform synagogues, thereby scorning the notion that Jerusalem alone was the sacred site of God's House. Rather than promote and celebrate Jewish difference, the new messianic aim of the Jewish People was the union of all the children of God.

Following Wellhausen, the Reformers hailed the prophets of ancient Israel for articulating this eschatological hope. The prophets served a dual function—they were credited as having in effect established a new universal religion of ethics that was different from the Judaism of the Torah, but they also provided the Reformers with a claim to continuity with the Jewish past. As Einhorn paradoxically announced, "Our views have entirely changed. We stand upon the ground of prophetic Judaism which aims at the universal worship of God by righteousness."[4] Notwithstanding this tension between new and old, at least one thing was clear: there was no longer any need for the Jews to look to return to the Land of Israel, because, it was now held, their exile was not a punishment. Rather, it heralded the commencement of their new mission: to teach this new universal religion to the gentiles in whose midst they lived. In time, the creed of this religion would be social justice.

The 1885 Pittsburgh Platform—a Reform credo that was christened by Wise as American Jews' "declaration of independence"—captured and succinctly expressed Reform's theological sentiments:

> We consider ourselves no longer a nation, but a religious community, and therefore expect neither a return to Palestine, nor a sacrificial worship under the sons of Aaron, nor the restoration of any of the laws concerning the Jewish state.

There went ritual and the dream of Zion. The Jews were now merely a religious community. And the platform went on to elaborate what the new religion of this community was. The final of the platform's eight tenets was the declaration that "the spirit of the Mosaic legislation" is "to regulate the relations between rich and poor" and hence that we deem it our duty to participate in the great task of modern times, to solve, on the basis of justice and righteousness, the problems presented by the contrasts and evils of the present organization of society.

The re-organization of society—which is a political objective—was the religious goal of this new faith. The term "social justice" with its current meaning was not yet in common usage, but the attitude it came to denote was evidently nascent in these early days of American Reform Judaism. The abandonment of Jewish ritual—exemplified by the non-kosher banquet—and repudiation of the historic Jewish attachment to Zion went hand in hand with the universalistic ethics that began to take the form of liberal and even socialistic politics. At first, this ideology was more a utopian hope than a guide to practical action. But in the early twentieth century mere faith began to give way to outright political agitation in the name of social justice.

Significantly, it was also in this era, during the rise of the Reform movement, that the lay leadership of American Jewry began to organize. A coterie of wealthy German Jewish families made critical contributions to the communal infrastructure and to the new establishments of Reform Judaism. Reform molded their attitudes and influenced the direction of the secular organizations they founded and led. These included the American Jewish Committee, which was the dominant voice of American Jewry for many years and is still influential today. And they also included the *New York Times*, whose owner, Adolph Ochs, was married to one of Wise's daughters. The ideology of Reform penetrated institutions that affected American society far beyond the boundaries of the Jewish community.

THE SOCIAL GOSPEL

Although Reform Judaism began to affect wider society, events outside the Jewish community still continued to shape the movement, as they had done back in Germany. Indeed the whole point of Reform was to mimic trends in its surrounding society—particularly in the Christian community—in order to appear less different. The principal influence drawing Reform Judaism away from mere utopian hope toward practical political action was the Social Gospel, a religious tradition that catapulted social justice to the forefront of American public discourse.

Social justice had been a religious ideology from its inception in the mid-nineteenth century. But back then it was a classically liberal notion (which today we would consider conservative). It took the form of a call by Catholic Italian nationalists for individual religious liberty and the protection of a strong religious civic society from the growing power of the state. Gradually, social justice became more focused on protections for the poor—an alternative to socialism. But by the turn of the nineteenth century and the rise of the Social Gospel, the politics of social justice had become almost indistinguishable from socialism, even as its expression remained religious.

The Social Gospel was a liberal Protestant movement that highlighted the religious underpinnings of Progressivism, which was at the height of its power in the first couple of decades of the twentieth century. Led by ministers and academics such as Walter Rauschenbusch, Washington Gladden, George Herron, and Richard Ely, the Social Gospel taught that the politics of Progressivism was "applied Christianity" (in Gladden's words). That is to say, the Social Gospel held that a certain political ideology was mandated by the Christian Bible, and good Christians would "apply" this teaching to society through politics. The Social Gospel was deeply statist, advocating what was called "coercive philanthropy"—the idea that many charitable services should be provided by the state.[5]

But whereas regular socialism was anti-religious, the Social Gospel took a different view. For Ely, the state wasn't just an important economic tool but was actually "religious in its essence." The state was the critical instrument by which religious eschatological (end-of-days) ambitions could be realized. "God works through the state in carrying out His purposes more universally than through any other institution," Ely wrote.[6] Indeed, he went so far as to teach that "if anything on earth is divine, it is the state."[7] Another leading Social Gospeller, Samuel Zane Batten, also spoke of the "divine meaning of the state."[8] Several leaders of the movement, including Herron and Ely, were so confident in the power of the state that they were openly socialist.

As with regular socialism, the statism of the Social Gospel represented a fundamental break from the contemporary organization of the economy. The Social Gospellers themselves embraced the revolutionary implications of their program—which they also understood and described in religious terms. Gladden said that the Social Gospel called for nothing short of a "new Reformation" in pursuit of the Kingdom of God.[9] Rauschenbusch explained that such a kingdom would "contain the *revolutionary* force of Christianity."[10] Why is it that the state was so holy for them and needed to be strengthened in such a far-reaching way? The Social Gospel was inspired by the this-worldly eschatology of Postmillennialism. This theory held that Christ could only return to rule in the end of days *after* a millennium of heavenly rule on earth. This period—an epoch of social justice—had to be achieved and sustained by man.[11] But to achieve this social justice, a radically different approach to public affairs was required. Only the state was powerful enough to deliver such a godly revolution—hence the state possessed the aura of the divine. Taking their cue from the Lord's Prayer ("Your kingdom come, Your will be done, on earth as it is in Heaven"), the Social Gospellers called for God's Kingdom to be established by man on earth.[12]

The Social Gospel had an indelible effect on Reform Judaism, rousing it from its utopian dreams to practical action. Indeed, Reform was so inspired by liberal Christianity that it eventually surpassed the gentiles in its zeal for social justice. And it wasn't just Reform that took its cue from the Social Gospel. So did another denomination—Reconstructionist Judaism—founded by the influential theologian Mordecai Kaplan.

Kaplan was born in Lithuania in 1881 to an Orthodox family. He immigrated to America as a child, and graduated from City College of New York. He emerged not from Reform Judaism but from Orthodoxy and Conservative Judaism. Reconstructionism was, like Conservative Judaism, something of a middle way between Orthodoxy and Reform. But like Reform, Reconstructionism rejected the idea of a chosen Jewish People and emphasized social justice. For Kaplan, Judaism was a civilization whose laws and rituals could be reconstructed to serve contemporary needs. Having grown up during the height of the Social Gospel, Kaplan understood those needs to include combatting economic inequality, political corruption, a failing education system, and the persistence of war. Kaplan understood religion as calling for us to "reconstruct the social order" and reconstruct Judaism in order to end these injustices.

THE RELAPSE OF THE REFORMERS

A century ago, those advocating for social justice in the Jewish community were fairly clear about how they were *changing* the Jewish religion: Judaism needed to be *reformed* or *reconstructed*. Sure, they might also have imagined they were rededicating themselves to the mission of the ancient prophets and a universal religion that these ancients supposedly preached—and this conflict between reform and rededication did create a tension in their ideology. But even the pretension of unearthing a long-forgotten "essence" of the Jewish religion was still—however paradoxically—in the context of trying something fundamentally *new*. Remember Einhorn's declaration: "Our views have entirely changed."

In light of this, you'd be forgiven for assuming that what became the Jewish social justice movement would have had less and less of an interest in the Hebrew Bible over the course of the twentieth century. After all, wasn't the idea behind the Reformist program and the enthusiasm for social justice to take the Jewish faith in a *different* direction—*away* from the ritualistic, legalistic, and particularistic Hebrew Bible?

Yet in recent decades we've seen not a diminution of Scripture in the Jewish social justice movement but a renaissance. Jewish social justice may have arisen from movements seeking a break with traditional Judaism, but today these same movements claim that they are *fulfilling* traditional Judaism—through their commitment to social justice. In fact, it's precisely the premise that the politics of *tikkun olam* are informed and shaped by the Hebrew Bible and rabbinic writings—the very things the old Reformers were so ready to jettison—that is today what makes Jewish social justice

Jewish. As David Saperstein, a leader in today's Reform movement, writes:

> Over and above its sociological and economic sources, the American Jewish commitment to social justice owes much to . . . the texts of traditional Judaism. From Torah text, we can cite the revolutionary social justice implications of Sinai and God's call to us to be a holy people (Leviticus 19) . . . These biblical injunctions led to the prophetic tradition, with its mix of particularistic and universal expressions of social justice. They led to the rabbinic . . . creation, in Talmudic times, of one of the world's first social welfare societies.[13]

According to contemporary Reform thinkers, it turns out that social justice is not, as American Jews were once taught to believe, merely some prophetic rebellion against the Mosaic Pentateuch, or something the rabbis forgot or deliberately suppressed, or some innovation in Jewish belief. Instead, we're now told it's always been a core part of Judaism—something everyone from Abraham to Isaiah and the rabbis of the Talmud endorsed. (Notice, by the way, how Saperstein echoes the Social Gospellers of a century earlier in speaking of the *revolutionary* implications of Scripture. Similarly, he goes on to present Reform's "belief in the perfectibility of human society and our embrace of a central role of the *public sector* in creating a more just and compassionate society.") This wasn't always the case, so when and why did this return to Scripture take place?

The horrors of the First World War challenged some of the optimism of early twentieth-century Progressivism (the era when Reformers became politically active), and the Second World War and the Holocaust shattered it—especially for the

Jews. American Jewry was reminded that even when it thought humanity was moving in the right direction, the Jews could not take their safety for granted. The world never lets Jews forget they're Jewish—and never stops punishing them for it. So after Reform's earlier eagerness to look outward, mid-twentieth-century events prompted a turn inward. One expression of this turn was Zionism, with certain influential figures in the Reform movement giving their blessing and support to this movement, especially as it pertained to saving European Jewry. Another was a return to ritual. We're not talking about strict legalistic Judaism, but some of the more extreme innovations of the earlier Reformers were reversed—you'd be hard-pressed, for instance, to find a Reform congregation anywhere today that holds its main service on a Sunday. This shift ended the era of what is known as Classical Reform—the late-nineteenth- and early twentieth-century Reform movement in America. The newer Reform that took its place did retain remnants of the old stridently universalistic ideology—especially Classical Reform's focus on social justice, which remains as central to the Reform movement as ever. But with particularism back in vogue in the community, Reform Jews wanted to express their ideology and politics in the language of the Bible.

Linked to these changes was the suburbanization of the descendants of Eastern European Jewish immigrants who had come to America in the decades around the turn of the nineteenth century. Unlike the German Jewish leadership of the community, these masses were residually Orthodox, and many of their children and grandchildren, upon moving out to the suburbs in the mid-twentieth century, affiliated to Conservative Judaism. This denomination, though not as stringent as Orthodoxy, nevertheless sustained ritualistic and legalistic Judaism in some form. It was founded by dissenters from Classical Reform who were alienated by its abandonment of ritual—the sort of folks who walked out of the non-kosher banquet. Even as they sought to adapt to contemporary American life, these Jews nonetheless wanted to *conserve* traditionalist Judaism—and that included Judaism's particularistic components. The Conservatives believed that Judaism needed to be updated for the modern era, but they still wanted it to be recognizably Jewish. So when social justice became a big thing in Conservative Judaism—which it did in the decades following the Second World War—it was expressed in Scriptural and rabbinic terms, rather than purely as a secular philosophy.

There was also a movement in and around the 1970s toward ethnicity across American society, and American Jews were not unaffected by this. In the Jewish community, one of its significant manifestations was the Havurah movement (Hebrew for "fellowship"). As the Conservative and Reform Jewish communities became more affluent and "bourgeois," their youth began to see their cavernous synagogues as reflecting the emptiness of their parents' religious commitment. The hippy Havurah movement criticized this suburban Jewish life, the monumental temples of Conservative and Reform Jews, and the established communal institutions. In their place, the movement launched alternative, local, post-denominational prayer and study groups, with some participants even inaugurating their own rural communes. These various Havurahs drew on the contemporaneous counterculture, felt the liberty to adapt Jewish law, and adhered to expressive individualism.[14] These were sincere efforts by uneducated Jewish youth to withdraw from the stagnating Judaism of their parents' communities and renew their attachment to the faith. Their interest in Judaism was prompted by the general turn toward minority identity in America at this time, particularly in the context of the Civil Rights and Black Power movements, but also by the amazement and ethnic Jewish pride surrounding Israel's startling victory over the armies of the Arab world in the Six-Day War of 1967. The Havurahs were expressions of a yearning for Jewish renewal. In fact, this movement also came to form the basis of a small Jewish denomination that was actually called Jewish Renewal.

Although these Jews wanted to cultivate their Jewish identities, they were steeped in ignorance. Lacking basic knowledge of Judaism or the tools to acquire it, they weren't prepared to commit to the years of study and practice that authentic Judaism requires—indeed they couldn't even grasp that this was necessary. Instead, they looked for guidance to the leaders of the Havurah movement—people who were more familiar with Eastern philosophy, political radicalism, and the American counterculture than they were with Judaism, such as activist Arthur Waskow. (The theologian Zalman Schachter-Shalomi, having grown up Hasidic but since estranged from Jewish Orthodoxy, was something of an exception). And so Jewish Renewal ended up simply reaffirming the attachment to what they had long been taught was the essence of Judaism—the campaign for social justice. By now, however, something had changed. The Classical Reformers had believed they were dedicating themselves to this same essence, but they still saw themselves as *reforming* the faith—fundamentally discontinuing what had come before. The idea of Jewish *renewal* was similar but the emphasis was reversed—the motivating presumption at this point was the continuation of what had always been real Judaism.

THE RISE OF THE RADICALS

Jewish Renewal was hardly the first appearance of radicals in the American Jewish community—where radicalism in fact has had a long pedigree. Much of the political activism in the Eastern European Jewish community in the early twentieth century took the form of socialism and communism, imported from Czarist Russia and nearby nations. Names like Daniel De Leon, the first Marxist firebrand in America, and the anarchist Emma Goldman come to mind. An influential figure in this activist camp was Abraham Cahan, a co-founder and longtime editor of the Yiddish *Forward*, a Jewish socialist newspaper. According to the sociologist Daniel Bell, the *Forward* "bound together the Jewish community and made it socialist," and Cahan famously (and somewhat optimistically) called socialism the new Torah of the Jews.[15] The *Forward* survives to this day (mostly in English) and, again illustrating the return to the language of Judaism among Jewish activists, its political orientation is now essentially that of contemporary Conservative and Reform Judaism—a Torah of social justice.

Nevertheless, radicalism in the early decades of the twentieth century remained fairly fringe—most Jews simply wanted to work hard and realize the American dream. They were much more taken by Franklin Delano Roosevelt, support for whom brought together the Eastern European and German Jewish communities, despite all their earlier differences. As the intellectual Irving Howe recalled, the enthusiasm for Roosevelt among the Jews was massive, ranging from working class to bourgeois, from East European to German, and from Right to Left. Jewish conservative Herbert London also recounted the feelings of his father: "To say anything negative about Roosevelt was a blasphemy that rarely went unpunished . . . For my father, God was a Democrat, and one didn't frivolously disagree with God's party."[16] Roosevelt united American Jews, and their zeal for him as a liberal reformer—and eventually as a savior of Jews in the Holocaust as well—was practically religious. Since then, American Jews have stayed overwhelmingly supportive of the Democratic Party.

In the 1960s radicalism among Jews re-emerged, however. Todd Gitlin, the president of the 1960s student protest group Students for a Democratic Society (SDS), was Jewish, as was Mark Rudd, the leader of its Columbia University chapter and a founder of the terrorist Weather Underground. So was Saul Alinsky, tutor to Cesar Chavez and originator of community organizing. Leaders of the counterculture such as Jerry Rubin, Abbie Hoffman, and Allen Ginsberg were Jewish. And three of the Chicago Seven—prosecuted for allegedly inciting a riot at the 1968 Democratic Party Convention—were Jewish. From Communists to anti-Vietnam activists and from feminists to civil rights campaigners, radical movements in America have always boasted a significant Jewish cohort. There was nothing particularly Jewish about most of these radicals—their activism in fact was usually predicated on rejection of such distinctions between peoples. But for our purposes, one radical Jewish mediocrity stands out: Michael Lerner.[17]

Lerner was born to a family of non-observant Jewish Democrats in New Jersey. He graduated from Columbia in 1964 and received a PhD from Berkeley, where he served as a teaching assistant to (Jewish) Marxist Herbert Marcuse and led the SDS branch. When his sister wedded a successful attorney, he interrupted the nuptials to denounce the guests—who included prominent politicians—as murderers with blood on their hands for not doing more to stop the war in Vietnam. When he himself got married, he and his wife exchanged rings extracted from the fuselage of an American aircraft downed over Vietnam and celebrated over a wedding cake decorated with the Weathermen motto, "Smash Monogamy." Unsurprisingly, the marriage lasted less than a year. While a professor at the University of Washington, Lerner founded the Seattle Liberation Front, which he later claimed was a nonviolent alternative to the Weathermen. He was arrested as a leader of the "Seattle Seven," but charges against him were eventually dropped, though J. Edgar Hoover dubbed him (rather hyperbolically) "one of the most dangerous criminals in America." Over the years, Lerner has drifted from vocation to vocation and fad to fad. After academia, he took an interest in mass psychology. In 1986, he launched a Jewish interest political magazine called *Tikkun* and in the early 1990s inspired then first lady Hillary Clinton's brief flirtation with his pseudo-profound "politics of meaning." In 1995, he dubiously became a rabbi.

Why do we care about Michael Lerner? He is an excellent example of another strand of American Jewish leftism that has fed into the community's interest in social justice: a secular radical who eventually turns to Judaism to express his or her politics. The Judaism that such radicals encountered was of course not traditionalist Judaism but the legacy of the Reformers—a Torah of social justice. The assimilation of left-wing politics into Judaism had taken place before these radicals decided to usurp the religion of Israel. But their contribution to this process, while more recent, has been no less consequential or adverse. For one thing, it was Lerner who popularized the name for American Jewish social justice: tikkun olam.

2

Repair the World

In 2003, when the United States was preparing to launch its assault on the regime of Saddam Hussein in Iraq, President George W. Bush traveled to the Azores to meet with world leaders and promote his cause. Thomas L. Friedman, a columnist for the *New York Times*, suggested that the president lacked a vision for the coming war, and that his leadership ought to be assigned to the British prime minister, Tony Blair, who did have such a vision. "Why?" he asked himself. "The only way I can explain it is by a concept from the Kabbalah called 'tikkun olam.' It means, 'to repair the world.'" Friedman elaborated, writing that unlike (the Republican) Bush, (the left-wing) Blair

> constantly puts the struggle for a better Iraq within a broader context of moral concerns. Tony Blair always leaves you with the impression that for him the Iraq war is just one hammer

and one nail in an effort to do tikkun olam, to repair the world.[1]

Friedman noted that Blair spoke passionately not just about Iraq but also about the Kyoto climate accords and the Arab-Israeli peace process, whereas Bush's interests seemed more parochial and, well, conservative.

This was interesting not merely because tikkun olam was being used to justify the War in Iraq (although that is certainly ironic) nor because this is a convenient illustration of the term's elasticity. Instead, this is notable because the phrase was featured at all in the newspaper of record. At that time, tikkun olam had not been around all that long, yet here was one of the most prominent columnists in the country not only referencing but elucidating it in one of the most widely read regular opinion pieces in the nation. As the Jewish language columnist Philologos wrote at the time:

> When a Hebrew expression that was unknown in the English language 20 years ago appears not once but twice in a column by Thomas Friedman about the war on Iraq, on the editorial page of *The New York Times*, *that's* a linguistic success story.[2]

So what is the story of tikkun olam?

The Jewish interest in social justice began some two hundred years ago in Germany and intensified in the United States over the last century. But whereas the liberal Protestant community gave its passion for social justice a distinctly Christian name— the Social Gospel—the Jews did not yet have a name of their own. Jewish social justice activists not only took political inspiration from the Social Gospel, but the Christian motif of a Kingdom of God on earth also impressed them. The Jews too wanted their religion to obligate humanity to build a socially just society in the world. Fortunately for them, a traditional Jewish prayer called Aleynu, recited at the conclusion of every service, seemed to contain exactly what they were looking for. Specifically, the liturgy makes a call "to perfect the world [le-takken olam] under the Kingdom of God."[3]

An early appropriation of Aleynu for this purpose is found in the work of Mordecai Kaplan, the founder of Reconstructionist Judaism, which as we've noted put social justice at the heart of its theology from the start. As with the Social Gospel, Kaplan was similarly skeptical that man could rely on other-worldly religion—religion that is mostly geared toward an afterlife in another world or a messianic era in this one initiated by God—to achieve "justice and peace." He therefore believed in the need to transform or reconstruct Judaism "from an other-worldly religion, offering to conduct the individual to life eternal" through observance of the laws of a divinely revealed Torah, "into a religion which can help Jews attain this-worldly salvation." It was not reasonable to leave this salvation up to God, Kaplan insisted. Rather, we have to work toward it ourselves. "We cannot consider ourselves servants of the Divine King," he wrote in the 1930s, invoking the Aleynu prayer, "unless we take upon ourselves the task 'to perfect the World under the Kingdom of the Almighty.'"[4] This "task" was a direct quotation from Aleynu, and it captured and Judaized the objective of the earlier Social Gospel.

The original usefulness of Aleynu to the cause of Jewish social justice was in its call for the establishment of a Kingdom of God on earth. But it was the other part of the phrase—the notion of perfecting the world, or tikkun olam—that eventually took on a life of its own.⁵ For a long time this process was slow. In the 1940s, a student of Kaplan's began to see tikkun olam as part of a broader vision for the American Jewish community. Alexander Dushkin, the executive director of the Jewish Education Committee of New York, wrote that man was a partner of God in *"tikkun ha-olam*—the continuous task of reconstructing the world." Dushkin included tikkun olam as one of seven "Common Elements" that should be taught in all Jewish schools.

Dushkin brought the idea of tikkun olam to hundreds of Jewish educators, and it was gradually taken up more widely after the Second World War. One of their number, the charismatic Shlomo Bardin, introduced the concept into the Brandeis Camp Institute in Simi Valley, California, which he had founded.⁶ A crucible of postwar West Coast Judaism, his non-denominational organization focused on experiential education. It reimagined Jewishness to make it more appealing to leisured Jewish Angelenos on the cusp of assimilation. Bardin promoted the tikkun olam of the Aleynu prayer as an expression of a Jewish mandate to work for a more perfect world. It was hoped that the notion of such an obligation could help to update "the great ethical heritage of Judaism" from something antiquated into a relevant and positive force in participants' lives.⁷

A couple of decades later, tikkun olam was adopted by other educators, this time in the Conservative movement. Troubled by trends of rebellion and apathy among Jewish youth, these educators called for significant reforms. A 1969 report by the movement's United Synagogue Commission on Jewish Education recommended curricula devoted to tikkun olam. This push culminated in the renaming of the youth wing's charitable program in the early 1970s as Social Action/Tikun Olam, or SATO.⁸

Although Reform and Conservative Judaism were already devoted to the ideals of social justice, this nonetheless appears to have been the first official use by a major Jewish denomination of tikkun olam as a phrase to denote social justice.

But generally in the decades immediately following the Second World War, use of tikkun olam to mean social justice was not widespread. The phrase didn't appear in any of the many introduction-to-Judaism books written after the war.[9] That began to change, though, with the release of the Jewish Catalog series. This publication grew out of the Havurah movement, which we discussed in the previous chapter. As we observed, many of the participants in this movement were countercultural Jews looking for some guidance on how to adopt and adapt traditional Jewish rituals and ideas. They looked to their radical leadership for answers, and the Jewish Catalog they produced was designed to be that guide.

The Jewish Catalog was a product of the Havurat Shalom of the Boston area, to which the first volume is dedicated. Inspired by the *Whole Earth Catalog*, which was an expression of the ecological counterculture of the era, the Jewish Catalog was originally envisioned as a directory of books and resources. But its authors quickly realized that a guide to Jewish life or do-it-yourself manual was more urgent than a directory, as so many young Jews were precisely looking to do it themselves.[10] The first volume, published in 1973, was a bestseller. Two more editions were published in later years. According to historian Jonathan Sarna, "few books in all of American Jewish history have ever been as influential."[11]

Tikkun olam made only a cameo appearance in the first edition of the Jewish Catalog. A chapter on bringing forth the messiah made passing reference to planting trees as "a small tikkun olam—fixing up the world—wherever the *olam* most needs it."[12] But the idea is not developed. In the *Third Jewish Catalog*, published in 1980, the idea of tikkun olam is elaborated:

> The Jewish ideal is in some senses a political one: not the perfection of individual souls, but *tikkun olam*—the repairing of the world. We are bound to commit ourselves to creating a more just, more whole world. This can take place only through the interactions between people and between communities, and so Jewish teachings have always been concerned with personal morality, social responsibility, and "political" questions of leadership, power, and control of property.[13]

Between the two catalogs, we can already see various elements of social justice being quietly associated with tikkun olam—ecology, utopian messianism, universalism, and politics. The later appearance in particular tied tikkun olam to the core concerns of social justice: politics, power, property, and the distribution of wealth. The Jewish Renewal movement itself never really amounted to much more than superficially Jewish ways to express the cultural and political whims of its leadership. So it's no coincidence that tikkun olam—a Hebrew and therefore distinctly *Jewish* way to express social justice—was popularized by radical Jews who participated in or were influenced by the Havurahs and Renewal.

Along with the third edition of the Jewish Catalog, there were other pertinent developments in the 1980s. A radical leftist group called New Jewish Agenda was founded in 1980 and adopted tikkun olam to summarize its objectives. The group's Founding Conference Unity Statement proclaimed:

We believe that Jewish experience and teachings can address the social, economic, political issues of our time. Our Jewish conviction requires that we give serious and consistent attention to the Jewish mandate of tikkun olam, the repair and moral improvement of the world.[14]

New Jewish Agenda's National Platform (adopted in 1982) further explained that "many of us base our convictions on the Jewish religious concept of tikkun olam (the just ordering of human society and the world) and the prophetic traditions of social justice." The platform promoted radical views on feminism; reproductive rights; gay rights; entitlement to employment, housing, education, and healthcare; easing life for the disabled; antisemitism; racism (particularly against Arabs and blacks); affirmative action; immigration; environmentalism; nuclear energy and weapons; economic justice and taxation; the labor movement; American-Israeli relations; the arms race; and conscientious objection. On every political issue, New Jewish Agenda took a liberal—and usually politically extreme—approach. It was in New Jewish Agenda and its offspring organizations that tikkun olam was properly married to social justice and radical leftist politics.

Major figures in the Jewish social justice movement back then were among the initiators of New Jewish Agenda and presenters at its founding conference—and many are still active today. They included: Michael Strassfeld, a co-editor of the Jewish Catalogs (recall that the third edition, which tied tikkun olam to politics, was published in the same year that New Jewish Agenda was founded); Arthur Waskow, a ubiquitous political radical and co-founder of Jewish Renewal; Michael Lerner; Samuel Norich, then the vice president of the World Jewish Congress and now the president of the *Forward* newspaper (the one founded by Abraham Cahan); Aviva Cantor, a founder of the Jewish feminist magazine *Lilith* and the Jewish Liberation Project, which sought to "radicalize and democratize the American Jewish community";[15] Gerry Serotta, who went on to become chair of Rabbis for Human Rights, North America; and Ruth Messinger, later the Democratic Party candidate for the New York City mayoralty and until recently the president of the American Jewish World Service.

New Jewish Agenda suffered from internecine struggles throughout its lifetime, including over the superficiality of its commitment to Judaism. Due to excessive debt, organizational weaknesses, infighting, and the rise of competing groups, the organization was disbanded in 1992.[16] Nevertheless, its influence has been significant because its members have gone on to assume positions in so many other organizations. As well as those just listed, they include the dovish Americans for Peace Now, Jewish Funds for Justice, the liberal lobby J Street, and the radical and antisemitic Jewish Voice for Peace. Another such organization was Michael Lerner's *Tikkun* magazine.

In 1986, Lerner, at this point a radical left-wing academic and activist turned psychotherapist, decided to become a magazine editor. He and his then-wife, Nan Fink, along with Peter Gabel, launched *Tikkun*, a quarterly publication inspired by the politics and vision of New Jewish Agenda. His magazine aimed "to heal, repair, and transform the world," hence its name—an abbreviation of tikkun olam. *Tikkun* was fueled by opposition to the Reagan administration, dissatisfaction with mainstream Jewish institutions, and protest and opposition toward the State of Israel. The magazine branded itself as "the liberal and progressive alternative to the voices of Jewish conservatism and the neo-cons," and in particular as a liberal alternative to the (by then) more conservative Jewish monthly *Commentary*.[17] Few other events or publications in the recent history of American Jewry did more to popularize the phrase "tikkun olam" and cement its association with social justice.

Having conquered the Jewish radical scene, tikkun olam then finally received recognition by the two major denominations. The youth arm of Conservative Judaism had given an early nod to tikkun olam already in the 1970s. But as these youths grew up, the movement as a whole properly endorsed it in 1988, when it published *Emet Ve'Emunah: Statement of Principles of Conservative Judaism*. This document was the first of its kind for the movement, and laid out its theological tenets. A subsection of the document called "Social Justice: Building a Better World" referred to social justice as "the prophetic ideal" and asserted that the Aleynu prayer captured the Jewish "impulse 'to mend and improve the world under God's Kingship.'" Naturally, this "impulse" required speaking out on the dangers of nuclear annihilation, racism, hunger, world poverty, and threats to the environment, and, if necessary, undertaking political action. The "ideal Conservative Jew" was, among other things, impelled by "the moral imperatives of our tradition . . . to universal concern and deeds of social justice."

In 1999, tikkun olam in a sense completed its journey, as the Reform movement followed Conservative Judaism in according tikkun olam a central position in a theological platform.[18] In its Pittsburgh Convention of that year (the same venue, you'll recall, as the 1885 Pittsburgh Platform), Reform's Central Conference of American Rabbis affirmed that we are "partners with God in tikkun olam, repairing the world." The obligation to pursue justice demanded engagement with a familiar roster of liberal political causes, and in committing to such engagement, "we reaffirm . . . social justice as a central prophetic focus of traditional Reform Jewish belief and practice."

This rapid rise of tikkun olam is astonishing. Remember, tikkun olam began as the junior partner to God's Kingdom in a liturgical phrase. It then became a modest concept at the experimental sidelines of mid-twentieth-century American Jewish education. Then it was adopted and promoted by a radical fringe. And now it has become an expression of the most central tenet of American Judaism, social justice. Tikkun olam today essentially defines the Reform, Reconstructionist, and Renewal movements, pervades Conservative Judaism, and is now even making inroads into Orthodoxy. It's one of the few Hebrew terms recognizable to the vast swaths of assimilated American Jews. And outside of the Jewish community it is American Judaism's most widely known teaching—referenced repeatedly by no less a figure than Barack Obama when he was president of the United States. One simply cannot begin to understand American Judaism today without understanding tikkun olam. And all said, this process didn't take all that long—a couple of generations, really. That's why Philologos could call this process "a linguistic success story."

A RELIGIOUS SUCCESS STORY?

The hegemony of tikkun olam in American Judaism may be a linguistic success story, but from the point of view of religion it is nothing to cheer about. Philologos went on to protest the political appropriation of the term as "an example of how authentic religious concepts can be cheapened when retooled and promoted for a mass audience." He feared that "the relevance we appear to give [the term] by decontextualizing it in this way comes at the expense . . . of honestly dealing with what tradition is trying to tell us."

This is true not just of the term "tikkun olam," but of Jewish social justice more generally. It was one thing for the Reformers to declare they were changing Judaism's direction. But, as we discovered in the previous chapter, Jewish social justice activists today aren't saying that that's what they're doing anymore. For the last few decades they've been saying this is authentic, traditional Judaism. That is, their liberal politics represent Judaism as it was always meant to be understood. Think about that. Isn't it just a little bit incredible for the teachings of the ancient faith of Judaism to happen to comprise without exception the agenda of the liberal wing of today's Democratic Party?[19] It's extraordinary just how few people have questioned how plausible this is.[20] And yet, as far as so many American Jews are concerned, Judaism means tikkun olam and tikkun olam means contemporary liberalism.

In order to demonstrate how Judaism means social justice, Jewish activists repeatedly point to a number of traditional Jewish texts that they believe bear out their liberal politics. Each of these sources reflects something inherited from Classical Reform and the Social Gospel. Specifically, these texts are the story of Creation in Genesis, which establishes universalism as the foundation of Jewish social justice; the appeal to God, also in Genesis, of the patriarch Abraham for the residents of Sodom and Gomorrah, an act of universalistic ethical selflessness that Jewish activists interpret as representing the very essence of what Judaism is about; the economic policies of Joseph in Egypt, which illustrate the indispensable and benevolent power of the state in achieving redemptive ends; the Israelite Exodus from Egypt in the second book of the Pentateuch, which underscores how fundamentally different the Kingdom of God is from our own society and the need for political revolution to get us from the one to the other; the Prophets, who supposedly eschewed ritual and overcame backward particularism and taught the universal religion of ethics; and, appearing in numerous rabbinic texts, tikkun olam itself, which captures what Jews mean when they talk about social justice. Together, this handful of passages forms the worldview of tikkun olam. These sources constitute Judaism's endorsement of the politics of social justice—they are what make Jewish social justice *Jewish*.

In his book *Why Are Jews Liberals?*, the neoconservative intellectual Norman Podhoretz wrote about how the Eastern European immigrants who got involved in labor activism and radical politics were effectively converting from Judaism to Marxism. Indeed the editor Abraham Cahan, as we mentioned earlier, declared that socialism is the new Torah. But the social justice movement has now in a sense reversed this process. Tikkun olam is not about turning Jews into Marxists. It's about rebranding Marxism as Judaism.

"The Marxists," Michael Lerner writes, "certainly didn't invent the challenge to private property. Anyone who has ever bothered to read the Torah knows that God claims the ownership of the world."[21] For too long, the tikkun olam movement's rebranding of Marxism as Judaism has been allowed to proceed unchallenged. Lerner and his cohort believe that anyone who has bothered to learn the traditional texts of Judaism must conclude that this religion endorses and even mandates the program of social justice. They are wrong. Dismally wrong. So let's take Lerner's challenge. Let's actually read the favorite Scriptural texts of the Jewish social justice movement. And let's find out if the God of Israel really is a Marxist.

3

In the Beginning

In the run-up to the United Nations Climate Change Conference in Paris in late 2015, news spread of the Pope's intention to issue an encyclical on the topic. This prompted a number of liberal American rabbis to get together to produce an epistle of their own. Their purpose was to "bring unique Jewish wisdom to the worldwide efforts to heal the world from climate disruption [and] to remind the Jewish community itself that practical wisdom about the relationships between human beings and the earth is encoded in the Torah."[1] The rambling letter, ultimately signed by some 425 rabbis, explained that "as Jews, we ask the question whether the sources of traditional Jewish wisdom can offer guidance to our political efforts to prevent disaster and heal our relationship with the Earth." The question was rhetorical. Their answer was that "the Unity of all means not only that all life is interwoven, but also that an aspect of God's Self partakes in the interwovenness."

Whatever exactly that meant, it required "the repair of social injustice." That repair would take the form of a reversal of the "worsening inequality of wealth, income, and political power" that allows "great Carbon Corporations [to] make their enormous profits from wounding the Earth [and] then use these profits to purchase elections and to fund fake science to prevent the public from acting to heal the wounds" while leaving "the poor in America and around the globe . . . to suffer from the typhoons, floods, droughts, and diseases brought on by climate chaos." The letter duly called "for a new sense of *eco-social justice*—a *tikkun olam* that includes . . . the healing of our planet." This healing involved opposition to fracking, coal burning, the Keystone XL Pipeline, and Arctic oil drilling, and support for government subsidies for renewable energy and a carbon tax.[2] As you'll recall, the 2015 conference culminated in the Paris Agreement, from which the Trump administration eventually withdrew the United States, provoking, as you can imagine, the fury of Jewish social justice campaigners.

The "source of traditional Jewish wisdom" cited by the rabbis in their letter was the idea of the "Unity" and "interwovenness" of all life. This esoteric notion—wildly popular in Jewish social justice circles—is a nod to the biblical story of Creation, which has always been the lynchpin of the movement's environmentalism. Ellen Bernstein, one of the signatories of the rabbis' climate letter, was an early promoter of Jewish ecology. Now a campus rabbi at Hampshire College, Bernstein founded Shomrei Adamah ("Keepers of the Earth") in 1988, an organization with ten local chapters that ran nature trips and held marches before closing in 1996 to make way for more politicized advocacy groups. Bernstein herself went on to join two such groups, Shomrei Bereishit ("Keepers of Genesis") and Aytzim ("Trees"). A nature lover from her youth, Bernstein was drawn to Judaism due to what she viewed as the Bible's commitment to environmentalism. She notes that Genesis teaches that humanity's dominion over nature came with a responsibility: we must "guard it and keep it" rather than exploit it, the Bible says.[3] Although we may have dominion over the earth, nevertheless, she counsels, "we are never allowed to own it." Bernstein takes this quite literally. Since the Bible also declares that "the land cannot be sold in perpetuity" (Lev. 25:23), she extrapolates that "the land is the commons, and it belongs to everyone equally and jointly." Since God owns the land and everything on it, it must be that private property does not exist. Humanity does not own the land; it is merely charged with managing it. This is the basis of Michael Lerner's belief that the Torah is a Marxist tract that opposes private property, a (faulty) proposition that opens the door to unlimited economic regulation, taxation, and expropriation.

(For that matter, it also invites even zanier schemes, such as the one Lerner advances, whereby, in lieu of private property, mankind establishes a sabbatical program of job rotations over six years, with every human assuming a new occupation every year and devoting the seventh year to rest. Conceding that such an economy would be far less productive than the present one, Lerner assures us that this is "a hardship which, if distributed fairly, people would quickly come to accept." After all, argues Lerner, because of the environmental costs of fossil fuel consumption and impending climate change, we need to make a fundamental change to our economy and society—we need a "transformative movement."[4])

Such liberal environmentalism is, of course, central to tik-kun olam. When people think of the repair of the world, often the first thing that comes to mind is the effort to stem and ulti-mately reverse the tide of human damage to the natural world. The Creation story is essential to this narrative. But Creation has other uses too. It is also frequently referenced in Jewish so-cial justice LGBT campaigns. In advocating for same-sex mar-riage, Reform Judaism, for example, is "guided by the basic belief that all human beings are created in the Divine image, as it says in Genesis 1:27."[5] The Reconstructionist movement too pro-claims that "because we see ourselves as embodying a spark of the divine (Genesis 1:26), we understand that every person has infinite worth."[6] Accordingly, it celebrated the Supreme Court's legalization of same-sex marriage nationwide.[7]

In fact, it's not just ecology and LGBT matters. Creation really encapsulates the Jewish social justice movement's concep-tion of humanity and the world. Although historically, the Classical Reformers looked to the Prophets when seeking to ground the new universal religion they were proselytizing in the Bible, today's Jewish activists are alive also to the potential of Genesis in furthering their universalistic message. The bibli-cal narrative we're talking about is very familiar: God creates the heavens and the earth over six days and rests on the seventh. He creates man from the dust of the earth in His image and divides him into two opposite—male and female—companions. In Eden, the snake induces the woman to eat the fruit of the forbidden tree and she gives of the fruit also to the man. Having eaten, they recognize their nakedness and make themselves clothes. God calls to them and they hide from Him in their shame. Dis-covering that they have eaten from the tree, God curses the snake and punishes the man and woman and evicts them from Eden.

From the biblical premise of God's creation of the world and the creation of humans in the image of God, the Jewish social justice movement makes three significant theological claims. The first is that all persons possess the same dignity, deserve the same opportunities, and are entitled to similar outcomes. The very nature of man demands the establishment of a society that guarantees its members the equality and respect appropriate to creatures who bear the image of the divine. According to these activists, the sort of society that gives everyone that respect and dignity can only be achieved through social justice.

Second, since God didn't create solely humans but all of nature, the environment has a streak of divinity of its own. We must therefore treat the natural world with suitable reverence, and seek to maintain and protect, rather than exploit, God's creation. Jewish social justice activists believe the way to discharge this responsibility is to campaign for "environmental justice"—for a comprehensive rethink of our energy and environmental policy through federal regulations and major legislative restrictions on Americans' economic behavior.

Third, there's a lesson in addition to human dignity and ecology that the Jewish social justice movement draws from the story of Creation. Although humanity reflects God's image, Genesis also teaches that man is brought forth from the dust of the earth. That means that mankind shares its origins with the rest of nature. Both are products of God's endeavors. Therefore there's a certain connectedness—an interwovenness—between humanity and nature, and this prompts the advocates of Jewish social justice to approach the natural world with an almost religious degree of veneration. After all, as the liberal rabbis' letter observed, "an aspect of God's Self partakes in the interwovenness." Repairing the world involves not just guaranteeing economic outcomes to ensure human dignity nor merely a monumental overhaul of the American economy to protect the natural world. It also urges recognition that nature itself is divine.

Because these ideas underlie the universalism of Jewish social justice, not to mention its concern for the environment and LGBT rights, they constitute the components of what we might call the theology of Jewish social justice. This theology is a contrived religious system, a sort of New Age mysticism that distorts the biblical Creation story and Kabbalistic (Jewish mystical) motifs in order to portray the politics of social justice as an organic Jewish teaching. Its purpose is to facilitate the quiet absorption of liberal politics—of social justice—into Judaism. This theology builds on the idea that all persons as well as nature share a common beginning. It is stridently universalistic, and at its core is the idea that everything—all mankind and all of nature—is connected. In the pithy words of the Reform rabbi and academic Lawrence Kushner, it's a theology that teaches "that everything and everyone is connected—that it's all One."[8]

The exemplar of this way of thinking is one of the initiators of the rabbis' climate letter, the liberal rabbi, academic, and activist Arthur Green—particularly in his book *Radical Judaism: Rethinking God and Tradition*.[9] Having gained rabbinical ordination from the Conservative Jewish Theological Seminary, Green is currently a professor at the more liberal Hebrew College and the founder and rector of its non-denominational rabbinical school. When he was in college, he encountered Zalman Schachter-Shalomi, who would become a leader of

Jewish Renewal and who remained a mentor to Green. In 1968, Green founded Havurat Shalom—the commune from which the Jewish Catalog emerged. He is a prominent figure in Jewish Renewal to this day, and a leading thinker in the Jewish social justice movement. Our investigation of the Jewish social justice reading of Creation—and the movement's theology—is therefore well served by an analysis of Green's thought.

In what follows, we will observe how social justice is a universalistic political ideology. Whereas traditional Judaism tends toward the particularistic—concepts such as the God of Israel, the Torah, and Jewish Peoplehood are central to the Jewish faith—social justice doesn't care much for distinctions between peoples. The challenge for *Radical Judaism* is how to incorporate the concepts of a particularistic faith into the theology of Jewish social justice, which is concerned not with difference but with sameness—with the interconnectedness of all people and nature.

RADICAL JUDAISM

Arthur Green's theology is bound up with his own experiences. He reminisces in his book that his younger faith in a personal God—the sort of God you learn about in Sunday school— eventually yielded to "theodicy and critical history." He doesn't seem hugely bothered by this development—actually, he was pretty relieved by "the death of my childhood God and the liberation from all that authority." But he didn't want to abandon the idea of God entirely. Instead, he considers himself a "religious humanist" and thinks our age is "a quest for meaning." The theology of *Radical Judaism* represents the fruits of his own quest for meaning—his quest for something else he could still call "God."

As well as being a "religious humanist," Green's "theological position," he explains, is that of a "mystical panentheist." That's someone "who believes that God is present throughout all of existence, that Being or Y-H-W-H [a superior name of the God of the Bible] underlies and unifies all that is." These, you'll surmise, are the beginnings of the theology of Jewish social justice, which deems everyone and everything to be connected, or interwoven. This isn't entirely original. There were elements of Hasidic thought that flirted with this way of thinking. Nevertheless, the idea of the "underlying oneness of being" is more redolent of Eastern mysticism. This is underscored by Green's assertion that there is no God, world, or self in his "unitive view of reality." There's "only one Being and its many faces." Green uses the terms "One," "Being," and "God" interchangeably.

Green's God is obviously not the personal God of the Bible. For one thing, his God doesn't have human-like consciousness or speak to the biblical patriarchs or the Jewish People—at least not in the way Jews and Christians have long understood. "The personified God" of traditional Western religion "is a mythical projection," Green announces. "A literal belief in a God who speaks the words of Torah is indeed far from what I have in mind."

So what exactly does Green have in mind? Although the One doesn't have "human-like consciousness," the One nevertheless contains "all mind and all consciousness ever to exist." Green's theology isn't about direct communication or a relationship with a personal God—which are what appear to feature in the Bible. Instead, his theology is based on those ineffable and inexpressible instants of fleeting connection to everyone and everything. We all have these sorts of moments—when we witness the awesomeness of nature or a child being born. These are "moment[s] of nakedness, a confrontation with a reality that we do not know how to put into language." But Green conceives of these moments as windows to a deeper reality. On these ephemeral occasions we connect with the One, Green says—we imagine that the One "inhabits each of us and binds us all together." This sentiment too is not original to Green. Such a description, you might have noticed, is quite suggestive of the effects of hallucinogenic drugs, which are also said to trigger feelings of unity, oneness, and connection to infinity. This observation might seem facetious but it's no joke—this foundation of Green's theology is a reminder of the "interwovenness" of tikkun olam and 1960s radicalism. (One is reminded also of Michael Lerner's description—somehow also not a joke—of one such hallucinogen, LSD, as a "progressive drug.")

We're all bound together, according to Green. All of reality is bound together. And if everyone and everything is connected, it follows that everyone and everything probably came from the same place. And that's exactly what Green wants us to think. He wants to "go all the way back to the Source." The "Source" is Creation—and Green becomes fixated on the idea and meaning of Creation.

Green's God is connected to the human and natural worlds, but he doesn't perceive this God as a Creator in the traditional sense. He explains his thinking as follows:

> I think of that underlying One in immanent terms, a Being or life force that dwells within the universe and all its forms, rather than a Creator from beyond who forms a world that is "other" and separate from its own Self. This One—the only

One that truly is—lies within and behind all the diverse forms of being that have existed since the beginning of time.

Just as Green's God didn't speak to Abraham and Moses like you imagined, this God also didn't create the world in the way you thought. He did not create a world separate from Himself, but rather this God is within all things—people and nature.

Given that the biblical God in Genesis—the one you're familiar with—is the personal God whom Green has rejected, he has to reconceptualize Creation as something different than how we usually imagine it. God has not created something separate from Himself, as the Bible seems to imply. But although the One may not be the Creator in the traditional sense, Green insists that He is still the Creator of sorts. The One, Green explains, is involved in an ongoing process of Creation—a process called evolution. He writes:

We would understand the entire course of evolution, from the simplest life forms millions of years ago, to the great complexity of the human brain (still now only barely understood), and proceeding onward into the unknown future, to be a meaningful process. There is a One that is ever revealing itself to us within and behind the great diversity of life.

There's a lot to unpack here. According to Green, Creation is evolution. And evolution is meaningful. In other words, Creation/evolution has a purpose. Evolution is not necessarily directed—but it still has a purpose. That purpose is the meaningful process by which the One reveals itself to us. Thus Creation/evolution is the gradual *revelation* of divinity. It's the process through which "the divine waits to be discovered."

Now, if Creation equals evolution, and evolution equals revelation, then—wait for it—Creation equals revelation. This elision is absolutely pivotal for Green. In traditional Jewish thought, Revelation—the Revelation of the Torah at Mount Sinai—is the wellspring of Jewish law and obligation. Since it was only the Jews who were present at Sinai, those laws and obligations mostly pertain only to the Jews. But Green doesn't like that. We know he doesn't like the law part—he was thrilled to be liberated from the authority of the Torah's law when he lost his belief in a personal God in his earlier years. But he also doesn't like the idea that the Jews alone are implicated in Revelation and its obligations.

Green therefore wants to identify the source of obligation (and we haven't yet identified what Green understands that obligation to be) in Creation. Since obligation in Judaism comes from Revelation, in order to achieve this Green has had to associate Revelation with Creation. He needs Creation to *be* Revelation. So he portrays Creation as an evolutionary process in which the One is *revealing* itself to us. The result is that "the oneness underlying 'Creation' and the oneness underlying 'revelation' are the same One."

Why is it so critical that obligation be rooted in Creation? Jewish social justice is a universalistic ideology, so if you want to say the Hebrew Bible endorses that ideology, the best way to do so is by emphasizing humanity's shared provenance—the creation of humans in the image of God. If Revelation is your starting point, then you end up with traditional Judaism. But if Creation is your starting point—as Green would like it to be— then the politics of tikkun olam might begin to make more theological sense. If all humans are created in the image of God, then maybe it does follow that every human being is entitled to

certain material and emotional dignities. These, of course, are
the outcomes which tikkun olam pursues. As Green puts it:

> That every human being is the image of God is Judaism's most
> basic moral truth . . . We need to help all humans to discover
> this dimension of their own existence in whatever terms they
> may choose to articulate it. We recognize that this truth may
> be depicted differently in the varied religious and sacred lan-
> guages of human culture. We do not require others to accept
> the language of Judaism, but we do see justice, decency, and
> civility to one another as universal human imperatives that
> stem directly from the reality that we call . . . the image of
> God. A person cannot be expected to discover the image
> of God within himself or herself as long as he or she is hun-
> gry, or as long as he or she is homeless or degraded by pov-
> erty, addictions, or the seemingly overwhelming burdens of
> everyday life . . . the forces that block out the light are quite
> concrete—social, political, or economic barriers—and they
> too have to become the object of our attention as people and
> communities of faith.

Green shows here how liberal politics—the politics of tikkun
olam—can flow from Creation. He explicitly mentions some of
the economic elements of social justice, such as the concern with
poverty and the need to overcome "economic barriers." But he's
attuned also to the social and ecological elements of social justice. He writes of the discovery of the image of God within all
of us "in whatever terms [we] may choose to articulate it" and
the truth behind "varied religious and sacred languages of
human culture," allusions to the importance of cultivating gen-

der, religious, and cultural diversity. Ecology is also present in Green's thought, of course—for example, in his statement in an earlier quotation that "there is a One that is ever revealing itself to us within and behind the great diversity of [all] life." It may indeed appear, therefore, that the politics of tikkun olam can flow from Creation. But Green and other Jewish social justice activists want to trick you into thinking these politics *necessarily* flow from Creation. This isn't so. There's no reason to assume that equality of economic outcomes or sexual permissiveness or an aversion to using the military are the best way to respect the dignity of human beings. Equally strong arguments can be made for the economic dignity of hard work, for sexual restraint to honor our divine image and potential, and for ensuring our safety and promoting our values around the world. The fact is that no particular contemporary politics necessarily flow from the Creation story in itself.

Green is nevertheless pushing the politics of tikkun olam, after all. And this brings us to obligation. We said that in traditional Judaism, obligation (the laws of the Torah) arise from Revelation—when the Torah was given to the Jews by God at Sinai. But Green made Revelation into Creation. So if there is a revelation—if there is obligation—in Green's theology, it's going to be in Creation. So what exactly is the obligation? What is the teaching of Green's Judaism? The answer is that humanity has a role in revealing divinity within everyone and everything. When Adam and Eve eat the fruit of the forbidden tree and learn of their nakedness, they hide. God calls out to Adam and asks, "Where are you?" The literal meaning is obvious. But Green intuits that there's a "silently spoken" meaning in this question. For him, the silent question beneath is the following:

"Where are you in helping Me to carry this project forward?"
Are you extending My work of self-manifestation, participat-
ing as you should in the ongoing evolutionary process, the
eternal reaching toward knowing and fulfilling the One that
is all of life's goal? That is why you are here, tumbling and
stumbling forward from one generation to the next! *What are
you doing about it?*

How exactly Adam and Eve were meant to fulfil this obligation
in Eden is not made clear. Nor, incidentally, is why Green
chooses to take some parts of the biblical Creation story—the
creation of human beings in the image of God and the eating
of the forbidden fruit—as portrayals accurate enough to teach
us something, but not the rest of the story. In any event, Green is
rooting obligation in the Creation story. And the reason he does
so is because if moral obligation is to be found in Creation, and
Creation implies liberal political activism (as we've just seen
Green suggest it does), then morality dictates liberalism. The
obligation of Creation/Revelation—of Judaism—is the liberal
politics of social justice, which is a religious imperative. Of
course, there's no real textual basis for Green's interpretation of
God's question to Adam and Eve, but this is nonetheless the
meaning of "commandment" and Torah in Green's Judaism.

In traditional Judaism, the commandments of the Torah
(the *mitzvoth*) are born of Revelation. They are the expression of
the covenant between God and His chosen people—the Jewish
People. Obligation and Jewish Peoplehood are thus bound up together. But if, as in Green's interpretation, Revelation is actually
merely part of Creation, and God's commandment is the political agenda of social justice, then what—or who—is the Jewish People? Astoundingly, Green rejects the idea of a distinct

Jewish People in toto. "I do not know a God who makes a covenant with Israel," he declares. The very notion is "too personifying and unduly particularistic" and "too narrow and chauvinistic" for him. The teaching of the Bible, in Green's view, cannot be the particularistic story of the Jewish People and its relationship with the God of Abraham. Instead, the lesson of Scripture is universalistic: "all of being is one in Y-H-W-H, and every person is in the image of God."

What, then, does Green make of the part of the Bible that talks about God giving the Torah to the Jews at Sinai? What was given to the Jews at Sinai, Green explains, was merely "awareness" of the Oneness of Being. That is the extent of the Jews' privilege. Otherwise, they received nothing more than any of the other peoples of the world who were not present at Sinai. But even this paltry excuse for the existence of the Jewish People is too much for Green to bear for long. Even the obligation to preach this awareness and its supposed moral and political meaning, Green avers, does not fall to the Jews alone. In other words, the Revelation at Sinai adds nothing whatsoever to what was already taught by Creation—because Revelation was already part of Creation. Accordingly, the Jews have no special place or role in the world. There is no covenant between God and the Jewish People. There is no need for the Jewish People.

But even if Green sees no need for the Jewish People, there are still Jews in the world (alas!). So what, according to Green, are they supposed to do? He advises that the Jews go "back to the single great story that unites us all"—the creation of human beings in the image of God. That is Judaism's "most essential teaching"—and it's the reason "Judaism still needs to exist." But this universalistic teaching is not Judaism's alone to teach and it doesn't impact the Jews alone. So whatever Green says, in truth this isn't really a compelling reason for why "Judaism still needs to exist." Not only that, but if the purpose of human existence is to recognize how we all come from the same place and ultimately are all the same, one wonders whether maintaining the Jews as a distinct people may not in fact actually be a hindrance to social justice.

A NATION FAITH

Without the personal and commanding God of Abraham, Isaac, and Jacob there is no covenant, and without a covenant there is no Jewish People. On this theory, moral obligation emanates not from the covenant but from the creation of human beings in the image of God, and it is universal. This universalism is the foundation of Jewish social justice, but it leaves the theology bereft of any cogent reason for Judaism to persist. If Jews and non-Jews are equally obligated to repair the world—to engage in social justice work—then what's special about the Jews? Sometimes it's said that the special role of the Jews is to teach the message of Creation to everyone—the message that we all have to do social justice—and we just saw Green halfheartedly make such a case. The Classical Reformers similarly claimed that the Jewish mission in the world was to teach the supposed universal religion of the prophets. But the discomfort felt by Classical Reform about any sort of Jewish distinction—which Jewish social justice activists continue to feel—is taken to its logical end by Green. For him, any Jewish difference is chauvinistic— even the modest calling to teach the universal lesson. But if Jews and gentiles come from the same place, have exactly the same rights and obligations, owe those obligations equally to everyone else, and share the same destiny as the rest of humanity, then there is nothing special, extraordinary, or even unusual about the Jews. There is nothing necessary about them either.

It's remarkable that such a theology could claim to originate in Scripture. The Hebrew Bible proclaims that the Jews "are a holy people to the Lord your God; the Lord your God chose you to be His treasured people from all the nations on the face of the earth" (Deut. 7:6). There's no getting around that. And yet, maybe the discomfort of Jewish social justice campaigners with the idea that the Jews are somehow separate from the rest of humanity is reasonable. Whatever the Bible may say, in this day and age it's simply not politically correct to think of oneself as different. So perhaps the Jewish social justice movement is right to reject this parochial and primitive mentality of Jewish chosenness?

Traditional Jewish thought and practice, however, have always depended on some sort of distinction between Jews and gentiles. It's a common misconception that this distinction necessarily means that the Jews are *better*—it doesn't. But it does mean they're a community apart. Actually, this isn't unique to Jews. Some sort of distinction is a critical characteristic of any religion or ethnicity—at least to some degree. For one thing, every religion considers itself *necessary*—otherwise why should its adherents make the sacrifices their religion demands? And if a religion is necessary, it will usually need to endure. In order to do that, it needs to keep itself somehow distinct from the rest of society. That's what traditional Judaism tries to do.

In fact, the similarities are even wider than that. Without differentiation, any identity grouping—religious or otherwise—will become diluted and dissolve. What would America be if every church, every state, and every community were exactly the same? If a group doesn't retain even cultural practices that are different from other groups, then it will disappear. Contemporary secularists, humanists, and cosmopolitans may, for their own philosophical or political reasons, welcome the disappearance of all groupings in society. But America was founded on freedom of religion and assembly—because the Founding Fathers recognized that it's a country of many different communities. As for the Jews, it has always been the faith of this people that their own separateness is divinely ordained and, ultimately, universally beneficial. It's this faith that Jewish social justice activists are abandoning.

To illustrate this, consider the biblical obligation to love your neighbor as yourself. The appropriations of this verse (and others) in the name of universalism and social justice are based on one big misunderstanding. Whereas Arthur Green grounds moral obligation in the creation of all human beings in the image of God, traditional Judaism roots obligation in the covenant between God and the Jewish People established at the Revelation at Sinai, endowing the creation of human beings in the image of God with a decidedly secondary status. The upshot of sourcing obligation in Revelation is that the Jews are a people apart. Laws such as the command to love your neighbor as yourself are legislated in the context of the covenant. The way to understand this injunction is in reference not to universalistic Creation but to particularistic Revelation. When Jews want to know who is obligated and to whom, they look to Revelation rather than to Creation. In other words, this biblical law does not have in mind all human beings created in the image of God but rather those particular humans who are bound by the laws of the covenant—i.e., Jews and their fellow Jews. Hence the traditional Jewish understanding of the Scriptural injunction to love your fellow as yourself means that a Jew must love his fellow Jew as himself.[10]

Although this may seem to jar with contemporary liberal sensibilities, within the context of Jewish thought it makes total sense. The Jewish People perceives itself as an extended family descended—biologically—from Abraham. He is literally the father of the Jewish People. Within this family, members are more greatly obligated to one another than to those outside of the family. This is just like in any family, where members will justifiably tend to their own first. It's only natural that siblings, for instance, look out for one another more than they would for strangers. Obligating the enhanced concern for fellow Jews is the Jewish way of expressing just such a familial bond. It doesn't mean Jews shouldn't treat gentiles well—just as siblings would be expected to show strangers decency and respect. But it does mean that they're expected to be especially good to their siblings.

Although Revelation is primary, Creation—and the universalism it implies—is still an important biblical teaching. But humanity's common origin doesn't mean that Jews (or indeed anyone) owe the same allegiance to everybody else. Consider this analogy: Americans are a generous and compassionate nation to citizens of other nations. But they don't believe they owe the same obligations to human beings on the other side of the world as they do to their fellow citizens. Foreigners living abroad are not enrolled into Medicaid and the U.S. military does not fight wars on behalf of other countries. That doesn't mean America doesn't trade with its neighbors or forge alliances with other nations or give foreign aid or provide humanitarian relief to those in need. It just means that fellow citizens are the priority. That's because they're more familiar to you and because they follow the same laws as you do—so you can expect the same from them. It's not so different with traditional Judaism. The Torah is essentially a constitution for a single people living in its own land under God, where obligations are designed to benefit the other citizens who have accepted the same laws and can be held to account for any lack of reciprocity. The amplified obligation Jews have toward their fellow Jews parallels the situation among citizens of all nations.

Judaism is also a parallel of other religions—in fact it's their forerunner. Other religions often prioritize obligations to coreligionists too. For example, Christians used to be prohibited from taking interest on loans to other Christians—and Jews and some Muslims still retain this restriction within their faith communities. The special obligation of Jews to their fellow Jews is not just familial but, like those other religions, it is also connected to their common relationship with God. The Jews are obligated to one another because they are also bound together to the Almighty. That is the nature of the covenant between the Jewish People and the God of Abraham.

The Jewish social justice movement ignores the limits that traditional Judaism placed on these various biblical injunctions, such as the command to love your neighbor. Liberal Jewish activists now apply them universally and obligate everyone to everyone else. But this undermines the covenantal connection between each Jew, and the Jews' distinction from gentiles, and the relationship between the Jewish People and God. To reiterate, if Jews and gentiles come from the same place, have exactly the same rights and obligations, owe those obligations equally to everyone else, and share the same destiny as the rest of humanity, then there is nothing special, extraordinary, or necessary about the Jews.

Yet for all this laudation of universalism, if Green read the Bible more honestly he might have observed and reckoned with the fact that there are two biblical epochs founded upon the creation of human beings in the image of God. The first is that commenced by Adam (Gen. 1:27) and the second initiated by Noah (Gen. 9:6). Both collapse spectacularly, one with the Deluge and the other with the Dispersion of Babel.[11] Establishing morality on the basis of the creation of human beings in the image of God, as Green does, is rather inauspicious. In fact, it is immediately after the failure of the second of these two eras that God's attention turns particularistic—to Abraham and his descendants. But such details are not for Green.

Clearly, nothing in Green's theology—the theology of Jewish social justice—bears resemblance to traditional Judaism. Green rejects the personal God of Abraham, Isaac, and Jacob in favor of a panentheistic Deity. He replaces the Torah and Jewish law with the liberal politics of social justice. And he abandons the covenant between God and the Jewish People in favor of an unexplained responsibility to promulgate a truth that is apparently accessible to everyone already anyway. Green has strayed very far indeed from Judaism as observed and understood by Jews for millennia.

Without a personal God interacting with the patriarchs in Canaan and with the Israelites at Sinai and making the former a promise and establishing a covenant with the latter, and without the transmission of a set of legal instructions to the People of Israel and some resulting differentiation between that people and the gentiles, there is no Judaism as traditionally conceived. Any suggestion to the contrary rings hollow in light of the very title of Green's work—*Radical Judaism: Rethinking God and Tradition*. Green's Judaism is radical and it is rethought.

As if a more explicit declaration of his break with traditional Jewish thought were needed, Green concludes by clarifying that "radical Judaism" means

> to rethink our most foundational concepts—God, Torah, and Israel and Creation, Revelation, and Redemption, to ask how they might work in the context of what we really believe in our age, and thus how they might speak to seekers in this century.

To make these foundational concepts relevant to our age really just means making them useful for Jewish social justice. Traditional Judaism has been deemed unfit for purpose and, in the spirit of tikkun olam, a new, radical theology has been made up almost out of whole cloth to suit the needs of liberal Jewish activists.

Only by emphasizing the creation of human beings in the image of God to the exclusion of everything else might the agenda of Jewish social justice possibly begin to make theological sense. This belief that everyone and everything is One isn't unique to Green—it's a theology that implicitly undergirds all of Jewish social justice. Although elements of Green's panentheism are not new in the annals of philosophy, this theology—with its elimination of the covenant and Jewish law—is not the traditional Jewish approach and runs counter to mainstream Jewish thought. This is the theology of Jewish social justice—and there is very little *Jewish* about it.

Abraham and the Meaning of Judaism

The patriarch Abraham truly became the father of the Jewish People when he heeded God's call to adopt the sacred purpose of spreading righteousness and social justice in the world. This is the view of Reconstructionist rabbi Sidney Schwarz. The figure behind a number of Jewish social justice organizations, Schwarz is considered by *Newsweek* to be among the most influential rabbis in the United States. Formerly the executive director of the Jewish Community Relations Council of Greater Washington, where he undertook public affairs work, he is also the founder of Panim: The Institute for Jewish Leadership and Values. Panim was launched in order to "ignite the passion of the next generation of Jews to repair a broken world," and has encouraged and trained over 15,000 Jewish teenagers to conduct political advocacy in the nation's capital.[1] At the heart of this advocacy is the ethos of Abraham.

Schwarz maintains that God's choice of Abraham signified that the Jewish People would not be "a people apart, a separate ethnic and political unit." Instead:

> They would be a people bound to a higher calling. According to God's covenant with Abraham, every Jew is called upon not simply to believe in the values of righteousness and justice, but to act on them: motivated by moral responsibility, to advocate—as Abraham did—on behalf of the vulnerable of all nations. Abraham lived in Canaan as a "stranger and a sojourner" (Gen. 23:4), but his sense of separateness and apartness did not prevent him from heeding a universalistic moral call—from behaving with altruistic compassion toward the people of Sodom and Gomorrah. This sense of higher calling—an altruistic urge to bring righteousness and justice into the world—is the Jewish legacy from Abraham.[2]

Abraham would not be disappointed. "Throughout their history," Schwarz observes,

> Jews have taken it for granted that Abraham's example with Sodom and Gomorrah was not to be considered the exception, but rather the rule. Ever since Abraham questioned God's moral judgment, there has been a longstanding Jewish tradition of advocacy on behalf of justice.

Upholding Abraham's legacy, exemplified by his protest at God's judgment of Sodom is, the theory goes, what it means to be a Jew. This "advocacy on behalf of justice" is the purpose of Judaism—to be Jewish is to pursue social justice. To borrow a phrase from the Social Gospel, social justice is "applied Judaism."

"The Jewish People are born," Schwarz explains in reference to the episode at Sodom, "when Abraham sets an example of righteousness and justice for his descendants, who will be called, in turn, to bring righteousness and justice into the world."

Sidney Schwarz is not the only one who believes the greatest zealots of this allegedly authentic Judaism are today's advocates of Jewish social justice. Aryeh Cohen concurs. Cohen is a professor of Rabbinic Literature at the American Jewish University in Los Angeles and has taught at the principal Reform and Reconstructionist seminaries in the United States. He used to sit on the board of Rabbis for Human Rights North America and was a founding member of Jews Against the War, two organizations premised on the wrongs of Israeli and American defense and security policies. Previously, he also served as the chair of the board of Progressive Jewish Alliance, a Californian Jewish social justice group that was formed by dissenters from the local chapter of a more mainstream national Jewish organization (the American Jewish Congress), which they considered insufficiently radical in its politics. Unlike Jews Against the War, Progressive Jewish Alliance was more interested in domestic issues such as economic justice. A few years ago, it merged with another group, Jewish Funds for Justice, to become Bend the Arc, which claims to be the largest Jewish social justice organization in America. Bend the Arc campaigns for higher taxes on the wealthy and higher minimum wages in the name of economic justice (although these days it seems to be engaged only in ceaseless protest against the Trump administration and fundraising to defeat congressional Republicans). The chairman of Bend the Arc is Alexander Soros, the son of the billionaire hedge funder and major backer of radical left-wing political causes, George Soros, and it has chapters across the nation. Aryeh Cohen is

Bend the Arc's rabbi-in-residence. He writes extensively on social justice, particularly as it pertains to economics. He too takes inspiration from Abraham, explaining:

> If by being Jewish one means connecting oneself to the wisdom of the Jewish tradition one would find that Jews who put social and economic justice at the heart of their concerns are tapping a deep vein. When God informs Abraham that God is going to destroy Sodom, Abraham challenges God: "Will the judge of all the world not do justice?"[3]

The "altruistic urge to bring righteousness and justice into the world" that Schwarz is talking about, and "the social and economic justice" of Aryeh Cohen, are demonstrated by Jewish activists in their promotion of higher taxes, minimum wages, and expanded entitlements to relieve poverty, single-payer healthcare to deliver universal medical coverage, big labor to protect workers and immigrants, and carbon taxes to repair the environment from the ravages of climate change. More broadly, it is evident in their aversion to capitalism. As Shmuly Yanklowitz, an Orthodox rabbi, founder of the Jewish social justice group Uri L'Tzedek, ranked one of *Newsweek*'s most influential rabbis in America, and formerly a staffer at Schwarz's Panim, laments: "In a globalized, unregulated market, we live in . . . a war of all against all." Accordingly, "Jews can certainly join in responding to [the] call for the immediate and passionate restructuring of our global economic priorities." In this context, he notes that "Abraham, chosen by God to be the first Jew, was given a mission to pursue justice."[4]

The Jewish social justice movement reads the story of Abraham at Sodom and Gomorrah as teaching that the purpose of Judaism and the mission of the Jews today is the pursuit of social justice. However, this reading of the biblical text and the conclusion these activists reach are pretty baseless. To understand why, we have to look at both the story and the social justice movement's interpretation more closely. So what, exactly, does the Scriptural passage actually say?

> And God said: "Shall I hide from Abraham what I am doing? After all, he will become a great and mighty nation and all the nations of the earth shall be blessed through him. For I have known him, that he will command his children and his house after him, that they will keep the way of God, to do righteousness [*tzedakah*] and justice [*mishpat*] such that God will bring upon Abraham what he Has said regarding him."

> And God said: "The cry of Sodom and Gomorrah is great and their sin is grievous. I will go down now, and see whether they have done according to the cry, and if not I will know" . . .
> But Abraham remained standing before God. And Abraham drew near and said: "Will You destroy the righteous/ guiltless [*tzaddik*] with the wicked? Perhaps there are fifty righteous in the city. Will You destroy and not forgive the place for the sake of the fifty righteous there? Far be it from You to act so, to slay the righteous with the wicked, rendering the righteous like the wicked. Far be it from You—will the Judge of all the world not do justice [mishpat]?"
> And God said: "If I find in Sodom fifty righteous within the city, I will forgive the entire place for their sake."

> And Abraham answered and said: "Behold, I have taken it upon me to speak to the Lord, yet I am but dust and ashes.

Perhaps there shall lack five from the fifty righteous. Will You destroy the entire city for the lack of five?"

And He said: "I shall not destroy if I find there forty-five."

And he spoke to Him again and said: "Perhaps there would be found there forty."

And He said: "I will not do it for the sake of the forty."

And he said: "Let not the Lord be angry, and I will speak. Perhaps there would be found there thirty."

And He said: "I will not do it if I find there thirty."

And he said, "Behold I have taken it upon myself to speak to the Lord. Perhaps there would be found there twenty."

And He said: "I will not destroy for the sake of the twenty."

And he said: "Let not the Lord be angry and I will speak this once more. Perhaps there would be found there ten."

And He said: "I will not destroy for the sake of the ten."

And God went as soon as He had finished speaking to Abraham. And Abraham returned to his place. (Gen. 18:17–33)

There are several elements of this passage that we need to consider. The first is the opening statement by God about Abraham doing righteousness and justice. To begin with, it should be noted that this is a difficult verse to decipher in the Hebrew—even in the English translation you can see that God starts by speaking in the first person but then shifts to the third person. But let's say that the above rendering is accurate enough. The question is then: What are the "way of God" and "righteousness and justice"? We have a tendency today, whenever we see the word "justice," to assume it means social justice. The Bible doesn't make that leap. There's nothing in this passage to suggest any endorsement of social justice in any political sense—nothing about collective bargaining rights or ending fossil fuel consumption. Instead, what we get is the impression that this statement about the "way of God" and "righteousness and justice" is a preface to a narrative that is going to tell us something about those things. But in part because this verse is cryptic, we don't know whether Abraham already exhibits these traits—and is displaying them in raising questions about God's impending judgment of Sodom—or whether Abraham has yet to learn them, and that God is confident that once Abraham has learned them he will inculcate them in his children. In other words, the "way of God" and "righteousness and justice" are somehow demonstrated in the story of Sodom, but it's not obvious how—is it by Abraham or is it by God?

The traditional rabbinic commentators on the Bible generally consider the appearance of these phrases here as drawing a contrast between Abraham, who will teach "the way of God" and "righteousness and justice" to his children, and Sodom, which has abandoned those ways. On this reading, the destruction of Sodom is to be an everlasting reminder for Abraham's children—who of course will in future reside in this very land—about the dangers of deviating from "the way of God" and "righteousness and justice" as Sodom did. This approach seems to play down the idea that Abraham's concern is what exemplifies "the way of God" or "righteousness and justice"; in fact they make his concerns harder to comprehend. A compelling solution to this dilemma is that the story is actually God's attempt to teach (or Abraham's attempt to learn) "the way of God" and "righteousness and justice"—and this includes the lesson that mercy has limits and is sometimes inappropriate. Having learned this, Abraham can then teach this "righteousness and justice" to his progeny, as God anticipates he will.

There is, of course, more to it. However little the traditional

Jewish commentators may think of Sodom, Abraham is not criticized for intervening on the city's behalf. The reason is clear: it was reasonable for him to show an interest in its inhabitants' welfare. Whether that's specifically because they were neighbors of his or more generally because they were human beings, there is no question that Jews should have regard for those around them. Schwarz, however, may be exaggerating when he contends that Abraham "models the individual whose concern does not begin and end with himself, his family, and his tribe," since Abraham's entire role in Jewish history is to beget his own family and tribe. (The story of Sodom is actually a lot more particularistic than Schwarz makes out. The only ones to survive the destruction of Sodom are Abraham's nephew, Lot, and Lot's two daughters—who almost certainly only survive because they are Abraham's kin. Moreover, Schwarz points out in the quotation earlier in this chapter that Abraham describes himself as a "stranger and a sojourner" in Canaan, but Schwarz doesn't mention that Abraham does so in the context of purchasing the first piece of land over which the Jews will be sovereign in the Land of Israel, and that Abraham then goes on to search for a wife for his son, insisting that he marry one of Abraham's own kith rather than one of the locals.) But that doesn't mean that Abraham—or his progeny—should not care about others. Indeed, as Jewish social justice activists rightly note, the Jewish tradition generally compares Abraham favorably to Noah (of the ark). For whereas Noah became aware of mankind's impending doom and said nothing on mankind's behalf, Abraham, when confronted with the prospect of the destruction of Sodom and Gomorrah, pleaded for them. (To be sure, the comparison with Noah is a little more complicated, as the two scenarios were quite different.[5] But the point still holds.) The problem with the

Jewish social justice reading of this episode is not that it's an example of Abraham caring about others—it's the belief that such care must translate into the leftist politics of social justice.

Let's look at that belief further. The focus on Abraham's queries and the assumption that it is these (rather than what God Himself is doing in the story) that illustrate the "way of God" is behind a popular view that the lesson of this story is the significance of protest. Abraham's challenge to God constitutes, as it were, truth-talk to the ultimate Power. This view is advanced, for instance, by Conservative rabbi Jill Jacobs, who observes that Abraham's plea for the condemned cities of Sodom and Gomorrah is among the most frequently cited of biblical stories that suggest a vision for a "just world." The reason for its popularity is, Jacobs suggests, that "Abraham embodies an obligation to protest injustice, even in situations in which victory seems impossible, and in which the potential victims are mostly strangers."[6] Joshua Stanton, then a rabbinical student at Hebrew Union College and now a congregational Reform rabbi, similarly writes that Abraham's plea here is a "testament to the sacred nature of protest."[7] This raises two issues: the first is the idea of Abraham protesting and the second is the purpose of that protest.

The claim that Abraham is engaging in a "protest" is something of an overstatement. After all, Abraham takes a pretty mild tone. Any sense that he's protesting is surely attenuated by the respectful language that he employs. He prefaces his supplications with phrases like "I am but dust and ashes," and the traditional Jewish commentators recognize and celebrate his attitude. They compare Abraham favorably to Job—for whereas Job, in his eponymous book of the Bible, objected to God over his myriad misfortunes in the form of statements, Abraham's concerns were expressed as questions.[8] The reverential form of

Abraham's remarks signal that this exchange is more one of hopeful entreaty than protest. As we've already suggested, it has even been argued by some traditional Jewish commentators that the entire conversation is a pedagogical exercise initiated by Abraham himself, who is curious to learn "the way of God." So the patriarch doesn't protest in any tangible fashion—it's not like he ties himself to the gates of Sodom to confront the impending fire and brimstone head-on. He voices his concerns respectfully and, assuaged and enlightened, simply returns home. Does anyone remember the last time a similarly peaceable model was adopted by protestors at UC Berkeley?

What's more interesting is what Abraham's "protest" is supposedly about. The presumption is that Abraham is the one demonstrating "righteousness and justice" and that he is calling on God to amend His plan so that it conforms to the dictates of justice, to which God can apparently be held to account. In other words, God's plan to destroy the cities is, as it were, theologically unacceptable to Abraham. That's because it violates justice—and so Abraham protests. Elliot Dorff, a leading Conservative rabbi, claims that Abraham's argument sets a precedent for "moral critiques of God's actions." In Dorff's view, this biblical passage "would [not] make sense unless one presume[s] that morality exists independent of God so that God can be morally called to account."[9] If there isn't some independent standard of justice or morality by which even God has to abide, then what's Abraham appealing to and how does he convince God? (Michael Lerner goes even further. He basically substitutes this independent morality in place of God Himself: "We can imagine," Lerner writes, "Abraham having this argument with *the voice of God within* as he witnesses what must otherwise have been the incomprehensible event of . . . destruction."[10]) When

such figures talk about justice, they mean of course social justice. And Schwarz tries to flesh this out, remarking that in
"challeng[ing] God's command," Abraham lodges "the first
human rights complaint in Jewish history." What interests
these writers and activists is the *politics* of Abraham's exchange
with God—the politics that form the purpose of the family and
faith that Abraham founds.

Again, the Jewish social justice movement has overreached.
On the face of it, their argument seems plausible—Abraham
pleads with the Judge of all the world to do justice. It really does
look like Abraham is appealing to some standard of justice that
exists independently of God to which He can be held to account.
But the problem with this reading lies in that part of the story
that the advocates of Jewish social justice largely ignore, which
is its conclusion: Sodom and Gomorrah *are* ultimately destroyed.
Abraham's pleas achieve nothing in practice. And this isn't
because God ignores those pleas—nobody thinks He's destroy-
ing the cities along with their righteous inhabitants. He's de-
stroying them because there are no righteous inhabitants
there. God's suspicion of the cities had in effect already accounted
for Abraham's pleas. To put it another way, it's not clear at all
that God originally intended to destroy the cities even if there
were fifty righteous residents there, or forty-five or thirty or
twenty or ten, nor is there any indication that Abraham somehow changes God's mind. In fact, God's mind doesn't seem to
change at all in the story. So the question of a standard of justice existing independently of God is left unanswered.

Let's say for a moment, however, that the Bible is in fact trying to tell us that there does exist an independent standard
of justice to which God can be held to account. In that case,
wouldn't it have made more sense to have shown God changing

His mind about Sodom based on Abraham's appeals? Shouldn't we be reading about God saying that Abraham is right and that He made a big mistake in planning to destroy the cities regardless of how many righteous folks live there? Surely that would have made the lesson much clearer for us. But of course this isn't what happens. Instead, God seems to anticipate each of Abraham's pleas in His original judgment. So from Abraham's perspective, the lesson of the story appears to be not that God is bound by some independent standard of justice. Rather, the lesson seems to be that God is just to begin with—despite any preconceptions to the contrary. "Will the Judge of all the world not do justice?" Abraham asks. Indeed He will, the patriarch learns. If Abraham had any doubts about God's justice to begin with, they are dispelled. This is also the view taken by prominent traditional Jewish commentators, who suggest that Abraham accepts God's judgment of Sodom and even joins in that judgment. (This confidence in God's justice may also explain why Abraham does not protest later on when God commands him to sacrifice his son Isaac.) And if God is just to begin with, the question of an independent standard of justice is left hanging—because it's superfluous. Those looking for a Jewish answer to the famous question posed in Plato's *Euthyphro* ("Is the pious loved by the gods because it is pious, or is it pious because it is loved by the gods?") will therefore be disappointed.

But let's allow that the story is about some sort of independent justice to which God is also subject. Is it really "social justice" that the Bible is talking about? It doesn't look that way. The agenda Abraham is pushing is about whether an innocent minority should be punished for the crimes of the guilty majority. That actually sounds a lot more like the justice of the courtroom than the politics of social justice. This brings us to Schwarz's contention that Abraham's appeal represents a "human rights complaint." Even leaving aside anachronism, this notion has no merit. To dispel it, you need only observe that Abraham's famous auction terminates at *ten* righteous persons. Since human rights refer to protections or benefits to which each *individual* is entitled, were Abraham defending the residents on the basis of human rights, surely he would have appealed for every last person. Instead, Abraham is appealing for what is apparently the smallest possible innocent or righteous *community*—and that doesn't really have much to do with human rights at all.

We opened this discussion by observing that, according to Jewish activists, Abraham establishes social justice as the purpose of Judaism and the mission of the Jewish People. So far, we've shown that this story actually doesn't really have all that much to do with social justice. That leaves the other part of the statement: Does the Bible present this story as in any way exemplifying the purpose (whatever that may be) of Judaism? To put this question another way: Is this story particularly important? Schwarz believes that by reacting to God's plan as he does, Abraham passes a "test." This success confirms his unshakeable commitment to justice and—crucially—seals God's covenant with him. This is significant for the destiny of the Jewish People. As we've seen, in Schwarz's view, "Abraham's status as ancestor of the Jewish People" depends on how he responds to God's judgment of Sodom, and "the Jewish People are born when Abraham sets an example of righteousness and justice for his descendants" by trying to defend the condemned city. The covenant made later in the Bible between God and all the Israelites at Sinai represents little more than the renewal and acceptance by the entire Jewish People of "Abraham's sense of moral purpose," demonstrated by his "altruistic advocacy for the residents of Sodom and Gomorrah." In connecting Abraham's appeal for these cities to the foundational event of Judaism—the covenant at Sinai—Schwarz underscores the pivotal significance of this Abrahamic episode to Judaism.

So is this event really a test for Abraham? Are Abraham's stature and God's covenant with the Jewish People somehow contingent on Abraham's performance here? Note that the term "test" is not used lightly, because the Jewish tradition associates Abraham with ten tests of faith.[11] Now, the traditional commentators disagree on the precise identity of these ten tests, so the several lists of tests that they've compiled over centuries of commentary comprise more than ten episodes in Abraham's life overall. But guess which story is conspicuously absent from every one of those tallies: that's right—Abraham's appeal to God for Sodom and Gomorrah.[12] Its consistent omission surely conveys that the Jewish tradition doesn't consider this episode to be a "test" of Abraham. Schwarz has gone out on a limb here.

If the story isn't a test in traditional Jewish thought, then it's also less likely that the covenant itself is somehow contingent on what Abraham does here. In fact, far from the covenant depending on Abraham's approach to the matter of Sodom, the Bible seems to suggest the opposite, as it has already recounted God's establishment of the covenant with Abraham and his descendants three chapters earlier in Genesis 15. Furthermore, the prophecy of the birth of Isaac—the child who is meant to and does inherit the covenant—has just been delivered literally right before Abraham's appeal for Sodom in this very chapter (Gen. 18:10). (Incidentally, this may bolster the argument that this story is more about God teaching Abraham the meaning of the "way of God" and "righteousness and justice" than it is about Abraham displaying those qualities.) There isn't really any textual evidence at all to link the covenant to Abraham's response to God's judgment of the cities.[13]

Unsurprisingly, therefore, whereas the Jewish social justice movement tries to make out that this story is pivotal to the establishment of the Jewish People and illustrates the purpose of Judaism, in traditional Jewish thought it has no such grandiose stature. The truth is that the passage is pretty abstruse and the traditional commentators are at pains to divine its meaning or significance. Consequently, they largely marginalize it. As we've said, unlike almost every other major moment in Abraham's life, this one is not viewed by the traditional commentators as a test. Contrary to the claims of the advocates of Jewish social justice there's little suggestion in the Jewish tradition that Abraham's appeal for the residents of Sodom is of consequential importance to the faith—nor does that appeal have much to do with social justice. The contention that this story is about social justice and somehow captures the meaning of Judaism and the mission of the Jewish People is totally untenable.

5

Joseph and the State

Back in the early years of the Obama administration, Jewish social justice groups across the country actively lobbied Congress to pass the bill colloquially known as Obamacare. "The time is long past to repair our broken system" of healthcare, they declared. No matter that—as many at the time warned—the proposals would fail to deliver on their promise and do little to "repair" the American health system but much to grow the burden of entitlements and intensify the public's dependence on government. Nor was it of much concern that the legislation was passed on strictly partisan lines. What did disappoint Jewish social justice activists instead was that there was no government-run public insurance option in the bill—let alone a greater involvement by the state in healthcare provision—and that there were more onerous restrictions on access to abortion than they would have liked. Nevertheless, for these groups, the passage of Obamacare was a "historic moment"—one for which they had campaigned hard in the name of tikkun olam.[1]

At that time, numerous Jewish activists presented rationales to justify their claim that Judaism endorsed their healthcare politics—rationales that still pertain. Among them were Sandra M. Fox and Martin I. Seltman. Fox is a licensed clinical social worker in private practice who chaired the Western Pennsylvania Coalition for Single-Payer Healthcare and was also chair of the Single-Payer Health Care Task Force of the Pittsburgh Interfaith Impact Network. Seltman is a doctor who was a member of Physicians for Social Responsibility, Physicians for a National Health Program, and the Western Pennsylvania Coalition for Single-Payer Healthcare. Together they penned a short essay for *Righteous Indignation* presenting the Jewish view (as they saw it) on American healthcare.[2]

Noting the statistics on uninsured and underinsured people in the United States, they lamented that "while some Americans continue to take pride in the U.S. health care system, believing it to be among the best in the world," the United States in fact not only had "a shameful record by international standards," but was also "doing abysmally by Jewish standards." Blaming the inflated prices of pharmaceuticals and the lack of regulation in the insurance industry for the high cost of healthcare, they observed that the drug and insurance companies themselves—and their executives—were doing very well. Confronted with this situation, they explained that "as Jews" they could not stand by and do nothing. And so they asked the multi-trillion dollar question: What sort of system can ensure the health of all Americans without putting the nation in financial jeopardy? Their answer: single-payer universal healthcare.

They were hardly the only activists making this argument.

Jill Jacobs, an influential Conservative rabbi and leading Jewish social justice writer and activist, also declared that "the first step in creating a new American health care system should involve restoring community—in this case, government—control over the system."[3] (How sad, incidentally, that Jewish social justice activists, whose work is conducted through the sort of civic and religious groups that make up civil society, are so often unable or unwilling to differentiate between "community" and "government.") Since 1975, Reform Judaism too has pushed for a "single-payer approach to national health care," which it views "as the most likely means of fulfilling the principles" of health-care reform long articulated by the movement.[4]

Fox and Seltman presented a number of traditional Jewish texts to substantiate their claim that Judaism supports the introduction of single-payer healthcare in contemporary America:

Is there a "Jewish position" on health care reform? Most of us can recite in our sleep the biblical commandment, "You shall not stand idly by the blood of your neighbor" (Lev. 19:16). What about our neighbor who is sick, but not yet bleeding? What about when the bleeding person is not a neighbor, but someone in a different town or state, of a different race or class background?

The Torah teaches that if a dead body is found abandoned in a field, the elders of the nearest town must prepare and bury the body, make a sacrifice, and pronounce a formula absolving them of any guilt. "Our hands did not shed this blood, nor did our eyes see it done" [Deut. 21:7]. The Rabbis [of the Talmud] rightly ask: Why must the elders make such a declaration, when no one would have suspected them of committing the crime in the first place? The rabbis explain that the elders need not proclaim that they are innocent of murder, but rather that they are innocent of ignoring a person at risk and in need. "He came not into our hands that we should have dismissed him without sustenance, and we did not see him and leave him without escort!" The town elders must swear that there was nothing they could have done to prevent this death. The implication is that if the elders had known about the danger, they would have been obligated to step in and prevent harm. The dead person could be a local or a foreigner, Jewish or non-Jewish, but unless we intervene, we are guilty.

For good measure, they add the famous biblical injunction: "'Remember the stranger, for you were once strangers in the land of Egypt.' Our tradition simply will not let us rest whilst illness threatens the lives of the most vulnerable among us." What are we to make of the contention that these biblical verses and passage endorse single-payer healthcare in the contemporary United States?

Plainly, this is gibberish. Both Leviticus 19:16 and Deuteronomy 21 are chiefly concerned with deaths by murder, wild beasts, and drowning, not with the establishment of a system of preemptive medicine—which in any case wouldn't prevent any of the deaths these verses are contemplating. As it happens, the authors seem to have second thoughts about having raised Deuteronomy 21 at all, advising that, in contrast to the elders and their sacrifice, "no ritual can absolve us to work toward a transformation of the U.S. health care system," a statement that rather undermines the entire analogy. But even if one were to accept that these verses mandate a concern for the medical wellbeing of one's fellow (which is already a stretch), why that concern needs to take the form of single-payer healthcare delivered by the federal government is never explained. As for the imperative to remember the stranger, why they bring it up in this context is anyone's guess.

There is, however, one additional biblical source that they cite that is especially interesting. This isn't because it actually endorses their take on American healthcare—it doesn't. But it is an illuminating insight into the Jewish social justice conception of government. The source is the story of Joseph in Egypt. Fox and Seltman write:

> In the book of Genesis, Joseph is thrown by his brothers into a pit, and then, transported to Egypt, he gets thrown into prison. There, Joseph transforms himself from self-centered adolescent to morally responsible adult. He *notices* and *asks* two of the prisoners why they appear sad, (Gen. 40:6, 7) signs that his own suffering has taught him empathy and compassion. He learns to listen to the dreams of others, not just his own. His compassion and wisdom save his life, when he is able to interpret Pharaoh's dreams. Ultimately, his careful listening, diagnosis, and responsible planning save the lives of countless Egyptians and his own estranged Israelite family during a grave famine.

The thesis here is that the juvenile Joseph thinks only of himself (like conservatives!), but following his own experience of suffering he becomes more empathetic and compassionate (liberal!) and this new "wisdom" not only saves his life but enables him to save the lives of untold numbers of Egyptians and his own family from famine. (In some societies, this sort of subtle insult is called a microaggression. But rather than take offense, shut down the debate, and track down the authors and set fire to their automobiles—which seems to be the response of "empathetic and compassionate" students on today's campuses—let's credit them for having a sense of humor and actually engage with what they're saying.) What interests us is the idea that Joseph's "responsible planning" is something that should be emulated—especially, Fox and Seltman conclude, in social justice efforts toward "a transformation of the U.S. health care system, so that it can truly serve the health of all, leaving no one behind."

The story of Joseph isn't just about healthcare. It's about the potential of an expanded role of government in our economy and society—a sentiment inherited from the Social Gospel. Jewish social justice activists are deeply inspired by Joseph. As Jill Jacobs observes, the story of Joseph is among the most frequently cited of the biblical "precedents" that "offer the seeds of a vision for a just world." This is because

> Joseph establishes a system for storing and rationing food so that the Egyptians will not starve to death during a time of famine. His example offers a lesson in using political authority to protect the lives of all members of society.[5]

Joseph's forecast of an immense famine and his establishment of a comprehensive and centralized system of food rationing to save the country and his family may indeed appear to represent a prime biblical example of the use of the power of the state to accomplish a daunting but necessary task for the common good. To the Jewish social justice movement, not only are Joseph's policies in Egypt a model for how the central planning of government can be used effectively to better the lives of ordinary

Americans, but they are also a strong indication of Judaism's endorsement of this "big government" approach.

This interpretation of the story, however, is utterly and dangerously wrong.

Let's remind ourselves of Joseph's biography in a little more detail. As the first son of Rachel, Jacob's favored wife, Joseph is his favorite son, and the patriarch's unabashed favoritism earns Joseph the ire of his brothers (Gen. 37). Joseph also has pretensions to fraternal leadership, dreaming of his parents' and brothers' prostration before him.[6] Eventually, Joseph's brothers become fed up with him and facilitate his sale into servitude in Egypt. In his new master's house Joseph is successful, but after refusing the sexual advances of his master's wife, he finds himself in prison. Sometime after accurately deciphering the dreams of two fellow inmates, he is released to interpret Pharaoh's dreams and warns the king that seven impending years of agricultural plenty in Egypt will be followed by seven years of famine. Accepting Joseph's premonition and impressed by his abilities, Pharaoh elevates Joseph to the position of viceroy, charging him to prepare for the years of scarcity by collecting grain from the people of Egypt during the years of plenty, in accordance with Joseph's prescription. Joseph dutifully does so, and redistributes the grain to the populace in the country's period of need.

But whereas the Jewish social justice movement sees Joseph's economic policies as a successful and inspirational use of central government, the real lesson of the story seems to be very different. In fact, it actually appears to present the very same warning that is repeated by opponents of "big government" in the United States today: state intervention creates dependency—and worse. How so?

Let's assume, as most people reasonably do, that the famine that Joseph forecasts was indeed to occur as he predicted.[7] Having hoarded grain by appropriating surplus from the Egyptian people during the years of plenty, it's commonly assumed that Joseph goes on to redistribute it to the people freely during the years of famine. Thus the country is saved from starvation. This is the way the story is often read, including by those who cite it as biblical evidence of social justice. But if you read the text more attentively, you realize that this isn't what happened.

Apparently not one to let a crisis go to waste, Joseph the viceroy takes the opportunity of the famine to enslave the Egyptian people to Pharaoh. Instead of returning the grain to the people during the years of scarcity, he *sells* it to them. First, the Egyptians expend all of their money for it, and then they exchange all of their cattle for it, and finally they offer their land and their very bodies to Pharaoh in return for sustenance (Gen. 47:13–26). Joseph readily accepts their proposition. And to establish beyond doubt that Pharaoh now owns the Egyptians and their land, Joseph conducts a mass population transfer of Egyptians across the country—a strategy used by authoritarian governments in more recent times as well.[8] Thus grain that Joseph had forcibly seized from the people of Egypt during the years of plenty was now returned to them in exchange for their servitude. This is the consequence of depending upon the government, the Bible seems to say. Joseph proclaims to the people: "Behold, I have bought you this day and your land for Pharaoh." And in response the people practically thank him for saving them, gratefully declaring themselves "slaves unto Pharaoh" (Gen. 47:23, 25). They have all but raced down the proverbial road to serfdom.

Joseph doesn't sustain only Egypt. He also feeds his estranged family, which descends to Egypt from Canaan having heard there is food there. Joseph welcomes his brothers to Egypt and grants them privileged access to grain. But they too become captive to Pharaoh. It seems that they're only able to leave Egypt to bury their late father, Jacob, in the Land of Canaan with Pharaoh's permission—the king sends with them a military escort and effectively holds their families and cattle hostage in Egypt to ensure their return (Gen. 50:7–9).[9] (This tactic becomes familiar when it forms the basis of offers the later biblical Pharaoh makes to Moses, when he tries to deliver the Israelites out of Egypt. Moses, however, recognizes such offers for what they are and rejects them.) And so, Joseph's family remains in Egypt long after the famine, as Joseph insists that he'll provide for everyone (Gen. 50:20–21). Dependency sets in. And, having become all but nominally enslaved, infamously the Israelites are also eventually forced into actual bondage themselves in Egypt.

By the way, Joseph himself is enslaved too—even unwittingly—as he's bidden entirely to Pharaoh. The first among slaves, Joseph is powerful—but he's enslaved nonetheless. And he may also have inadvertently brought about the eventual enslavement of his own people as well.[10] (It should be added that this doesn't necessarily mean that Joseph is to *blame* for the fate of the Israelites; for one thing, it may equally have been his brothers' earlier facilitation of Joseph's sale into slavery that set in motion this series of events. Either way, the plight and bondage of the Israelites had been prophesied by God earlier still in the Bible, and appears throughout Genesis to have been a part of His redemptive plan [Gen. 15:13].)

This assessment hardly presents Joseph's endeavors in Egypt in the most positive light. You might raise an objection to this treatment by recalling that Joseph is sometimes described by classical Jewish commentators as a *tzaddik* ("righteous man"), which could be taken to affirm the policies that he enacts. However, this accolade is due to other events in Joseph's life, in particular his refusal of the sexual advances of his master's wife during his first years in Egypt, and not to his political activity and economic policies.[11] In any case, we're not really interested in casting blame around. The point we're making is instead to simply show that a passage cited by Jewish social justice activists to teach the supposedly unmitigated benefits of giving the government enormous economic power in fact, when read properly, actually seems to warn precisely against such centralized power.

In view of what the Bible actually says, then, if this story indeed offers "the seeds of a vision for a just world," as Jacobs proposes, then that "just world" truly is a frightening one. It is so astonishing that anyone could point to this narrative and claim it "offers a lesson in using political authority to protect the lives of all members of society," that you just have to assume they've misread it. Not only is the "lesson" of the Joseph story not what these activists wish it were, but, remarkably, its real lesson seems to be the very opposite: reliance on government leads to dependency, and dependency can lead to much worse. To use this story as an argument *in favor* of expanding entitlements in today's America is breathtaking.

Few would disagree with Fox and Seltman that healthcare in the United States needs reform—but just because people may disagree with their prescription doesn't make such people selfish or uncaring, and it certainly doesn't make them ignorant of the Bible. Fox and Seltman may be right to assess Joseph's scheme as "leaving no one behind," but read in context that's no good thing. In his zeal to execute his plan and ensure the short-term wellbeing of the Egyptian people as he saw it, Joseph wrought long-term catastrophe. The Jewish social justice movement ought to take that insight a lot more seriously.

Interestingly, this point is not entirely lost on all Jewish activists. Micha Odenheimer, an Orthodox rabbi from Los Angeles now based in Israel, does notice and criticize the enslavement of the Egyptian people and the "centralization of power and resources in the hands of Pharaoh" that Joseph brings about.[12] But for him, the "juxtaposition of slavery and accumulation" in this story and the association of "the concentration of capital . . . with oppression and poverty" convey a different lesson. To wit, "faithful Jews" should combat "the accumulation of wealth by multinational corporations." In Odenheimer's telling, the system of capitalist globalization itself is recast as the "Pharaoh" that is oppressing and enslaving the world's poor.

How malleable are Thy works! Jewish social justice activists are somehow able to celebrate Joseph's concentration of power at the same time as they critique his accumulation of resources. The difference is that the concentration of power is apparently fine when government is the beneficiary, but not when it is private enterprise and business. Okay, you respond, that's just their politics—they're left-wing and they think government uses power to benefit everyone while corporations abuse power to enrich only their executives and shareholders. What's wrong with that? What's wrong with it is this: whether or not the story of Joseph is about the accumulation of resources *in general* is debatable, but what's not debatable is that it is expressly dealing with the concentration of power specifically in the hands of *government*. Yet that is precisely the scenario that these activists are inverting to their advantage. Odenheimer has at least understood what's happening in the story and tried to generalize it for his political purposes. Fox, Seltman, and Jacobs have either not understood what is happening and consequently reached a dangerous conclusion—or they've deliberately misconstrued the story.

The story of Joseph's efforts in Egypt to alleviate the effects of famine does not represent an endorsement of extensive government involvement in the provision of important services today, contrary to what the Jewish social justice movement wants you to believe. Although Joseph does indeed save Egypt from famine, whether this required an unprecedented expansion of the authority of central government is unclear. But what is clear is that this expansion had grave consequences—and exactly those feared by opponents of such expansion in the contemporary United States. To suggest that the story of Joseph's activities in Egypt is somehow a "precedent" for positive governmental activism is therefore founded on a dangerously mistaken reading of the Bible.

Exodus and Revolution

On the third day of the Jewish spring festival of Passover in 1969, 800 people—half of them Jews and the other half African-American and White Christians—sat down for a Seder. Traditionally, the Seder night—a ceremonial dinner of songs, props, and visual aids accompanied by the recitation of various biblical and rabbinic passages recounting the Israelite Exodus from Egypt—is held on the first night of Passover and, outside of Israel, also on the second night. But this Seder (a word that means "order" in Hebrew) was hardly traditional. This gathering dispensed with the traditional Haggadah—the collection of readings and rituals for the meal. In its place, they read a new volume called *The Freedom Seder: A New Haggadah for Passover*. That night was different from all other nights—and *The Freedom Seder* was certainly different from all other Haggadahs.

The idea for *The Freedom Seder* came to its author, Arthur

Waskow, a year earlier, he says. It was a few days after Reverend Martin Luther King Jr. had been killed on April 4, 1968. Riots had broken out in cities across America, prompting the deployment of the military—including in Washington, DC. Waskow was walking home for Passover and observed the armaments on his block. "This is Pharaoh's army!" he thought to himself. He wrote *The Freedom Seder*—borrowing some traditional readings and mixing them with paeans to the labor movement and references to various "liberation struggles," ranging from the more militant elements of the Civil Rights Movement to the vicious campaign of the Vietcong.

Waskow himself—in his mid-thirties at the time—was a political agitator active in civil rights and protests against the Vietnam War. He earned a doctorate in history, focusing on the Chicago Race Riot of 1919, and worked as a Democratic congressional aide. In 1963, he co-founded the Institute for Policy Studies, a radical institution long suspected of harboring pro-Communist sympathies, if not of acting as a proper Soviet propagandist. Waskow participated in numerous sit-ins and protests during the 1960s, was an alternate delegate to the disastrous 1968 Democratic Party Convention, and promoted resistance to the draft and even to taxation as long as the United States remained involved in Vietnam. He was a contributing editor at the leftist magazine *Ramparts*, the outlet that published *The Freedom Seder*.

Like Michael Lerner, Waskow turned to religion primarily as a vehicle for his existing leftist politics. *The Freedom Seder* is a perfect example but hardly the only one. Waskow went on to become involved in the Havurah movement in the 1970s, helped found Jewish Renewal and several of its organs, participated in the anti-Israel group Breira, and was a central figure in radical

1980s associations such as New Jewish Agenda. In 1983, he also founded the Jewish social justice organization, The Shalom Center, "a prophetic voice in Jewish, multireligious, and American life," which was originally geared toward opposition to nuclear weapons. Also in the 1980s, he served on the faculty of the Reconstructionist Rabbinical College, and in 1995 he finally received some form of rabbinical ordination himself. He has been honored by various liberal Jewish institutions, including the *Forward* newspaper, the Reconstructionists, and T'ruah. He has also been listed by *Newsweek* as one of the fifty most influential rabbis in America. His numerous books and activism attest to the shifting focus of his political ire over the decades from race to the Vietnam War to nuclear weapons to climate change.

Truly, Waskow's influence has been widely felt. One of his greatest contributions to the Jewish social justice movement has been the appropriation of Jewish festivals to advance political causes. *The Freedom Seder* represented the first major foray into this area, but as Waskow's interests shifted, so did those appropriations. In the 1980s, New Jewish Agenda recast the Ninth of Av, the most solemn day in the Jewish calendar, which commemorates the destruction of the two ancient Temples in Jerusalem, as a memorial to the dropping of the atomic bomb on Nagasaki. The group also reconceived the ritual booth of the festival of Tabernacles (or Sukkot) to promote disarmament across the street from the White House.[1] Then, when Waskow became more interested in the environment, so did his festivals. In 1998, for example, he reimagined the ritualistic beating of willow branches on the festival of Hoshanah Rabbah as a protest against General Electric's environmental practices.[2] Today, this sort of thing has become routine in the social justice

Judaism of the Reform, Conservative, Reconstructionist, and Renewal denominations. But it is Passover—and especially the Seder night—that has proven most popular in—and most useful to—the Jewish social justice movement. And that's thanks to Waskow and *The Freedom Seder*.

In 1968, Reverend King was due to join the famed Jewish theologian Abraham Joshua Heschel for the Seder night ten days following his murder. When Passover came that year, Waskow conceived of *The Freedom Seder*, and it was held the next year in the basement of Lincoln Temple, an African-American church in Washington, DC, in an event sponsored by a group called Jews for Urban Justice (a group active in the nation's capital in the late 1960s) and broadcast on the radio. *The Freedom Seder* wasn't just for the Jews, nor was it much of a commemoration of the Jewish Exodus from Egypt. Instead, it was meant to be a Haggadah for everyone. "This Haggadah," Waskow explained, "is deeply Jewish, but not only Jewish." In fact, however, the tasteless composition was barely Jewish at all.

"In our world," Waskow tells us in his Haggadah, no doubt with the American military in mind, "we all live under Pharaohs who could exterminate us any moment, and so enslave us all the time." As this was a Haggadah for everyone, *The Freedom Seder* couldn't be about the Jews—it had to reimagine the Exodus as a timeless and universal tale of "liberation." The liberation of workers, women, blacks, the third world—you name it. In brief, Waskow's version of the Exodus saw the Israelites redeemed from slavery because Moses recognized the employment abuses of the "boss," Pharaoh, and sought to do something about it. Initially, Moses encountered opposition from the Israelites themselves, since "slaves do not always welcome their deliverers." Rather, Waskow laments, invoking another

Marxist sentiment, "they get accustomed to being slaves." But eventually Moses became a proto-union leader, organized his people, and, singing "Solidarity Forever," led them to freedom.

In Waskow's telling, Moses is a militant trade unionist and God plays practically no role at all—He's nothing more than a figure of speech. Waskow writes:

> the work was [the Israelites'] own; the profound Conversation between the Lord our God, blessed be He, and the people of Israel was the conversation between the Promise and the Work, the Vision and the Creation; freedom, justice, sustenance, and law were all made real by their own hands.

Within the context of Jewish social justice, this makes total sense. You'll recall how the Social Gospel taught that social justice must be brought about by man. Waskow took the same approach—social justice has to be made real by our own hands.

As far as the Jews are concerned, Waskow conceives of their role in the world rather like the Classical Reformers did. The Jews have a mission to set an example for others and to bring to them ethics and justice as part of a universal religion. Waskow writes that God "hast commanded us [the Jews], even against our will to become a beacon for justice and freedom for them all." Jewish election (or chosenness) is not discussed, and neither are the covenant or the Jews' special relationship with God. Echoing the "universal religion" of Classical Reform, Waskow's Exodus teaches that being religious means "to build brotherhood in freedom—because that is what men, the children of God, were created to do!"

Some parts of The Freedom Seder are amusing, reflecting the

political hysteria and lack of any sense of proportion that typically accompany leftist radicalism. "We must end the genocide," Waskow urges, referring to Vietnam, while advising in a footnote, in recognition that the war in Vietnam would not last forever, the following: "Insert any genocide that is current . . . depending on the situation." In other words, whenever you live, if you haven't discovered genocide somewhere, then you're just not looking hard enough. The critic Robert Alter observes another example of this lack of perspective, writing of Waskow's *Freedom Seder*: "We are asked, apparently, to see a complete identity between the literal enslavement and mass infanticide reported in the biblical story, and the sundry institutional ills and inequities of contemporary America."[3]

Other parts of this Haggadah are more pathetic. The traditional Jewish Seder includes a song, "Dayeinu," in which participants thank God for the abundant goodness that He bestowed upon their Jewish ancestors during the Exodus by exclaiming that each beneficent act alone would have sufficed and yet God did more and more for them. Waskow, however, adds his own version of the song. His new rendition replaces God with "we" (naturally), and grateful praise with *dissatisfaction*, as each enumerated accomplishment "would not be sufficient." With oppression apparently so rampant and no gratitude shown for the blessings that we do enjoy, inevitably ever more desperate revolutions are necessary. "We and our children speak of the departure from Egypt because we and they know that in their generation too it will be necessary to seek liberation," Waskow says. He goes on to warn ominously that "the struggle may not be bloodless during the next generation."

Since *The Freedom Seder*, Arthur Waskow has remained in the Haggadah trade—co-opting the Seder for a variety of other political causes. In 1984 he composed *The Rainbow Seder*, which focused on nuclear disarmament and environmental concerns,[4] and in 2004 he produced yet another Haggadah calling for freedom from the "new Pharaohs" of big oil and environmental degradation. But he no longer has a monopoly on the market. *The Freedom Seder* inspired a veritable industry of Jewish social justice Haggadahs by other authors, each devoted to a specific element of the tikkun olam agenda, including feminism, homosexuality, outmarriage (where a Jew weds a non-Jew), interfaith, the Arab-Israeli conflict, solidarity with Latin-American dissidents, ecology, and vegetarianism. Some Haggadahs try to incorporate several elements of the agenda. The Jewish Social Justice Network's "Passover Social Justice Resources," for example, was published in 2003 to provide "alternative readings for the Passover Seder." Over ten Jewish social justice organizations contributed readings to this pamphlet on themes including the rights of undocumented immigrants, labor abuses, same-sex marriage, and disobedience, protest, and rebellion.[5] In 2017, the social justice organization American Jewish World Service published the second edition of its "Next Year in a Just World" Haggadah to proselytize on refugees, malnutrition, poverty, sexist violence, and persecution of minorities.[6] This is the context of the Passover Seders of the Obama White House, where the president introduced the reading of the Emancipation Proclamation.

The unifying feature of all these attempts to change the Haggadah's focus is, as the author and radio host Michael Medved has observed, "the grim tone that often creeps in . . . [which] brings a distinctly sour note to a holiday generally perceived as joyous and . . . almost euphoric."[7] Or, as Robert Alter has put it, the "sweeping of all real and suspected grievances onto the Seder plate [has] the effect of converting the Season of Our Rejoicing into a feast of resentment."[8] These Jewish social justice Seders serve as occasions to bemoan the state of the world from liberal and radical political perspectives—rather than to celebrate the divine redemption of the Israelites. Everything, it seems, is worthy of discussion on the Seder night except the actual Exodus and what it has traditionally meant to the Jewish People.

That traditional meaning is the divine rescue of the Israelites from bondage in Egypt, and the Revelation of the Torah and the covenant struck between God and the Jewish People at Mount Sinai, beginning the tale that sees the Israelites return to and inherit the Land of Israel—as God had pledged to the patriarchs. Genesis may contain the promises God makes to Abraham, Isaac, and Jacob, but Exodus—the second of the five books of Moses—is the start of the fulfilment of those promises. As the pivotal story of the Hebrew Bible, the Exodus is remembered by observant Jews daily in their prayers and, in a wider sense, in all the religious laws they observe as part of the covenant between the Jewish People and God established at Sinai— in particular the rituals of Passover, such as the Seder night.

Since the Exodus is so important to Judaism, it makes sense that Jewish social justice activists should wish to find some relevant meaning in it.[9] What they are looking for above all is the revolutionary fervor of Judaism. You'll recall that the Social Gospel, the religious Christian movement for social justice a century ago, had a subversive impulse—it sought a new Reformation to create a Kingdom of God that contained the *revolutionary* force of Christianity. Campaigners for Jewish social justice today believe that Judaism has its own revolutionary force—a force that compels fundamental alterations to our economy and society. They think that it's in the Israelite

Exodus from Egypt that this revolutionary force can be found.

To see how, we have to explore a book published in 1985 that's very popular in Jewish activist circles, titled *Exodus and Revolution*.[10] The book's author is Michael Walzer, a political philosopher and longtime co-editor of the socialist magazine *Dissent* (now edited by a former member of the terrorist Weathermen faction). Known in academic circles as a proponent of communitarian theory, Walzer has taken an interest in the political questions posed by immigration, minorities, and toleration, and has also written on just war theory and, most pertinent to our investigation, the Bible.

To establish the connection between Exodus and the idea of revolution, Walzer explores how themes from the Exodus have been adopted by revolutionary factions and partisans throughout the ages. These partisans included African-Americans campaigning for civil rights, parliamentarians in the English Civil War, French revolutionaries, Marxists, Boers, black anti-apartheid South Africans, Latin American preachers of Liberation Theology, leaders of the German Peasants' Revolt, Protestant Reformers, and, of course, the Founding Fathers of the United States.

Walzer is ostensibly interested in these appropriations of the story because he wants "to discover [the Exodus's] meaning in what it has meant." That's a subtle way of saying that he wants to take the partisan meanings *attributed* to the text of the Exodus by these historic fighters and to *superimpose* those meanings upon the biblical narrative. The effect is to make their revolutionary agendas part of the text's original meaning and purpose. "Revolution," Walzer writes, "has often been imagined as an enactment of the Exodus and the Exodus has often been imagined as a program for revolution." Therefore the biblical text itself can be "plausibly understood in political terms, as a liberation and a revolution . . . a paradigm of revolutionary politics."

Walzer isn't alone in conceptualizing the Exodus as a political revolution. Leading Conservative rabbi Elliot Dorff writes that "the Exodus from Egypt . . . articulates powerfully the need to redeem people from their various forms of slavery . . . so that they can reshape their lives."[11] And Michael Lerner also draws from the Exodus a "revolutionary message."[12] Since everyone agrees that the Exodus is Judaism's central event, if the Exodus is a model of revolution then it follows that Judaism must be a revolutionary faith.

Seeing the Exodus as a general how-to guide for political revolution requires some creative license, however. The particular elements of the story—those parts of it that are specifically about the Jewish People—must be downplayed. Egypt, for example, cannot be merely the place where the Israelites were enslaved, nor can the Promised Land be simply the Land of Israel. In the Jewish social justice interpretation of the Exodus, "Egypt" and the "Promised Land" become metaphors—one for the condition of every oppressed people and the other for their liberation. The Exodus is thus transformed from a particular story about the Jews to a universal template for political revolt. Walzer develops this idea most clearly. He disconnects the slavery, redemption, and Promised Land of the Bible from their Jewish uniqueness and portrays them instead as the generic chronological components—beginning/problem, middle/struggle, and end/resolution—of any revolution.

The "problem" is identified by Walzer not as the particular oppression visited by Pharaoh upon the Israelites that happens to take the form of slavery, but rather as the universal wrongs of slavery and injustice. The oppression of the Israelites is interesting to him only to the extent that it's illustrative of the persecutions of minorities at all times and places. Thus in the "beginning," the significance of the Israelites in the Exodus is diminished.

In the "middle" or "struggle" component of the story, Walzer manages, like Waskow, to exorcise God as well. Walzer views the Exodus as "a realistic account, in which miracles play a part but which is not itself miraculous" (whatever that means). This is despite the plain reading of the Bible, which clearly portrays God as the agent of the Israelite redemption from bondage. After all, not only is it God who directs Moses to perform miracles on His behalf, but in fact the message that the miracles broadcasted to Egypt and the world about their false gods is a crucial part of the story's meaning. Yet Walzer understands this "struggle" phase of the revolutionary process as the part when the people—without divine help—rebel against the oppressive authority. For him, the story isn't about God's redemption of the Israelites at all. Instead, it's about a straightforward maturation of the Israelites as they learn that they "could become free only insofar as they accepted the discipline of freedom, the obligation to live up to a common standard, and to take responsibility for their own actions." No Torah. No laws. No covenant. For the freed Israelites, the goal of their "struggle" is apparently to establish some form of godless communitarianism. Without the divine intervention that characterizes the Exodus (and Scripture more generally), the redemptive responsibility falls entirely to man. As with the Social Gospel, injustice must be combatted without any expectation of heavenly assistance.

The "resolution" of the Exodus is also recast by Walzer to

exclude the fulfilment of the divine covenant with the Israelites. In the Bible, the Exodus leads to the Israelite entry into the
Promised Land—so called because God pledged that territory
to the patriarchs in Genesis—and ultimately to the construction
of the Temple in Jerusalem some generations later. But Walzer
depicts the "resolution" part of the Exodus "revolution" differ-
ently. He contends that since the Israelites never fully observe
the laws of the covenant, they fall short of the ideal. In a sense,
they never completely possess the land—it "still remains a
promised land." Not only do the Israelites fall short of fully in-
heriting the Promised Land by their sinful behavior, but their
conduct, he argues, actually transforms that land into yet another Egypt—complete with its own oppression. Consequently,
yet another revolution is required. Walzer's Exodus ends back
where it started.

For Walzer, if there is a Promised Land to be reached, it isn't
literal but figurative. He sees the Promised Land not as a territory to be possessed but as an ethical condition to be realized.
The achievement of the Promised Land "is not a matter of where
we plant our feet," he writes, "but of how we cultivate our spir-
its." This way, the biblical Exodus can be reconciled with, for
example, Latin American Liberation Theology, whose preachers "describe the Promised Land as a society free at last from
'exploitation.'"

The same formula is evident throughout the Jewish social
justice Haggadahs as well, which routinely replace the traditional declaration of "next year in Jerusalem" with "next year
in a world of justice and peace." In *The Freedom Seder*, Waskow
writes that what it means "to get out of Egypt and into Canaan"
is the process of building brotherhood. And although he concedes that "the tradition says . . . this year we celebrate here, but

the next year we hope to celebrate in the land of Israel," he immediately corrects himself, adding, "as another tradition says, '*Ubi libertas, ibi patria*'—where there is liberty, that is my country. That is my Israel." Like Walzer, Waskow jettisons the particular Jewish relationship to the actual Land of Israel. Whereas "this year, all mankind eat as aliens in a land not wholly theirs, next year we hope all mankind will celebrate in 'the land of Israel'—that is, in a world made one and a world made free." In other words: "Liberation Now! Next year in a world of freedom." Another tradition indeed.

It's interesting to note that the transformation of the Promised Land and specifically of its capital, Jerusalem, to a spiritual condition is not a Jewish concept but a Christian innovation that goes back to St. Augustine. Meanwhile, downplaying the territorial aspect of Scripture also enables Walzer et al. to sidestep the apparent biblical mandate to rid the Promised Land of its Canaanite inhabitants, the implications of which rather complicate the Jewish social justice view of the Exodus.

In any event, although Walzer reconceives the Promised Land as an ethical condition to be realized, he's skeptical that that condition can actually ever be truly fulfilled. Thus, in a telling passage at the end of his book, he captures the Jewish social justice movement's take on the Exodus story:

So Pharaonic oppression, deliverance, Sinai, and Canaan are still with us, powerful memories shaping our perceptions of the political world. The "door of hope" is still open; things are not what they might be—even when what they might be isn't totally different from what they are. This is a central theme in Western thought, always present though elaborated in many different ways. We still believe, or many of us do, what the Exodus first taught, or what it has commonly been taken to teach, about the meaning and possibility of politics and about its proper form:

- first, that wherever you live, it is probably Egypt;
- second, that there is a better place, a world more attractive, a promised land;
- and third, that "the way to the land is through the wilderness." There is no way to get from here to there except by joining together and marching.

All this—as you might have noticed—is a radical departure from the text. It's also totally foreign to the traditional Jewish understanding of the Exodus, which is actually more modest and certainly more specific.

In the first place, the traditional reading is primarily concerned not with slavery in the abstract but with the specific slaves in particular. God hears the Israelites' cries not merely because they are an enslaved people per se, but because they are *Israelites*— His chosen People. The fact that their cries are due to their *enslavement* is, in an important sense, secondary. After all, the Bible is not in principle averse to slavery, so reading the Exodus as a condemnation of that practice is undermined by later biblical passages. As the Bible scholar Jon D. Levenson has written:

In modern times, the tendency is to see the Exodus from Egypt as rooted in God's principled opposition to slavery. In point of fact, however, there is no such opposition in the Hebrew Bible . . . and the motivation for the Exodus actually lies in the special relationship of Israel to God.[13]

Jewish social justice activists try to reframe the Exodus as a polemic against slavery and oppression in general in order to maximize its relevance to their political agenda. But in doing so, they sabotage the story's particularly Jewish character—which has always been the emphasis of traditional Jewish thought.

It follows that the role of God as the Redeemer is also fundamental to the biblical narrative. The fulfilment of God's promises to the patriarchs and the Revelation of the Torah at Sinai to their progeny are ordinarily recognized as the purpose of the Exodus. It's often quoted that Moses pleaded to Pharaoh to "Let My People go"—but that's only half the quotation. Moses demanded that the Egyptian king release God's chosen People in order "that they may serve Me." Indeed the Israelites are even described later in the Bible as "slaves" (or "servants") to God (Ex. 8:16 and Lev. 25:42). The Jewish social justice movement seeks to marginalize God in order to claim that the redemptive responsibility to achieve social justice falls to man—just as the Social Gospellers preached a hundred years ago. But to diminish the role of God in Scripture is a perversion of the story.

The other advantage of minimizing God's part in the Exodus for Jewish social justice campaigners is that the more of God that you see, the more you're reminded that the story's message is the fulfilment of His promises to the patriarchs and the Revelation of the Torah at Sinai. These are very Jewish things. The more they're emphasized, the less relevant the Exodus becomes as a universal model for revolution everywhere. The covenant at Sinai and the concrete laws of the Torah have to be transformed into abstract principles and empty platitudes such as "freedom," "a common standard," and "responsibility"— and to do this, you need to get rid of God. In the process, the

Jewish social justice movement has missed the very thing the Exodus, and indeed the Hebrew Bible, is actually about—the particular relationship between God and the Jewish People.

As for the Promised Land, in the Bible it's no metaphor. It's a *real* territory that has been known as the Land of Israel for millennia. Walzer may be right to observe that the Israelites fail fully to live up to the covenant once they arrive and settle there. But in the Bible the punishment for their disobedience is foreign occupation or exile—always followed by a redemptive victory and return to *the same actual land*. To disavow that—as Walzer does—means subverting also the particular relationship of the Jewish People to the Land of Israel.

In substituting the biblical Promised Land for an unrealizable ethical condition, Walzer reaches a conclusion with confusing—and worrying—implications by any reckoning. To assume that our society is *probably* Egypt—its virtues be damned—encourages gross ingratitude for the blessings that we do receive. You'll recall Waskow's version of "Dayeinu," which replaced grateful praise with expressions of *dissatisfaction*. Is that really what we want Jewish and American children to be taught?

And by the way, a society perpetually searching for oppression, even where it might not exist (again, recall Waskow's "insert genocide here" footnote), is actually quite likely to miss it where it does. Just witness what's going on at colleges around the country, where students are forcing out professors for the most insignificant supposed transgressions while doing nothing to stop Jewish students being served mock eviction notices on the basis of their ethnicity.[14]

The mentality Walzer is encouraging, moreover, generates restlessness for constant—and probably ill-considered—political change. It distorts the linearity of the biblical Exodus into a cyclical process of iterated, or permanent, revolution that never achieves its goals.[15] If this is what the Jewish social justice movement believes the Bible is really about, then no wonder Michael Lerner thinks the Marxists were plagiarizing Scripture.

There is a dear price to be paid by the Jewish People for this reading of the Exodus. In their desperation to universalize the story, Jewish social justice activists have expunged everything about it that is particular to the Jews. The cause of the Jews' redemption from Egypt is not their special election but their generic misery. Their covenant with God is replaced with ethical and political platitudes. And their deep connection to the Land of Israel is interpreted out of existence.

It's one thing to observe proudly how imagery from the Exodus has inspired non-Jewish peoples struggling for a better future. But it's quite another, from the point of view of traditional Judaism, to suggest that those appropriations of the story are somehow its essential meaning—or to suggest that the text somehow commands such revolutions. Whatever the Jewish social justice movement tries to claim, this is simply not the traditional Jewish understanding of the Exodus—nor, frankly, is it the simple meaning of the text. By focusing so much on the appropriations of the story by gentile revolutionaries rather than on its traditional or even plain meaning, Walzer is reading the Exodus like a non-Jew. In advancing a left-wing revolutionary agenda by seeking to discover the Exodus's "meaning in what it has meant," Walzer and his cohort have managed to celebrate every meaning of the Exodus but the Jewish one.

The Prophetic Legacy

On September 17, 2011, a protest began in Zuccotti Park in New York City's Financial District that called itself Occupy Wall Street. This protest, which lasted two months and inspired concurrent simulations across the United States and in cities abroad, was concerned with perceived social and economic inequality and greed of the corporate and financial sectors. Billing themselves "the 99 percent," these anarchic demonstrators bewailed the allegedly exploitative practices of the richest one percent of the population. Adopting as their logo an image of a ballerina balancing atop the iconic Wall Street Charging Bull statue, the protestors called for action against the supposedly excessive wealth of the one percent and their nefarious political and financial influence. Along with its sister protests, Occupy Wall Street "would become marred with incidents of murder and suicide, sexual assault and rape, violence, drug use, theft, bullying, public defecation, indecent exposure, defacement of American flags, littering, and disease—even tuberculosis."[1] It was an archetypal protest of the radical left.

On the evening of Yom Kippur (the holy Jewish Day of Atonement) that year, hundreds of leftist Jews gathered in Zuccotti Park in solidarity with the protestors and held the evening Kol Nidre prayer service there. This would be followed a few days later by the erection of ritualistic tabernacles (tents or booths) for the festival of Sukkot, and then a celebration of Simchat Torah (when the annual cycle of Torah readings is completed), as well as Sabbath dinners and a prayer to mark the onset of the new Jewish month. (In fact, the tabernacles played a decisive role in sustaining the entire protest, as previously all tents had been removed by police, but the cops demurred from dismantling a "religious" tent and thus a precedent was set.) The appropriation of these Jewish festivals in aid of a radical—and antisemitic[2]—left-wing protest was the brainchild of none other than Arthur Waskow, but in conjunction with a younger Jewish social justice activist named Daniel Sieradski.

A writer, web designer, and activist, Sieradski is the founder of the liberal Jewish blog Jewschool, and was the national organizer of Jews for Bernie—in support of Senator Bernie Sanders' 2016 presidential campaign. Described as the "most prominent Jew" in Antifa, the violent left-wing faction, he has been hailed by various Jewish media outlets, including the liberal *Forward* newspaper, as a rising star in the community.[3] His most notable achievement was the launch, during the Occupy Wall Street protest, of Occupy Judaism. Although other Jewish social justice groups supported the demonstrators in Zuccotti

Park, including Waskow's Shalom Center, Jewish Funds for Justice/Progressive Jewish Alliance (the precursor organizations to Alexander Soros' Bend the Arc), and the Jewish Labor Committee, it was Occupy Judaism that took center stage among Jewish activists. Describing itself as "an occupation progressive Jews can get behind," the group's logo adapted that of Occupy Wall Street, replacing the ballerina balancing on the Wall Street Bull with the fiddler from the famous Jewish musical *Fiddler on the Roof.* (It was apparently lost on these Jewish anti-capitalists that the musical's most famous tune is called "If I Were a Rich Man," itself based, even more egregiously, on the Sholem Aleichem monologue, "If I Were a Rothschild.")

The purpose of Occupy Judaism was to inject Jewish social justice into Occupy Wall Street (and thereby also provide the protest with cover from accusations of antisemitism). This was evident, to take one example, in Occupy Judaism's most acclaimed feat: the Yom Kippur service. Traditionally, Jews spend the Day of Atonement in synagogue, abstaining from food and drink. In his defense of Jews who chose Zuccotti Park over a Jewish house of worship, Sieradski quoted from chapter 58 of Isaiah, one of the biblical readings in the liturgy of the day:

> Is it such a fast that I have chosen? A day for man to afflict his soul? Is it to bow down his head as a bulrush, and to spread sackcloth and ashes under him? Will you call this a fast, and an acceptable day to the Lord? Is not this the fast that I have chosen: To loosen the bands of wickedness, to undo the heavy burdens, and to let the oppressed go free, and that you break every yoke? Is it not to deal your bread to the hungry, and that you bring the poor that are cast out to your house? When you see the naked, that you cover him?

Sieradski deduced: "A real fast—a fast of Isaiah—is one in which you fast from your capitalist lifestyle and pour out love and compassion for your fellow man, putting people over profit." Sieradski understood Isaiah to be saying that showing ethical solidarity with the other social justice protestors was preferable to actually fasting and certainly to attending ritualistic services at a synagogue.[4] In a sense, this was a culmination of the vision of the Classical Reformers, who, also appealing to the prophets of the Bible, had called in their Pittsburgh Platform for a movement away from ritual and toward the search for a solution to the "contrasts and evils of the present organization of society."

Notwithstanding the shift in attitudes toward the Bible between the Classical Reformers and the tikkun olam movement of today, as we observed earlier the Prophets have remained consistently popular. The Reformers pointed to these texts as the apparent Scriptural basis for a universal religion of ethics that had no need for the antiquated rituals of the Jews. This new religion was more suited than traditional Judaism to the enlightened Germany of Kant and Wellhausen, who abhorred Jewish ritual, and to nineteenth-century America. The Jewish social justice movement, which has inherited this preference for ethics over ritual, still lauds the prophets as the greatest articulators of the essence of the Jewish faith. The movement's literature and activities are replete with references to prophetic figures—especially Isaiah, Jeremiah, Amos, and Micah. Two of them even have Jewish social justice fellowships bearing their name.[5]

The essence of Judaism that the prophets are thought to have uncovered and propagated is so indebted to them that it has become known as the "prophetic spirit" or "prophetic legacy." For Michael Lerner, the prophets were "attempting to bring back the people to the essence of the religion."[6] For Sidney Schwarz, "it was the prophets who interpreted what God wanted from the Jewish people" and "reminded the Jewish people of the Torah's core values."[7] Schwarz declares in no uncertain terms that the "prophetic legacy is why the Jewish people were put on this earth."[8] The prophetic legacy—the essence of Judaism—is a universal religion of ethics: the politics of social justice. This legacy has two components, which we should explore in a little more detail: first, the emphasis on ethics over ritual; and second, the rejection of particularism in favor of universalism.

Let's begin with ritual. The prophets are famous for denouncing the Israelites' stringency in matters of ritual when such scrupulousness was accompanied by indifference to ethical imperatives. Take the opening chapter of Isaiah, one of the most prominent prophets in the Bible:

> "To what purpose is the multitude of your sacrifices to me?" says the Lord: "I am full of the burnt offerings of rams, and the fat of fed beasts; and I do not delight in the blood of bullocks, or of lambs, or of he-goats. When you come to appear before Me, who has requested at your hand, to tread My courts? Bring no more vain oblations; incense is an abomination to me; the new moons and Sabbaths, the calling of assemblies, I cannot endure; it is iniquity, even the solemn meeting. Your new moons and your appointed feasts My soul hates; they are a trouble to Me; I am weary to bear them . . . Learn to do well; seek judgment, relieve the oppressed, judge the fatherless, plead for the widow."

No wonder this passage is frequently cited by Jewish social justice advocates. God seems to be rejecting the rituals of sacrifices,

Sabbaths, and incense in favor of ethics—standing up for the oppressed, orphans, and widows. Chapter 58 of Isaiah, quoted by Sieradski and cited above, gives a similar impression. Consequently, the prophets were "the embodiment of one of humanity's finest qualities—moral judgment, the ability to distinguish between right and wrong," Sidney Schwarz writes.[9] They "became the lasting moral and ethical voice of Judaism."

Michael Lerner explains why the shift from ritual to ethics was so important to the prophets. "The ritualization of Judaism," he expounds, could

> quickly lead away from the revolutionary message and into an absorption in the details of ritual life. How easy to turn away from the Biblical injunction "Justice, justice shalt thou pursue" and instead focus exclusively on questions of ritual purity and other details of the law. This, of course, was one of the central complaints of the prophets . . . who denounced what they saw as a perversion of Judaism.[10]

The danger of ritual, according to Lerner, is that it distracts you from being ethical. Fixation on the performance of ritual leads to neglect of ethics, which is bad enough. But it's especially problematic because it can cause you to miss the political core of Judaism—its "revolutionary message."[11] That's no small thing—as we know, revolution is foundational to social justice as learned from the Social Gospel. "For the prophets," Lerner writes, "it seemed obvious that the point of the whole enterprise [of Judaism] was to be witnesses to the possibility of *a very different social order*."[12] When the prophets of ancient Israel looked at their society, Lerner imagines that what they saw was this disregard of the revolutionary politics of social justice. They made their names—and their legacy—inveighing against this evil, demanding their fellow Jews abandon ritual in favor of establishing a righteous (liberal) society.

The plea to abandon ritual for ethics is one side of the prophetic coin. The other is the call to forsake the particular in favor of the universal—another thrust of Jewish social justice. We've already seen this most powerfully in the weight accorded by Jewish activists to Creation and in their reading of the Exodus, which tried to play down the Jewishness of the story in favor of something more relevant to everyone. The emphasis on the universal is especially linked to ethics, however, because ethics apply to one's relations with everyone else. Ethics are inherently concerned with the universal. By contrast, ritual, which is usually confined to a specific religion or culture—holy days, dietary laws, a sacrificial order, and so on—tends to be particularistic. Hence, if the prophets were denigrating ritual, they were ipso facto relegating the particular. That too fits neatly into the Jewish social justice worldview, which also tries to diminish the particularly Jewish in favor of the universally applicable.

At this point, you might be sensing a dilemma. You'll recall that we noted in an earlier chapter how the rejection of Jewish ritual by the Classical Reform movement gave way in the mid-twentieth century to something of a return to ritual in modern Reform Judaism. Ritual was always retained to some degree by the Conservative movement, and Jewish Renewal also tried to revive some ritual—albeit usually for political ends (as exemplified by Arthur Waskow's use of the festivals). At the same time, these denominations remain unwaveringly committed to Jewish social justice—a dogma they maintain was promoted by the ancient prophets. But these prophets, we now learn, apparently weren't themselves big fans of Jewish ritual. So how is it that the major American Jewish denominations have become more interested in ritual while upholding an ideology—Jewish social justice—that isn't especially keen on ritual at all (notably in its prophetic expression)? The answer is provided in a telling passage by Conservative rabbi and activist Jill Jacobs. After expressing some uncommon skepticism toward the popular conception of the prophets as opponents of ritual, she goes on to argue that

> the goal of ritual behavior, Isaiah argues, is to bring about an increased awareness of your surroundings, and not to substitute for ethical practices. The experience of fasting should attenuate the faster to the suffering of those who regularly lack food and should inspire a type of reflection that makes you feel more—and not less—obligated to act in the world . . . the commandments are useless unless they sharpen our awareness of the condition of the world . . . and engage us in working toward the biblical vision of a redeemed world.[13]

Jacobs wants to make the case for a Judaism that can accommodate ritual—the Judaism of contemporary America as opposed to that of Classical Reform. But ritual emanates from and fosters particularism. So she has to find a way out from these particularistic implications of the ritualism she is defending. Accordingly, she reconceives ritual as practical lessons in ethics (rather than as practices with their own integrity). She declares that rituals are futile unless they foster an ethical awareness. That ethical awareness must be universal—it is not simply about, say, the state of the Jewish community, but about the "condition of the world." Ultimately, this ethical awareness ought to lead to the implicitly political campaign of "working toward the biblical vision of a redeemed world"—or, as Schwarz puts it, "a world healed through justice and holiness." This is the same argument that Michael Lerner makes, albeit more subtly.

To summarize the Jewish social justice conception of the prophets, they were ancient personalities who perceived that the essence of Judaism was its ethical teachings. The particularism of ritual, they preached, was a distraction from the universal religion of ethics that is the real message of the Bible. Ritual is therefore undesirable—unless it helps to cultivate a universalistic ethical awareness. That awareness, when properly matured, should prompt a revolutionary political effort to repair the world. It is thus only natural that Jewish social justice figures and outlets, such as Michael Lerner's *Tikkun* magazine, should regularly be described as "prophetic voices."[14]

This Jewish social justice interpretation of the Prophets was summed up well by the neoconservative intellectual Norman Podhoretz, who panned it as "liberological."[15] A close reading of the Bible puts paid to this brazen attempt to enlist the prophets of Israel into the leftist brigade. Jewish activists have characteristically resorted to highly selective readings or misreadings of the Prophetic books to claim the prophets for themselves. Let's see how.

To begin with, the contention that the prophets don't like ritual very much doesn't hold water. Let's return to the passage we quoted above from Isaiah 1. We read how God appears entirely to reject the rituals of Israel, such as sacrifices and Sabbaths, preferring good deeds and ethical behavior instead. Yet a closer examination of the context yields a rather different and more profound message. Rather than ritual being undesired—or even being independent of ethics—Isaiah's point is that ritual and ethical practices are both elements of obedience to God and the Israelite covenant with Him. What is unacceptable, he preaches, is doing one and not the other. In this text, Isaiah's complaint is not about ritual in itself, but about ritualistic repentance that is accompanied by corrupt behavior. It is this hollow ritual that he declares futile and undesired by God. Following the passage quoted above, Isaiah goes on to say:

> And when you spread forth your hands, I will hide My eyes from you: when you make many prayers, I will not hear.

Why will God not heed the Israelites' rituals and prayers? Not because God doesn't like rituals—after all, some of these are the very rituals He commanded in the Pentateuch. Instead, He won't heed these rituals and prayers because, Isaiah explains, "your hands are full of blood." The Israelites' ritual is unwanted because it is hypocritical—the blood of bullocks won't wash away the blood on your hands.[16] It would, therefore, be wrong to conclude from this that ritual is wholly undesired. What is desired is complete obedience to all aspects of the covenant:

> though your sins be as scarlet, they shall be as white as snow; though they be red like crimson, they shall be as wool. If you be willing and obedient.

The prophets railed against hypocritical and hollow ritual. Sincere ritual, on the other hand, *was* desired. Elsewhere in Isaiah, for example, God is explicitly nostalgic for sacrifices:

> You have not brought Me the small cattle of your burnt offerings; neither have you honored Me with your sacrifices. I have not caused you to serve with an offering, nor wearied you

with incense. You have bought Me no sweet cane with money,
neither have you filled Me with the fat of your sacrifices
(Isaiah 43:23–24).

You can't read passages such as these honestly and blithely conclude that the prophets weren't in favor of ritual.

Moreover, the reward promised by the prophets to the people
for their obedience is itself ritualistic. Already in chapter 1, after
warning the people against hypocritical offerings, Isaiah assures
the people that if they are obedient, they

> shall eat the good of the land . . . And I will restore your judges
> as at first, and your councilors as at the beginning: afterward
> you shall be called, the city of righteousness, the faithful city.

The "city of righteousness" is Jerusalem, which God will restore
to glory. As Isaiah goes on to clarify, this means God will establish and exalt His Temple there:

> And it shall come to pass in the last days that the mountain of
> the Lord's house shall be established at the top of the moun-
> tains (Isaiah 2:2).

References to Jerusalem and especially to "the Lord's house" are
allusions to the ancient Temple of Israel. This is significant
because pretty much everything to do with the Temple is
ritualistic—the sacrifices, the incense, the showbread, the me-
norah (candelabrum), the prayers, and even the priestly caste itself. If the prophets were really concerned only with ethics and
not with ritual, then why would the reward they guarantee to
Israel for good behavior be the sacrificial order of worship at the

Temple—the most ritualistic of all Jewish practices? Jeremiah gives the same assurance, this time in reference to the ritualistic observance of the Sabbath:

> And it shall be that if you listen to me, says God, not to bring in any burden through the gates of this city [Jerusalem] on the Sabbath day, and sanctify the Sabbath and not engage in any labors, then kings and princes sitting upon the throne of David shall come through these gates riding in chariots and on horses, they, men of Judah and inhabitants of Jerusalem. And this city shall be inhabited forever. And they shall come from the cities of Judah and the environs of Jerusalem and from the land of Benjamin, and from the lowlands and from the mountains and from the south, bringing elevation offerings and sacrifices and meal offerings and frankincense and thanksgiving offerings in the house of God (Jer. 17:24–26).

It's a little odd that prophets who were supposedly so opposed to ritual should have tried to inspire the people to good behavior by reference to a ritual bonanza. Surely it's a stretch to argue that ethics represent the prophetic "essence" of Judaism if the vision of the prophets was in fact a society pervaded by ritual.

What the prophets were saying was therefore not that ritual is inherently undesired. It's that ritual—and especially empty ritual—cannot compensate for disobedience to other aspects of the covenant. Moreover, it's not just corrupted ritual that is unwanted: ethical behavior alone is also insufficient. It is ritual performed by the pious in a framework of complete obedience to God that is desired. In Isaiah's words:

> Keep judgment, and do justice: for My salvation is near to come, and My righteousness to be revealed. Blessed is the man who does this, and the son of man who lays hold of it; who keeps the Sabbath from polluting it, and keeps his hand from doing any evil (Isaiah 56:1–2).

There you have it. God wants the "ethics" of keeping judgment, doing justice, and avoiding evil. And He also wants the ritual of the Sabbath. The Jew who does all these things is blessed. You get the same impression from Isaiah 58. That's the portion read on the Day of Atonement and cited by Daniel Sieradski to justify attendance at Zuccotti Park rather than at synagogue, and a "fast from your capitalist lifestyle." The verses that immediately follow the cited portion suggest a different meaning:

> If you turn away your foot from the Sabbath, from doing your pleasure on My holy day; and call the Sabbath a delight, the holy of the Lord, honorable; and shall honor Him, not doing your own ways, nor finding your own pleasure, nor speaking your own words: Then shall you delight yourself in the Lord; and I will cause you to ride upon the high places of the earth, and feed you with the heritage of Jacob your father (Isaiah 58:13–14).

When you read the whole chapter, rather than a deceptively selected bit of it, you see that God isn't after ethical behavior alone but wants the rituals too. Both together represent obedience to His law.[17] It's not about prioritizing ethics over ritual or vice versa—they're both essential parts of the covenant. They're almost indistinct.

This being the case, you might wonder why the prophets have a reputation for being concerned with ethics. Notwithstanding the exaggerations of Jewish social justice activists, the prophets were indeed exasperated by the behavior of the Israelites toward their brethren. They preached obedience to all parts of the covenant, but found that it was those laws governing behavior between Jew and Jew (rather than between Jews and God) that were being neglected. But that did not mean that they encouraged abandonment of ritual worship of God.

Consider by analogy a father and his children. When the father's child behaves well toward him but badly toward her sibling, the good behavior toward the father feels hollow—even insulting. The father would much prefer to see the children behaving well toward one another. But that doesn't mean the father doesn't care how they behave toward him. The father wants his children to behave well toward one another because of the familial relationship that they share—a relationship that connects them not only to one another but also to him, toward whom they should also behave well. The expectation between God and the Jewish People is similar. The Jews are in a covenantal relationship with God and with one another. The prophets preached the message of the God of Israel that He desired their good behavior toward one another (what some readers choose to categorize as "ethics") and also toward Himself (the ritual). That's not to say that meaningful ritual can't also have the effect of encouraging good behavior toward others (but contrary to Jacobs, that is not its primary purpose), and it's certainly not the case that good behavior toward others has no bearing on one's relationship with God, who commands such behavior in the Bible. The distinction between ethics and ritual is more blurred than some try to make out—which, again, is why the opportunity for ritual worship in the Temple can be presented by the prophets as a reward for good behavior toward one's fellow.

Since the relationship between ethics and ritual in the Prophets is more complicated than the Jewish social justice movement tries to maintain, it follows that the supposed dichotomy between the universal and the particular—of which ethics and ritual are expressions—is also not straightforward. Generally speaking, when the prophets show concern for behavior toward one's fellow, their target is most immediately the behavior of Israel alone. The analogy between father and children pertains here too. The obligation to behave well toward one another is not borne primarily of some universal characteristic shared by every human being, but rather from the covenantal and familial connection between each Israelite and every other Israelite. In Jeremiah 11, for example, when the prophet witnesses bad behavior, he doesn't curse humanity in general but rather the disobedient Israelite:

> The word that came to Jeremiah from God saying: "hear the words of this covenant and speak to the men of Judah and the inhabitants of Jerusalem and say to them: thus says the Lord God of Israel, cursed is the man who does not listen to the words of this covenant, which I commanded your fathers when I brought them out from the land of Egypt, out of the iron furnace, saying: listen to My voice and do them, according to all I have commanded you, and you will be to Me a People and I will be to you God" (Jer. 11:1–4).

Jeremiah is lambasting those Israelites who are not obeying the laws of the covenant that God commanded the Jews (alone) at Sinai. Those laws stamped the Israelites as the Jewish People and the God of Abraham as their God. They are being cursed for not upholding that code of law that makes them particular—that connects them to one another as distinct from other peoples. Jeremiah's concern is not for the whole world but for the Israelites exclusively. Someone who sums up the logic here well is—of all people—Michael Walzer, in a more recent book of his on the Bible. Jeremiah and the other prophets are narrowly interested in the Israelites rather than all of humanity because the Israelites are part of a covenant with one another and with God. As Walzer observes, "the covenant, if it is serious, ought to give rise to obligations shared by all Israelites and to a pervasive fellow feeling."[18] Israelites are part of a covenant and if that means anything, it has to mean they have additional, special obligations to one another.

So when the prophets are famously aggravated by the suffering of widows and orphans, they are *Israelite* widows and orphans. The reason that their suffering is so frustrating to the prophets is because the covenant demands that each Israelite show concern for every other Israelite. The prophetic rebukes aren't statements made for a universal audience as such. The prophets of Israel are concerned with the behavior of Israelites—because those Israelites have a sacred responsibility to one another as they are bound together in covenant. That covenant does not extend to other peoples. So even what Jewish social justice activists think is the prophets' concern for ethics is actually less about universal ethics than it is about the particularistic covenant.

The messages of the prophets are most immediately particularistic. But when they start talking about reward, the conversation is both particularistic and also universalistic. The reward the prophets anticipate is redemption. First of all this is about the Jews specifically. It's forecasted across the Prophetic writings that the Jewish People will be ingathered from exile to the Land of Israel. Jeremiah assures Israel that God "will gather the remnant of My flock out of all countries whither I have driven them" (Jer. 23:3), and that God will return "every man to his heritage, and every man to his land" (Jer. 12:15). Amos too proclaims that God "will bring again the captivity of My people Israel" (Amos 9:14).

But through the particular redemption of Israel, a universal redemption is also achieved. Consider the most famous of all "universalistic" prophetic visions in Isaiah. Only the middle verse is plastered on the "Isaiah Wall" of the United Nations, but the fuller context makes a different impression:

> And it shall come to pass in the last days, that the mountain of the Lord's house shall be established at the top of the mountains, and shall be exalted above the hills; and all na-tions shall flow to it. And many people shall go and say, Come, and let us go up to the mountain of the Lord, to the house of the God of Jacob; and He will teach us of His ways; and we will walk in His paths: for out of Zion shall go forth the law, and the word of the Lord from Jerusalem. And he shall judge among the nations, and shall rebuke many people: and they shall beat their swords into plowshares, and their spears into pruning-hooks: nation shall not lift up sword against nation, neither shall they learn war any more. O house of Jacob, come, and let us walk in the light of the Lord (Isaiah 2:2–5).

Israel's redemption brings about global redemption. From the eschatological perspective, the distinction between particular and universal is collapsed.[19] Israel's charge in the Books of the Prophets is obedience to all aspects of its particular covenant with God, and that obedience shall be a boon to all mankind.

Michael Lerner was of the view (shared by other Jewish social justice activists, if sometimes more implicitly) that the prophets had a political—revolutionary—agenda. That agenda was the politics of social justice, the goal of which is to heal the world. As it happens, the prophets don't make any linguistic reference to *tikkun olam* or a healed or transformed world in any of the books that bear their names. But can it at least be argued that their concern for widows and orphans (even if they are Israelite widows and orphans in particular) led them to call for the establishment of a socialist economic system in ancient Israel? There is no indication that this is what they are doing. Undoubtedly, they are urging genuine care for their fellow Israelites and are pushing for efforts to mitigate suffering. But that's it. They don't call for higher taxes on the rich or a welfare state or single-payer healthcare. For example, when the prophet Amos tells off the wealthy Israelites for their indifference to the plight of the poor around them, he's not bothered with inequality per se. He's pointedly indignant that the privileged are not showing fraternal sympathy—they "are not grieved for the affliction of Joseph" (Amos 6:6).[20] It's this failure to care for their brethren that provokes them—not low taxes.

Aryeh Cohen of Bend the Arc has offered a specific Prophetic verse to make his case for the pursuit of the politics of social justice today. He quotes Jeremiah 29:7:

Seek the peace of the city to which I have exiled you, and pray to the Lord on its behalf, for in its peace you will have peace.

Cohen understands Jeremiah to be urging exiled Jews not merely to advance their own narrow interests but also to promote social justice in their communities. "Most American Jews feel the call of the tradition to create cities wherein [social] justice lies," he writes. "As a community," he goes on, "we should demand that when politicians speak about Jewish issues, they speak about the issues that really matter to us, issues of social and economic justice," rather than simply declaring support for the State of Israel—a quintessentially Jewish issue.[21] But Cohen's reading is problematic. Jeremiah isn't intending that Jews agitate politically for social justice in the lands of their dispersion so that they can find peace there in perpetuity. Instead, the context of his statement is God's directive to the Jews exiled in Babylon to live their lives as normal and in harmony with their new neighbors—with the assurance that after seventy years they'll be restored to the Land of Israel (Jer. 29:4–14). (As it happens, God also warns the people not to believe false prophets in their midst who tell them that they will not or need not return to the Land of Israel in due time—a warning the Jewish social justice movement and, as we shall later see, Aryeh Cohen in particular, should heed.) In other words, Jeremiah's instruction to the Jewish People in exile is to do what is necessary for their own security and survival in expectation of an eventual return to the Land of Israel.

A similar sentiment is found in a statement from the Talmudic sage Rabbi Haninah:

Pray for the welfare of the kingdom, for without fear thereof a man would swallow his fellow alive.[22]

Jeremiah may be going further than Rabbi Haninah in hinting at action rather than just prayer, but both adages are self-serving:

for Jeremiah, the city's peace is a prerequisite to Jewish peace, while Rabbi Haninah recommends praying for political stability because that is more likely to favor the survival of the exiled Jews.[23] (Indeed for this reason the Orthodox scholar Jacob J. Schacter renders the Talmudic statement as follows: "Pray for the welfare of the kingdom, for without fear thereof *the gentiles* would swallow the Jews alive.") So much for being revolutionary—this Talmudic exhortation to loyalty to the status quo is almost Hobbesian.[24]

For all the talk of political social justice and revolution, the truth is that the ambitions of the prophets were, strange as it may seem, much more modest. They taught that Israelite obedience to the covenant can assist in bringing about redemption—but that redemption is, at the end of the day, in God's hands. As Podhoretz writes:

> One must . . . accept that it is only in His power to perform these miracles, and not in the power of mere mortals like ourselves. In sharp contrast to [modern] revolutionaries . . . the classical prophets were thoroughly imbued with this truth . . . that neither kings nor priests—nor, for that matter, prophets—could on their own build the utopia of their eschatological visions.

Although the prophets call for the Israelites to obey God's word in order to bring about the redemption, they are very careful to insist that the redemption remains up to God. We've seen how the Jewish social justice movement tries to make it seem like the Israelites' redemption from Egypt in the Exodus was achieved by the Israelites themselves and not by God. Here too the advocates of Jewish social justice want you to think that the prophets are calling upon mankind to establish the Kingdom of God—a healed world—on earth. But that's not what the prophets actually say. For all their righteous indignation, Jewish social justice activists lack appreciation for the prophetic medium or message and consequently risk just being the next in a long line of utopians who believe they speak in God's name. The Shalom Center, *Tikkun* magazine, and other entities and personalities in the Jewish social justice movement may be lauded (or laud themselves) as "prophetic voices," but this sort of "assumption of the prophetic burden" is, as the critic Robert Alter wrote, "self-important and spiritually vacuous." Alter goes on to observe that "such a politics of preachment, moreover, tends to assume, even without mentioning God's name, a quasi-divine and hence absolute authority for its own particular view of contemporary problems—always a dangerous assumption."[25]

According to Scripture, prophecy was a phenomenon of the biblical era whereby a message was received and promulgated within certain parameters. That message urged obedience to all aspects of the covenant between Israel and its God—and not simply those that are politically useful or seem to make sense. It wasn't without prudence that the rabbis insisted that, following the prophetic epoch, prophecy is suspended. This is because prophetic pretensions are conceited and can easily become hazardous. The prophets carried God's message to the Jewish People to mend their ways, not the world, and He will do the rest.

8

Tikkun Olam

With thirty-seven years at the pulpit behind him, Robert Barr is the longest-serving community rabbi in Cincinnati. Although he grew up Conservative and was ordained in the seminary of Reform Judaism, his Congregation Beth Adam is not affiliated with any of the main Jewish denominations—but it's still firmly within the mainstream when it comes to Jewish social justice. Part of the synagogue's ethos is engaging in tikkun olam—and even the synagogue's name, referencing Creation, is a nod to universalism.[1] Now, Barr intends to run for Congress, in order to protect and advance Obamacare, promote campaign finance reform, and repair the environment. (You can probably guess which party's nomination he'll seek.) Having dedicated himself to tikkun olam long ago, Barr doesn't see the move from pulpit to Congress as much of a change. "What drove me to become a rabbi was my sense, following the Jewish tradition, that we have a responsibility to repair the world," he declared to the *Forward*. "I've been doing that and working within that framework of repairing the world in my rabbinic career. Running for Congress is really an extension of that."[2] And to the *Washington Post*: "37 years I have been a rabbi, been trying to repair the world, and I have a responsibility to run now."[3] For Barr, as for the many other Jewish social justice activists, tikkun olam is a religious imperative to be political—to be liberal.

However important the other sources we've looked at may be—Creation, Abraham, Joseph, the Exodus, and the Prophets— our investigation of the favored texts of the Jewish social justice movement could not, of course, be complete without a treatment of tikkun olam. As we've seen, early Jewish social justice activists witnessed the Social Gospel with its aspiration to establish a Kingdom of God on earth, and they found a similar notion in the Jewish prayer of Aleynu, which yearned for the "perfecting of the world under the Kingdom of God." Eventually, the motif of perfecting (or repairing) the world attracted Jewish radicals, and they popularized it through their publications and organizations. Finally, the major Jewish denominations officially adopted tikkun olam to describe their existing Jewish social justice programs, and today it has totally taken over American Judaism. As if the political nature of tikkun olam needed any further demonstration, now it is aptly being cited by a rabbi to explain and justify his decision to run for Congress.[4]

The Jewish social justice movement has pointed to Aleynu and other appearances of tikkun olam in the traditional Jewish canon to claim that social justice has always been a part of Judaism. In the view of these Jewish activists, Judaism requires Jews to repair or perfect the world and bring about God's Kingdom by human hands. This mandate to pursue social justice is so important that tikkun olam is variously described as a "tenet" of Judaism, a "Jewish ideal," a "prophetic value," a Jewish "imperative"—even a "commandment."[5] For many it has even become a substitute for all other religious observance and, ultimately, for God.[6] But is tikkun olam really that important in traditional Judaism? And if we "look more deeply within Jewish tradition at the roots of the phrase tikkun olam," can it, as leading Conservative rabbi and a professor of rabbinics at Hebrew College Jane Kanarek hopes, offer us "real guidance for social justice efforts"?[7]

The answer is: no. As we shall see presently, tikkun olam in traditional Judaism has no connection to tax rates, the labor movement, abortion, immigration reform, healthcare provision, education concerns, environmentalism, or any of the many other political issues in which social justice is interested. Tikkun olam does not express or even resemble the political philosophy of social justice in any real sense. Tikkun olam in the Jewish tradition has never referred to or meant social justice at all. It doesn't have any rational connection to modern social justice whatsoever.

TIKKUN AND OLAM

Before we dive into the texts, we should take this opportunity to say something about the phrase "tikkun olam" itself. Specifically, note that the two words in the phrase—"tikkun" and "olam"—convey little on their own. This is not because each word has no meaning in isolation, but because they have too many meanings. So far, we've translated "tikkun" as "repair" and "perfect" and (more poetically) "heal," as these are the most common renderings—and you could also add "rectify" and "improve." But notice that "repair" and "perfect" are not the same thing. You only repair things that are broken. You could "perfect" something that's broken, sure—but usually you perfect something that is satisfactory but could be better still. So already there's a tension: Are we repairing a broken world or are we making a satisfactory one perfect? If it's broken, why is it broken and when did the breaking happen?

"Tikkun" can also mean other things too. In fact, Gilbert S. Rosenthal has observed that t-k-n, the root of "tikkun," is one of the most flexible words in Rabbinic Hebrew.[8] (The conjugation of words in Hebrew, which is a Semitic language, occurs through a process of nonconcatenative morphology of usually trilateral (three-letter) roots, such as t-k-n. Essentially, you use the same consonants in the same order but with different vowels to indicate different tenses or even to mean slightly different things.) In rabbinic literature t-k-n can refer to the establishment of legal ordinances—which are called *takkanot*—or can be used to connote preparing for something. It has also been used by rabbis to refer to things as mundane as the repair of shoes and the fixing of one's hair, as well as to the complicated and consequential process of determining festival dates. In more mystical writings the word can be used to denote spiritual corrections.[9] Meanwhile, the volume used by a Torah chanter to prepare his reading and by a scribe to prepare the writing of a Torah scroll is called a tikkun. So t-k-n has no single intrinsic meaning and it certainly has no exclusive attachment to contemporary notions of tikkun olam.

Turning to the word "olam," it can definitely mean "world," as it does in the usual translation of "tikkun olam." Alternatively, it can refer to "all the people" or "the community." But the word is deeper too. It collapses space and time and signifies not only the geography or demography of the world but also "eternity," "perpetuity," and "forever."

It's worthwhile noting the various meanings of these two words so that it is understood that the phrase "tikkun olam" doesn't tell us very much on its own. The words are simply too ambiguous to assume that the phrase is going to mean the same thing everywhere it comes up. The first lesson we need to keep in mind, therefore, is that the phrase needs to be read in the contexts in which it appears. We have to identify where it's mentioned in Jewish texts and try to understand its meaning in each of those places.

Speaking of where the phrase appears, there's something else you should know. For all the excitement about tikkun olam in the Jewish social justice movement and how important everyone thinks it is in Judaism, it actually appears relatively rarely in traditional Jewish writings. It emerges in a few different guises, but they're not thematically related to one another. Again, this means we need to examine context carefully. But it also means that tikkun olam isn't as big a deal in traditional Judaism as Jewish social justice campaigners want you to think it is.

THE BIBLE

We'll come to the Aleynu prayer in just a moment, but first we should investigate whether tikkun olam is mentioned at all in the Hebrew Bible. You'd have thought a concept supposedly as central to Judaism as tikkun olam ought to appear—

prominently—in the faith's primary document. Yet it's entirely absent. That's right—tikkun olam isn't mentioned in the Bible anywhere. This is remarkable, since significant religious ideas, such as Creation, the Exodus, the Revelation, the Temple in Jerusalem, and even the messianic age, all feature somewhere in the Bible—as you would expect.

Beyond the phrase "tikkun olam," even the usually ubiquitous t-k-n is mentioned only three times in all of Scripture. All three appearances are in the Book of Ecclesiastes:

That which is crooked cannot be made straight (*litkon*) (Ecc. 1:15);

Consider the work of God: for who can make that straight (*l'takken*), which He has made crooked? (Ecc. 7:13);

Because the preacher (Kohelet) was wise, he still taught the people knowledge; yea, he gave good heed, and sought out, and set in order (*tikken*) many proverbs (Ecc. 12:9).

Of the three appearances, none has normative implications: the first is proverbial, the second is abstract, and the third is hagiographical. And none appears to bear any relevance to tikkun olam. Quite the contrary, actually, since the author of Ecclesiastes (in characteristic fashion) seems to regard tikkun as futile—which is of course the opposite of what the Jewish social justice movement believes. As a result, liberal Jewish activists don't point to the Bible as a direct source of tikkun olam—because they can't. We haven't even got to Aleynu or the other sources, and yet it already seems like the grandiose stature of tikkun olam in contemporary American Judaism is questionable.

ALEYNU

The Jewish social justice movement doesn't get tikkun olam from the Bible, because it isn't there. Instead, it comes from Aleynu. Although the other places where the phrase appears are also important, Aleynu is the movement's original source. The familiar line, "to perfect the world under the Kingdom of God" (*"l'taken olam be'malchut Shaddai"*), was likely initially appealing because of the reference to the Kingdom of God, which echoed the aspiration of the Social Gospel. But eventually everyone's focus shifted to the perfecting/repairing part.

Aleynu has appeared in a section of the New Year (Rosh Hashanah) and Day of Atonement (Yom Kippur) prayer services called Mussaf perhaps since ancient times. Later it was incorporated into the three daily services recited all year round. Observant Jews who pray regularly are therefore very accustomed to this liturgy. Aleynu, which is in Hebrew, is divided into two paragraphs. The first paragraph recounts the greatness of God and His particular relationship with the Jewish People. The second introduces the promise that divine sovereignty will eventually encompass the entire world. The pertinent verse, "to perfect the world under the Kingdom of God," appears in the second section, which translated in its entirety reads as follows:

> Therefore we put our hope in You, Adonai our God, to see soon the glory of Your strength, to remove all idols from the Earth, and to cut off completely all false gods; *to perfect the world under the Kingdom of God.* And all living flesh will call Your name, and all the wicked of the Earth will turn to You. May all the world's inhabitants recognize and know that to You every knee must bend and every tongue must swear loy-

alty. Before You, Adonai, our God, they will bow down, and give honor to Your precious Name, and may all take upon themselves the yoke of Your rule. And may You soon reign over them forever. Because all kingship is Yours, and You will rule forever and ever. As it is written in Your Torah: "Adonai will reign forever and ever." And it is said: "Adonai will be Ruler over the whole Earth, and on that day, God will be one, and God's Name will be one."

It's a beautiful and powerful hymn, and you can see why it started out in the Kingship portions of the New Year and Day of Atonement prayers. The plain meaning of this second paragraph seems to point to the elimination of all other forms of religious practice in favor of the exclusive and universal worship of the God of Israel. It's in that context that the call to perfect the world under the Kingdom of God is made.

Jill Jacobs, a conservative rabbi and prominent campaigner for Jewish social justice, has given more attention to interpreting this prayer than others have. But she's troubled by what Aleynu seems to be advocating. She feels that "to our contemporary pluralist ears, the rejection of other religions appears intolerant and proselytizing."[10] For this reason, some non-Orthodox Jewish congregations do not recite Aleynu at all—which is rather ironic, given the extent of their devotion to the concept of tikkun olam, which was originally lifted from this very prayer. Jacobs thinks omitting Aleynu from prayer services entirely is a little drastic. Instead, she wants us to interpret the tikkun olam in Aleynu to mean "working toward the manifestation of divinity in every corner of the world." This manifestation, she explains, depends on "the establishment of Godly qualities throughout the world." Regrettably, these qualities are being

blocked by "poverty and discrimination." So for Jacobs, the tikkun olam of Aleynu refers to the amplification of divinity in the
world through our eradication of economic inequality and social prejudice in American society—which is what Jewish social
justice is all about.

There are thus three things you're meant to think about the
verse "to perfect the world under the Kingdom of God." First,
you're supposed to believe the line refers to the perfection (or
repair) of the world, and that it's reasonable for American Jews
to connect Aleynu to tikkun olam, at least semantically. Second,
you're meant to come away thinking the line is directed at man—
that it's humanity that has to do the perfecting. Third, you
ought to conclude that perfecting the world apparently requires
the elimination of poverty and discrimination. This is how Jewish social justice activists understand and utilize this prayer. But
all three of these assertions are faulty. Let's take each in turn.

The first query concerns the phrase itself—the reference to
repairing the world. This seems to be a no-brainer—of course
Aleynu talks about tikkun olam! Or does it? Is it possible that,
despite what we think we know, the prayer in fact makes no reference to tikkun olam at all? That is what Mitchell First has
compellingly argued.[11] It is very likely that the original phrase
was not "letaken [לתקן] olam be'malchut shaddai," as it is read
today, but rather "letakhen [לתכן] olam be'malchut shaddai" ("to
establish the world under the Kingdom of God"). This construction appears in multiple historical versions of Aleynu, particularly in the Middle Eastern and North African tradition, and it
survives in Yemenite Jewish prayer books to this day. Furthermore, this phrasing has several biblical and liturgical precedents,
which further indicate that it's the correct rendering.[12] It also

has one additional advantage, which is the most important: it makes much more sense! Kingdoms are *established*, not perfected.

The prayer is calling for the establishment of the Kingdom of God over the whole world. It's pretty likely that the text has been corrupted over time from "establish" to "perfect"—and given how close the Hebrew spellings and pronunciations of these two words are, this theory is hardly implausible. Now, we're not talking about a fundamental difference in the meaning of the prayer. The paragraph is essentially the same either way—it's depicting the initiation of God's kingship over the whole world. But if the proper phrasing is not "perfect" but rather "establish," then the semantic association of Aleynu with tikkun olam is severed. This would mean that Aleynu is not actually a source for tikkun olam at all. That's surely a startling revelation. Although the original attraction to this line was the "Kingdom of God" part, which remains, it's the "perfecting" part that has become the watchword of American Judaism—and it's probably not even correct! If the Jewish social justice movement has got the name wrong, that's pretty embarrassing.

Let's be charitable, though. For the sake of argument, let's assume that the more well-known version of the line in Aleynu is accurate and therefore that the prayer does in fact speak of "perfecting" the world under the Kingdom of God. Our next query concerns the agent of the repair: Who is supposed to do the repairing? It's commonly supposed that it's the Jewish People (or perhaps humanity in general) that are charged with fixing the world under God's sovereignty—and this is what Jewish social justice campaigners want you to think. After all, the whole point of the Social Gospel, and indeed the Jewish social justice movement today, is that it's humanity (or at least, in the case of Jewish activists, the Jews) that has to engage in tikkun olam. But, in fact, the agent implored to perfect the world under the king-ship of God in Aleynu isn't man at all. It's God Himself. This is clear from the paragraph's opening line, which reads, "There-fore we put our hope *in You*." This is also consistent with the pattern of the High Holy Days liturgy from which Aleynu is taken.[13] Pace the Jewish social justice activists, Aleynu does not urge human effort toward the repair of the world. This too is remarkable. The whole point of the Social Gospel—and the Jewish social justice movement that it helped inspire—was the notion that it fell to humanity to build God's Kingdom on earth. Jewish activists chose Aleynu as their banner because it seemed to dovetail with the theology of the Social Gospel. Yet in fact Aleynu expressly calls for God—not man—to establish God's Kingdom. It's the opposite of what Jewish social justice is about.

The conservative Jewish politico Jeffrey Ballabon has kindly tried to help the liberals out. He contends that the omission of an explicit call to the Jewish People to perfect the world in Aleynu is not quite a "disqualifying flaw" in the assumptions of Jewish social justice. It's conceivable, he allows, that although God is the primary agent of the perfection, the Jewish People might possess an acceleratory prerogative. In other words, even if God is doing most of the perfecting, the Jews (or humanity) can still make a contribution to the perfection that can hasten the outcome. This is a bit like Religious Zionism, he observes, which as an ideology and as a movement appears to hold that human activity can have just such an acceleratory effect on the Redemption—which will still ultimately come from God.[14] Just because it's God who is beseeched to perfect the world under His own kingship doesn't mean that the Jews do not nonetheless possess the capacity to contribute to that endeavor. Fair enough. But even if we can't say that tikkun olam in Aleynu is not for the Jews (or humanity) to pursue, we can say that it's not *primarily* for them. This still runs counter to the entire ethos of Jewish social justice as inherited from the Social Gospel. Moreover, certainly nobody could infer any *obligation* to undertake tikkun olam from Aleynu.

Oh dear. Not only might Aleynu not be about tikkun olam at all, but even if it is, it's also not demanding that humanity do the perfecting. Those are two pretty serious holes in the hull of Jewish social justice. But it hasn't sunk yet. If we assume "tikkun olam" is the original and proper phraseology, and also that Aleynu does in fact invite the Jews or humanity to engage in perfecting the world, then our third query concerns the activity that would constitute such perfection. We've seen that for Jacobs, it's about working to end "poverty and discrimination." She desperately needs this interpretation to work, otherwise no liberal Jew is going to bother with Aleynu at all. But alas, her interpretation is completely unfounded. Where on earth did she get it from? It has no basis in the paragraph or anywhere else in the prayer. In fact, if you read the verse in context, ending discrimination is practically the opposite of the prayer's exhortation! Jacobs is right to worry that the second paragraph of Aleynu challenges pluralism—its every line declares that the God of Israel is alone worthy of worship and that eventually the whole wide world will recognize this. The universalistic motif of this second paragraph of Aleynu thus complements and completes the particularistic theme of chosenness elaborated in the first, calling for the unchallenged kingship of the God of Israel over the entire world. Perhaps Aleynu invites Jews to begin to perfect the world in order to bring about the Redemption, but if so, it doesn't seem like the advocates of Jewish social justice would be prepared to accept the literal iconoclasm that the prayer propagates.

Aleynu is the reason people call Jewish social justice "tikkun olam." Maybe Abraham, Joseph, the Exodus, and the Prophets were too much for them to ask for, but you'd have thought Jewish social justice campaigners could at least get this one right. Yet we've seen that the phrase "tikkun olam" probably isn't meant to be in Aleynu at all, and that there's no obligation in this prayer calling for mankind to establish God's Kingdom on earth, and that the prayer has nothing to do with the agenda of Jewish social justice. It's almost comical how everything they pinned on this prayer has come loose. Remember that lesson about context? You can't understand tikkun olam unless you examine the context in which it appears carefully. Clearly, the Jewish social justice movement has failed to do that. Only by isolating tikkun olam from the rest of Aleynu and arbitrarily associating it with a call for social justice did radical Jewish activists manage to persuade everyone that Aleynu supports their cause. It doesn't.

THE TALMUD AND THE LEGAL RESPONSA

The Talmud is a mammoth collection of Jewish legal discussions from two thousand to fifteen hundred years ago. It too makes important references to tikkun olam that are cited by Jewish activists. The Talmud is divided into two sections. There's the slightly older—and for that reason more authoritative—Mishnah, which is an anthology of laws and legal statements. And there's the Gemara, which comprises discussion of those laws. The phrase *"mipenei tikkun ha'olam"* ("for the sake of tikkun

ha'olam") appears a number of times in the Mishnah as a rationale for the adjustment of various pre-existing laws, principally
divorce law.

For example, imagine a man wants to divorce his wife, but
they're not in the same place. So he sends a writ of divorce to
her via an emissary. But then he decides, after the emissary has
departed but before the man's wife receives the writ, to revoke
it. The emissary and the man's wife will be oblivious. She'll receive the writ and when she does she'll reasonably assume herself to be divorced. Legally, however, she's still married and
shouldn't marry again. But neither she nor anyone else knows
that she's still married, and so she might remarry. For various
reasons, this jeopardizes the status of any children she has in
this new marriage. Therefore this scenario must be avoided
at all costs. Hence a leading Talmudic sage prohibited this sort
of revocation on the husband's part, "for the sake of tikkun
ha'olam."

Based on these kinds of appearances of the phrase in the
Mishnah, Jane Kanarek concludes:

> The discussions of tikkun ha'olam in the Mishnah and Talmud
> teach us the importance of creating systemic change through
> law. In the Jewish tradition, law is an essential instrument for
> recalibrating the world to be a more just society. As we pur-
> sue tikkun olam in the contemporary world, we follow the
> path of our ancestors when we re-examine our laws to make
> sure that they are helping to achieve the world we want.
> We should ask ourselves: Are our existing laws helping to
> end poverty? To provide universal health care? To tackle hun-
> ger? How are our laws fostering justice and equality in race,
> gender, and class?

Talmudic tikkun olam, according to Kanarek, requires us to take a step back and observe "that the world is out of balance." It compels us to reconsider the laws on which our society—with its systemic injustices—is founded. Only by asking "the big structural questions" can we achieve what Talmudic tikkun olam aims at: a "recalibrating of the world." You can see why Talmudic tikkun olam would be useful to the Jewish social justice movement. But is this really a fair assessment of tikkun olam as it features in the Talmud?

When we try to understand the tikkun olam of the Talmud, the first difficulty we encounter is the precise meaning of the phrase, "mipenei tikkun ha'olam." It's quite enigmatic. The Hebrew is hard to decipher, and so there's no definitive English translation. It has variously been presented as "for the sake of the public weal," "for the sake of the public good," "for the sake of the social order," "to prevent abuses," "for the better ordering of society," and "for the benefit of society."[15] These translations may not be all that dissimilar from one another, but they're still fairly vague. Anything, it seems, could be justified using this rationale. Yet the Talmud doesn't use it to justify anything and everything—it uses the rationale sparingly. We should therefore consider the contexts in which the phrase arises.

"Mipenei tikkun ha'olam" appears primarily in the Mishnah, almost exclusively in the tractate of Gittin (one of sixty-three tractates in the Talmud), and almost all in the fourth chapter (of nine). It's not a particularly widespread formula in Talmudic discourse—and therefore not especially significant either. Even though the rationale appears like it could be broad and very useful, it's not actually used in the Talmud very much. That being said, the rationale is brought to bear on quite a wide variety of concerns. In addition to the divorce scenario we already mentioned, it's used in order to justify a measure that minimizes confusion over the authorship of documents, in order to grant freedom to slaves in certain circumstances, and in order to prohibit the purchase of overpriced Judaica from idolaters. It's also used to justify the enactment of the *Prozbul*, a technical device designed to spur lending to the poor in the sixth year of the septennial *shemitta* cycle, in the seventh year of which all debts are canceled. (Since all personal debts are forgiven every seventh year, creditors might fear lending in the sixth year lest debtors be unable to pay in time. The Prozbul offers a technical solution.[16]) These scenarios don't share much in common, making "mipenei tikkun ha'olam" challenging to even comprehend, let alone translate.

For assistance in understanding concepts like these that come up in the Mishnah, you'd usually turn to the Gemara. That's the part of the Talmud that comments on the Mishnah and typically elucidates these sorts of concepts. Yet even the Gemara, on those few occasions when it does inquire into the meaning of "mipenei tikkun ha'olam," avoids providing a general interpretation.[17] Not only is this phrase hard to decipher in isolation, but even when we regard the contexts in which it arises it's still tough to understand.

So where does that leave us? What can be said of "mipenei tikkun ha'olam" and the Jewish social justice interpretation of it? For one thing, we can say that the reality is far more modest than Kanarek suggests. It's used in the Talmud as a basis for mostly minor legal adjustments to safeguard the existing system—but that's all. It's not teaching us "the importance of creating systemic change" (a revolutionary sentiment, you might have noticed), since the whole point of these adjustments is to *uphold* the system. To return to the divorce example above, nothing about the procedure of rabbinic divorce is upended—the legal amendment is simply to prevent confusion in order to sustain the existing practices. Even Jill Jacobs finds herself rendering the phrase "mipenei tikkun ha'olam" as "for the sake of the preservation of the system as a whole" (which she concedes sounds rather "conservative").[18] Pace Kanarek, there really is no indication that Talmudic tikkun olam reflects any sort of concession that "the world is out of balance," or that it's about "recalibrating the world," or that it invites us to "ask the big structural questions." Quite the opposite: the goal of the minor legal adjustments made in the name of tikkun olam (whatever its precise meaning) is to *sustain* the existing "system."

Kanarek is wrong on another count too. Notice that she reads Talmudic tikkun olam as suggesting the *world* is out of balance, and that there needs to be a recalibration of the *world*. Jewish social justice campaigners are always keen to try to universalize local Jewish ideas and practices in order to put them to political use in the contemporary United States. But this is a problem. Talmudic tikkun olam isn't concerned about the world. The "system" that Talmudic tikkun olam is upholding is a specifically Jewish society—and, in the case of the Mishnah, that of ancient Israel in particular. There's no suggestion that the Talmud means tikkun olam to be applied to any society other than a Jewish one.[19] What evidence is there that the Talmud has this narrower perspective? For the essayist and translator Hillel Halkin, it's obvious that the Talmud's intentions were particularistic—because the rabbis' authority to enforce laws did not extend beyond the Jews.[20]

But one could go further. It's clear that Talmudic tikkun olam is limited to Jewish affairs from the circumstances in which it's brought up. Almost invariably it's invoked to tweak specifically *Jewish* practices, such as lending to fellow Jews, the first fruits offering, the purchase of Judaica by Jews, and the avoidance of bearing children who will be stigmatized due to their mother's incomplete Jewish divorce from her previous husband (as in the example above). The Talmud is clearly talking about a Jewish society. So is it even reasonable for the Jewish social justice movement to try to introduce the concept of Talmudic tikkun olam into contemporary American political discourse at all? It doesn't seem so. In fact, in her PhD dissertation on the earliest appearances of the phrase "tikkun olam" in Hebrew literature, Sagit Mor concludes that "olam" in Talmudic tikkun olam refers to "Jewish culture and civilization," rather than to either universal humankind or the natural world.[21] (You'll recall from our discussion of the meaning of "olam" earlier that the term can mean many different things.)

Mor is not alone. Scholars from a range of backgrounds who have looked at this phrase have come to the same conclusion. Eugene Lipman, a leader of Reform Jewry in the last century, wrote that nothing he saw in the Talmudic literature "could serve to bring me to the conclusion that the Talmudic sages were speaking of all humanity in their enactments." Levi Cooper, an Orthodox researcher, also believes that "the legal justification [of tikkun olam] . . . was offered for the inner workings of the Jewish community" alone.[22] The Jewish social justice reading of Talmudic tikkun olam therefore rather exaggerates not only tikkun olam's aims, but also its purview.

To linger a little more in the Jewish legal genre, it should be noted that tikkun olam also appears several times in the rabbinic responsa. This is the vast corpus of legal rulings issued by rabbis over the past fifteen hundred years since the sealing of the Talmud. Most of these tikkun olam cameos, which are few in number, don't represent groundbreaking reforms and aren't at all germane to the agenda of Jewish social justice. Hence they're rarely cited by activists.[23] In fact, given the malleability of the concept and its potential usefulness, this rabbinic aversion to using it is itself revealing. As Eugene Lipman exclaims, he is "struck by the degree to which the medieval commentators followed the Talmudic sages in not discussing the phrase or making an issue of it."[24]

But there is one notable exception. It's a twentieth-century ruling by the leading Zionist rabbi, Abraham Isaac Hakohen Kook. It is quoted by On1Foot, a Jewish social justice educational website that is a project of the American Jewish World Service, and also, among other places, by Arieh Lebowitz of the Jewish Labor Committee in his essay "Why a Labor Movement Matters." They translate this Hebrew ruling as follows:

> Within the workers' organization, which is formed for the purpose of guarding and protecting the work conditions, there is an aspect of righteousness and uprightness and tikkun olam. The workers' organization may sue both the employer and the worker who cause this [problem], for unorganized labor brings damage and loss of money to workers. For the unorganized worker works under worse conditions, both in regard to wages and in regard to working hours, etc. And this is likely to make working conditions worse in general.[25]

Finally we've found a traditional rabbinic source that seems to connect tikkun olam with at least one aspect of contemporary social justice! Moreover, this source is authored by a respected traditionalist rabbinic authority and appears to mandate compulsory union membership, a common demand of labor unions that is supported by the Jewish social justice movement. This would make it one of the very few occasions that tikkun olam is associated with an item on the social justice agenda and actually endorses the prescriptions of that agenda. It's an impressive and popular source.

However, it's actually not nearly as convincing as the advocates of Jewish social justice wish to believe—for several reasons. To begin with, the ruling was delivered orally (and reported in the press) rather than being recorded in a formal, written responsum as one would have expected of a serious ruling.[26] Much more significantly, the extract quoted by these Jewish social justice activists is only an excerpt—it's not the whole statement.[27] The ruling goes on to clarify that a labor union must submit all disputes to a *beth din* (a Jewish court) before taking strike action. Only if the employer refuses to submit to the court's judgment are the workers permitted to strike. It's in this scenario that strikebreaking is proscribed, because the "union" is, as it were, an enforcement agent of the court, tasked with forcing the employer to comply with the court's decision.[28] This isn't quite what Jewish social justice activists have in mind when they quote this source—and one wonders if they cut the quotation short deliberately.

There's more. The unionization and the striking and the strikebreaking have nothing to do with tikkun olam. The ruling cites tikkun olam not because it has any substantive relevance to the agenda of social justice—it isn't invoked in reference to union rights per se. It's mentioned in connection with the implementation of a judicial decision—a clarification in a situation where there might be confusion. This reflects the use of tikkun olam in the Talmud, and indeed Rabbi Kook, in the original Hebrew, uses the Talmudic "tikkum ha'olam." That Rabbi Kook's use of tikkun olam in this instance happens to concern employer-employee relations—an issue with which social justice is concerned—is merely coincidental. Hence, even Jacobs admits that Kook probably did not have contemporary notions of tikkun olam in mind when issuing this ruling.[29]

Talmudic tikkun olam—and its echoes in the rabbinic responsa—is not interested in overhauling the structure of society or recalibrating the world. To the contrary, it's about upholding and sustaining that structure and society as they currently exist through minor adjustments. There's also no indication that Talmudic tikkun olam is applicable beyond the Jewish community. Finally—and this point cannot be understated—it's a comparatively unimportant concept in the huge rabbinic legal genre. As Gilbert Rosenthal observes in his study of the subject, the appearances of the phrase amount to "remarkably few exceptions to the phenomenon that a potentially broadly applicable principle of law was essentially ignored for centuries by jurists and codifiers." Levi Cooper too concludes that "it is difficult to see it as a guiding notion of the Jewish legal system."[30] When it comes to the Talmud and rabbinic responsa, Jewish social justice activists have a lot less to point to than they would like you to think.

THE MIDRASH

The Midrash is a literary category comprising homiletical rabbinic teachings—mostly from a similar era as the Talmud. They're commentaries that build on nuances, ambiguities, discrepancies, and other textual anomalies in the Bible to make more general theological, mystical, or normative claims that often depart radically from the plain meaning of the words of the biblical text. This exegetical process will become clear as we explore a couple of examples.

There are lots of these sorts of commentaries, and a very small number of them mention tikkun olam. Jill Jacobs derives from these few a more "literalist" understanding of tikkun olam as denoting the physical repair or stabilization of the natural world—literally a repair of the natural world and the environment. Jewish social justice advocates hope that these appearances of tikkun olam in the Midrash can demonstrate that liberal ecology—a prime facet of Jewish social justice—has long been a concern in rabbinic thought. It's also a back door into the Bible, since, as we saw, tikkun olam isn't mentioned anywhere in the Bible. Although the Midrash is a collection of rabbinical commentaries, they're commentaries that draw out theological meaning from Scripture. So if the Jewish social justice movement can show that tikkun olam is part of the Midrash, they can also make a subtle association of the concept with the Bible.

One such commentary that Jacobs cites is Genesis Rabbah 4:6. It explores the division of the waters (the sea and the sky) on the second day of the Creation story. God creates the seas and the skies by division—He divides the lower waters (the seas) and the upper waters (the skies). But whereas on every other day of the Creation story God declares that His creation is "good," on this second day He does not say that. The commentary picks up on this:

> "And let it divide the waters." Rabbi Tabyomi said: If "for it was good" is not written in connection with that day, even

though that division was made for *tikkuno shel olam* ["the stability of the world"] and its orderliness, then how much more
so should this apply to a division which leads to its [the world's]
confusion!

This is an example of a midrash noticing an omission—the second day of Creation is the only day in the story on which God
does not compliment His creation (He doesn't say that "it was
good"). From this omission the commentary draws a moral lesson: if God refrains from praising even a beneficial division, it
must be that division in general, especially among people, is a
bad thing. What interests Jacobs is less the substance of this
commentary than the use of the phrase "tikkun olam." She observes that this commentary understands tikkun olam as a
necessary undertaking for the good of the natural world—the
division of the firmament was required as part of the creation
of the environment. There is here a "more literal understanding of tikkun olam as the physical repair or stabilization of the
world," she observes. "The world is 'fixed' when it is physically
viable." She infers from this commentary that tikkun olam can
mean the physical preservation of the environment, and that
therefore the ecological agenda of social justice is endorsed by
the rabbis.

Is the reading advanced by Jacobs a fair one? Semantically,
it's correct to read "tikkun olam" in this specific instance as referring to the "stabilization of the world." But Jacobs subtly slips
in "repair" and "fixed" too. These make much less sense in context, because of course in the story the world was only just in
the process of being created. So why would it be in need of repair or fixing? The commentary gives no indication that it does.
If Jewish social justice is about repairing or perfecting the world,

a text that talks only about the stabilization of the world isn't all that useful. This isn't just a minor quibble—it shows how Jewish social justice activists deliberately misinterpret passages to make them seem like they're saying something they're not.

There's also no political inference to be drawn from this commentary. First of all, the tikkun olam here doesn't refer to a human activity but rather to a divine one—this is part of God's creation of the world. So much for tikkun olam being something man needs to do. Meanwhile, the substance of the *tikkun* is the division of the firmament. This is hardly a replicable operation and it's certainly not one with obvious normative ecological ramifications. Finally, the commentary isn't making an ecological point at all, but an ethical one: if a schism with even a positive purpose isn't considered "good," then surely we shouldn't ever desire a schism with a negative purpose, such as between people. This commentary isn't actually interested in ecology at all.[31]

Let's take one other example. The Coalition on the Environment and Jewish Life (COEJL) is one of a number of Jewish social justice organizations that focus on ecology. The COEJL "seeks to expand the contemporary understanding of such Jewish values as tikkun olam . . . to include the protection of both people and other species from environmental degradation." Its priorities "are to mobilize the Jewish community to address the climate crisis through advocacy for appropriate legislation as well as action to reduce our own greenhouse gas emissions."[32] This means challenging public officials and corporations, helping to ease poverty, protecting the underdeveloped world, and advocating for sustainable policies in order to bring about "environmental justice."[33]

All this is very urgent. If we don't act now, it'll be too late. How do we know? The COEJL presents a commentary from the

Midrash to prove its point. This commentary interprets one of the three verses where t-k-n appears in the Bible, which you'll recall from earlier on. "Consider the work of God: for who can make that straight (*l'takken*), which He has made crooked?" The solitary source the COEJL references to back up its "Covenant Campaign Declaration" is Ecclesiastes Rabbah 7:13, a commentary on that biblical verse. What does the commentary say?

> Look at My works! See how beautiful they are, how excellent! For your sake I created them all. See to it that you do not spoil and destroy My world, for if you do, there will be no one after you to repair it.[34]

The commentary is teaching the importance of safeguarding the world that God has created. The teaching doesn't seem all that dissimilar to the ethos of environmental justice espoused by the Jewish social justice movement—on the surface. But if you look closer, you'll see it doesn't quite say what the COEJL wants to claim.

Notice that the message of the commentary is entirely uncontroversial. Pace the more hysterical liberal ecologists, no reasonable person supports causing needless harm to the environment. Today's ecological debate centers on the parameters of balancing human need and environmental conservation. That is the real dilemma, and the commentary provides no practical guidance. Should we build cities that damage the natural terrain? Should we refrain from burning needed fossil fuels to preserve the environment? The commentary doesn't answer either of these or any other ecological questions. It's not an agenda but a warning. It's an important warning, to be sure. It cautions against complacency—but it doesn't offer any instruction or any endorsement of the radical ecological ideas of Jewish social justice campaigners. This midrash teaches vigilance.

More importantly, though, the COEJL tries to use this commentary to underscore the urgency of repairing the damage that humanity has done to the natural world. "We [the Jews] are a people of menders, of healers," the Jewish Energy Covenant Campaign Declaration proclaims, and "our fractured planet . . . cries out for healing."[35] But, hang on! What does the commentary actually say? It cautions that if man destroys God's world, *there will be nobody to repair it.* In other words, we have to avoid a situation where repair becomes necessary, because repair is *futile* (futility is one of the main themes of Ecclesiastes, remember). If repair were not futile, the midrash's warning would be totally blunted. It isn't telling us to be careful because fixing is difficult; it's warning us to be careful because fixing is impossible. If, as the COEJL claims, the planet is already "fractured" and "cries out for healing," then according to the logic of this commentary we're too late. So for the COEJL to cite this source as being about the need to fix things makes absolutely no sense. (In fact, if these activists had bothered to read the rest of this midrash, which talks about how sometimes it's unavoidable that even the best of us can still suffer for the mistakes of our ancestors, they might have realized that the ecological point of the commentary is to warn us against irreparable damage that will affect future generations regardless of what they do.) The COEJL is quoting this commentary in support of a campaign of repair that the commentary itself insists would be useless. The organization has completely misunderstood the text and defeated its own implorations.

Tikkun olam features in a miniscule number of the hundreds of commentaries in the Midrash. Not only do these appearances of the phrase not say what the Jewish social justice movement thinks they do. Sometimes, it turns out, they say the exact opposite.

LURIANIC KABBALAH

Finally, there is the tikkun olam of Lurianic Kabbalah, which is also a very popular traditional source in Jewish social justice circles. This is the mystical system of Isaac Luria (1534–1572). Jane Kanarek contrasts tikkun olam's appearances in the Talmud and in Lurianic mysticism as follows: whereas Talmudic tikkun olam is interested in communal remedies to social problems, Lurianic tikkun olam emphasizes the power of the individual to repair a shattered world. In the Lurianic system, a mending (tikkun) takes place "through a Jew's performance of *mitzvoth* [commandments], study of Torah, worship of God, and righteous actions." These are all actions of the individual Jew. But what fascinates Kanarek is that Luria propounded "the audacious idea that human actions have the potential to affect and heal the Divine." God Himself needs the Jewish People to engage in tikkun olam—which gives the concept a powerful eschatological feel.

The academic Howard Schwartz underscores the distinctly human role in the process of tikkun granted by Lurianic thought. He notes that rather than God being the sole agent of repair, Luria "was the first to propose that the Jewish people are God's partners in repairing the world."[36] The Jewish social justice movement is eager to find a source that calls for a human contribution to the repair of the world in order to match the power of the Social Gospel, which was based on the idea that man had to establish the Kingdom of God on earth. It turns out that Aleynu does not endorse the idea of humanity getting involved in tikkun olam as strongly as the Jewish liberals had hoped. But maybe Lurianic Kabbalah is their answer?

A summary of Lurianic tikkun is in order.[37] Luria taught that prior to Creation, the cosmos was entirely filled with the presence of God, imagined as limitless divine light. Luria framed Creation as *tsimtsum*, a metaphysical withdrawal or "contraction" of the infinite God into Himself. The result was the creation of a metaphysical space into which He could emanate and a purely spiritual creation could come into existence. However, some divine residue remained in the metaphysical space, and that residue formed into vessels. These vessels were to serve as containers for the divine emanation. However, that emanated light was too great for the vessels to endure, and they shattered, leaving only shards, which became the basis of material reality. Most of the light contained in the vessels returned to its divine source, but some sparks remained trapped, clinging to the shards. These sparks longed for reunion with the divine source. In the wake of this event, divinity sought to mend itself through a series of complicated processes of tikkun, whereby the procedure of emanation was repeated. This time, the emanations were clustered and therefore more resilient. The process was largely successful and most of the sparks were returned.

All of this occurred before the creation of Adam, the first human being, hence this first round of Lurianic tikkun was a purely Divine activity. When Adam was eventually created, he was an entirely spiritual being. His sin in Eden paralleled the shattering of the vessels. Future souls, and within them sparks, became trapped in what became the material world. The goal of tikkun now—a process in which man is now implicated—is to retrieve the sparks of divine light and restore them to their divine source. This process is performed by gentiles through the fulfilment of the seven laws the Jewish tradition teaches were given to Noah and his descendants, known in Judaism as the Noahide laws. And it's performed by Jews in exile through the fulfilment of the mitzvoth and the recitation of prayer with appropriate intention and concentration. Lurianic tikkun, which is entirely spiritual, is therefore an eschatological enterprise that fulfils God's initial intention for Creation. "The restoration of the ideal order, which forms the original aim of creation," wrote the eminent scholar of Jewish mysticism Gershom Scholem, "is also the secret purpose of existence."

So is the Jewish social justice take on Lurianic Kabbalah accurate? Well, Lurianic mysticism does rely upon individuals—and in certain ways more so than some of the other formulations of tikkun olam that we've looked at. And Kanarek is on solid ground in observing that Lurianic tikkun is "particularly Jewish work. For the Kabbalists, living Jewishly, performing commandments, and studying Torah are all part of the fabric of creating a better world."

But how do Jewish social justice activists get from "living Jewishly, performing commandments, and studying Torah" to the liberal political agenda of contemporary Jewish social justice? Lurianic Kabbalah never had anything like political activism in mind. In fact, Luria, a mystic who lived several centuries ago, was not even talking about the material world at all. For him, tikkun was an entirely spiritual enterprise. Its goal was repair not of this physical world but of other, spiritual worlds. It's fundamentally not a material endeavor—and that is crucial to bear in mind. As Scholem warns, "one is easily tempted to forget that for Luria [tikkun and the restoration of the scattered lights of God] refer to purely spiritual processes."[38] This is entirely unlike the vision of Jewish social justice activists—their goal is a material one achieved through political advocacy. That's the whole point of social justice work—to create a just society (as they see it) *in this world*. Whereas Jewish social justice urges comprehensive political reform to achieve essentially this-worldly objectives, Lurianic tikkun refers to other-worldly repair and is achieved through particular Jewish religious practices. The two ideas bear very little relation to one another.

For this reason, the Orthodox writer Yitzchok Adlerstein has sardonically but justifiably noted that when Adam and Eve were evicted from Eden following their sin, there were not yet any wars or famine or social oppression, no holes in the ozone layer or threats to blue whales or excessive greenhouse gas emissions, and yet, according to Lurianic thought, "no moment in history better defined the need for tikkun olam than that one."[39] Even Jacobs concedes that the "emphasis on realizing divine perfection, rather than on improving the condition of humanity, complicates the application of the mystical concept of tikkun to contemporary social justice work."[40] That, of course, is a deceptive way of saying that Lurianic tikkun and contemporary tikkun olam actually have nothing to do with one another.

IS TIKKUN OLAM STILL RELEVANT?

In this chapter, we've seen that tikkun olam doesn't feature in the Bible at all, and that its appearances in Aleynu, the Talmud, the Midrash, and Lurianic Kabbalah aren't actually pertinent to contemporary liberal Jewish activism. Tikkun olam, as it appears in rabbinic texts, has no connection to the various causes on the agenda of social justice. These texts provide no advice or instruction as to how contemporary America should approach these political questions—and there's certainly no endorsement of liberal or radical proposals of the sort promoted by Jewish social justice campaigners. Sadly for Kanarek, traditional tikkun olam simply does not provide any "real guidance for social justice efforts" at all.

In fact, tikkun olam can scarcely be said to constitute a coherent concept in the traditional Jewish sources. It appears here and there and serves totally dissimilar functions. Although the ideology of social justice has certain qualities—statism, universalism, a revolutionary impulse, and so on—the same isn't true of tikkun olam. Its various occurrences are just too different to make easy generalizations. That being said, each appearance of the concept does exhibit certain traits unto itself. For example, Aleynu's tikkun olam might be said to be universalistic—but only insofar as it envisions uniform worship of the God of Israel, which is a state of affairs considered antithetical by advocates of Jewish social justice. No version of tikkun olam encourages structural change—in fact, Talmudic tikkun olam takes the opposite approach, seeking to protect the existing system through minor adjustments. There's also little evidence of a revolutionary impulse in traditional tikkun olam—no notion that we need drastic reform or reconstruction or revolution. Fulfilment of the radical vision of Aleynu ultimately depends upon God, while Luria called for continued and more fervent observance of the traditional mitzvoth. Traditional tikkun olam may harbor certain eschatological ambitions in Aleynu and in Lurianic Kabbalah—but in neither case does the anticipated messianic era resemble the political aims of the Jewish social justice movement. It's odd that tikkun olam should have become the Jewish name for social justice, because it has no resemblance to social justice whatsoever.

Tikkun olam also can't be said to represent a central concept in traditional Judaism. It is omitted from the Bible, it lacks thematic consistency, and it appears overall comparatively rarely in the enormous Jewish canon. In fact, before radical activists popularized it in the United States, tikkun olam had never been believed to be a central concept in Judaism. It doesn't constitute a "Jewish ideal" or "tenet" or "imperative" or "prophetic value" or "commandment." Most fatally, it has no legal status in traditional Judaism—which is a profoundly legalistic religion. Put simply, tikkun olam is not a *mitzvah*. As the Orthodox rabbi and academic Michael J. Broyde has observed, tikkun olam has "never been treated as a mandatory Jewish law principle in the same way as any general religious obligation . . . [It was] never deemed to be a mitzvah and has never been formulated as any sort of a Jewish religious imperative."[41] Tikkun olam is a huge deal in contemporary American Judaism—but there's no basis for that in traditional Jewish thought.

The colossal disparity between the traditional and modern uses of the phrase yields no conclusion other than that today's tikkun olam is alien to Judaism as traditionally understood and practiced. The modern use of tikkun olam to denote social justice is not only an entirely recent phenomenon, as we know, but we've now learned that it's also without any basis in the Jewish tradition. This assessment may be surprising to many in the American Jewish community and beyond, but it's not as controversial as it may seem. In fact, some major figures in the Jewish social justice movement have validated it.

Leonard Fein, the founder of *Moment* magazine and the Jewish social justice organization Mazon, described tikkun olam as "a formulated meaning for American Jews." He elaborated that "the shattering of old ways, of the traditional culture with its implicit understandings and connections, *requires that in our time it be formulated anew, explicitly.*"[42] Fein thus recognized that the attachment of tikkun olam to social justice is a novel and deliberate development. Meanwhile, Arthur Green, the prominent theologian we met earlier on, defines "tikkun olam" as "an ancient Hebrew phrase that has taken on *new life* in the past few decades." He too admits that, although he believes the values that it expresses are "deeply rooted in the Jewish tradition" (not true), nevertheless "associating these ideals with tikkun olam may be *a recent innovation.*"[43] Eugene Borowitz, the late leading Reform theologian, has also written that the invocation of tikkun olam as a Jewish call to ethical action is "anomalous" and a "remarkable transformation" of the term. He goes on to remark that

> today's tikkun olam has little or nothing to do with [Jewish legal] adjustments or mystical intentions. Rather, it summons us to Jewish ethical duty, most often of a universal cast—but in keeping with our intensified postmodern particularity; *it legitimates this remnant of modernity by cloaking it in a classic Jewish term.*[44]

Contemporary tikkun olam is a "modern" idea "cloaked" in a classic Jewish term. Such cloaking is necessary because social justice is not easily located in the traditional Jewish sources. Ironically, it's even less easily located in the sources that explicitly mention tikkun olam.

Some leading advocates of Jewish social justice seem to have grasped that modern tikkun olam lacks any traditional basis and that it has now just become a go-to phrase to justify any liberal political aspiration. Some of them have criticized or discarded the term altogether. Margie Klein, a Jewish social justice activist in Boston, has reportedly deemed the phrase cliché.[45] Aryeh Cohen has described it as "rote and meaningless" and avoided mentioning it in his book *Justice in the City*.[46] Jill Jacobs has also admitted that the term is trite and as much reviled in Jewish social justice circles as it is beloved—but she believes it can yet be salvaged. Others have gone further. Arnold Jacob Wolf, the late Reform rabbi and a leading figure in the Jewish social justice movement in past decades, delivered a particularly damning indictment, blasting tikkun olam as a "strange and half-understood notion [which has become] a huge umbrella under which our petty moral concerns and political panaceas can come in out of the rain."[47]

These internal evaluations notwithstanding, *tikkun olam* remains the favored descriptor of Jewish social justice campaigners to label their work. Therefore it's surely legitimate for us to have investigated it. But Aryeh Cohen thinks that questioning the validity of Jewish social justice by pointing out that tikkun olam "has been misused or misunderstood"—a contention he agrees with—is a "bait and switch." This is because "the argument that Jews are obligated to work towards a more just world is not dependent on a single phrase [but] on a consistent and coherent reading of an unbroken tradition."[48] But it's Cohen who has, in fact, missed the point. "Tikkun olam" didn't become the recognized Jewish nomenclature for social justice for no reason. It's totally bound up with the history of the Jewish social justice movement. The phrase captures a movement whose origins are in Classical Reform, which, Cohen apparently needs reminding, was predicated precisely on "breaking" the tradition. That movement—and the adoption of the phrase—was influenced by the Social Gospel, which is another tradition entirely. The movement was then shaped by the American Jewish return to ritual and Hebraic expression—hence the phrase "tikkun olam," which is, obviously, in Hebrew, became more accepted. (Or maybe it's not so obvious. One is reminded of the joke in which an American Jew, stereotypically ignorant of his heritage, arrives in Israel and asks how you say "tikkun olam" in Hebrew.) And then the secular Jewish radicals entered into the communal conversation and popularized the term. If Cohen accepts that tikkun olam is misunderstood, perhaps he should be more open to the possibility that that's because the people who propagated it—the champions of Jewish social justice—did not themselves understand Judaism. Tikkun olam isn't just a name—it's a reminder of where Jewish social justice came from. But maybe that's why some of these activists are so eager to set it aside.

How Not to Read the Bible

What the Bible says and what the Jewish social justice movement thinks it says diverge. Abraham's appeals for Sodom are not the purpose of Judaism. The story of Joseph is not a straightforward example of benevolent government. The Exodus from Egypt is not reducible to political revolution. The "prophetic legacy" is not social justice. And tikkun olam itself has never meant what American Jews now understand the term to mean.

We've seen how this phenomenon has come about historically—it's the product of a shift from Classical Reform to modern non-Orthodoxy. The Classical Reformers were generally of the view that they were changing the Jewish religion. Halfhearted claims to be rediscovering the essence of the faith notwithstanding, they were still consciously *reforming* Judaism—making it into something else. Today's activists have retained the political ideology of their forebears, but differ insofar as they now claim that they're not innovating but are remaining true to the Jewish tradition. The Reform, Conservative, Reconstructionist, and Renewal denominations make out that their obsession with social justice is in fact not a new thing but a very old thing—something present in the Bible and rabbinic Judaism since time immemorial. But this raises a difficulty—the Classical Reformers obviously felt that their politics and objectives were not expressed in traditional Jewish practice and belief—hence the need to reform them. So how can contemporary Jewish social justice activists, largely keeping with those politics and objectives, now argue that the practices and beliefs of old do contain this ideology? For some insight, let's turn to Margie Klein, one of the co-editors of *Righteous Indignation*.

Klein attended Hebrew College Rabbinical School and is now the minister at Sha'arei Shalom Synagogue in Ashland, Massachusetts. She is involved in various social justice campaigns, such as for a living wage and protection of immigrant communities, and was the founder of Moishe Kavod Jewish Social Justice House in Boston, part of the national network of Moishe Houses which house and serve local young Jewish professionals. Klein has grappled with the question of the connection between her politics and traditional Jewish texts. In her experience, she explains, the politics of social justice are a given. The biblical sources, she implies, are simply appropriated for political advantage. She writes:

> Personally, I began to care about social justice because I went to a justice-conscious Jewish day school, and was taught that that's what Jews do. There, I came to believe that our shared story of liberation inspires us to dream of liberation in every generation. And through further journeying, I came to feel

called by our mystical traditions, the idea that God/Every-
thing is One, that we are all interconnected, and therefore all
responsible for one another. Those ideas set me on a path, but
then were strengthened and given form by the contemporary
progressive values of my family and community.[1]

American Jewish families, communities, and schooling are
geared toward social justice from the start. Schools are not simply Jewish—they are "justice-conscious." This isn't necessarily
because this is what Judaism actually teaches—it's simply
because it's "what Jews do." Naturally, the justice-consciousness
of these communities and schools defines the teaching of texts
and religion, the encounter with which is therefore really just
to reinforce the political conceptions that Jewish kids get from
their liberal parents. As an example of this, Klein points to "our
shared story of liberation," a reference to the Exodus. As we saw
earlier, the Exodus in traditional Jewish thought is not merely
or even primarily a story of liberation from slavery or general
oppression—but that's the interpretation that American Jewish
children are taught because it has the greatest usefulness to the
politics of social justice. In order to tie this and other dubious
biblical readings together, there is a turn to "mystical traditions."
This is the theology of Jewish social justice arising from the
movement's reading of Creation—the upshot of which is that
humanity is undifferentiated and all humans are equally obligated to one another. This pedagogy does not suggest there is
an honest encounter with Jewish texts going on.

In fact, Klein is more explicit. Impressed by a Talmudic source
about healthcare, for example, she clarifies that "while I was glad
to know that the rabbis thought about these issues, I was also
clear that my own commitment to [health]care . . . would have

remained even if I learned that the Talmud taught otherwise." Evidently, what the Talmud says isn't actually all that important, and the same goes for the Bible. Jill Jacobs, among others, may insist that the wisdom of Jewish sacred texts "can inform our own approaches to current issues, challenge our assumptions, and force us to consider alternative approaches," but there is no indication that any Jewish social justice assumptions have been substantively revised in the light of traditional sources.[2] These activists care about social justice independently of Jewish texts, from which they have no interest in actually learning. As the essayist and translator Hillel Halkin has written:

> Judaism has value to such Jews to the extent that it is useful, and it is useful to the extent that it can be made to conform to whatever beliefs and opinions they would have even if Judaism had never existed.[3]

We have seen this process of making Judaism conform to the politics of social justice over the past several chapters. We have seen how traditional Judaism does not endorse the political views of Jewish social justice activists. Consequently, they dispense with actual exegesis (the drawing of meaning from a text). Instead, they're doing something else. What they're doing is called eisegesis—they're imposing their preconceived views and biases onto the Bible. As Margie Klein herself readily observes, advocates of Jewish social justice were committed to their cause—to their political views and biases—long before they opened the Bible or Talmud. Nothing about their encounter with these texts is meant to change their mind. To the contrary—it is their mind that is meant to change the meaning of the texts.

Sometimes this eisegesis is done subtly, such as when Jill Jacobs surreptitiously suggests that the Aleynu prayer calls for an end to poverty—an inference that is totally unfounded. But sometimes it's more explicit. Aryeh Cohen, for example, introduces his book on Jewish social justice by writing that "This theory of justice that I seek to propose is significantly drawn from that textual tradition [of rabbinic discourse], while it is also based on a contemporary ethical and philosophical framework."[4] Cohen is openly stating that his theory of Jewish social justice—the theory he uses to advance his political worldview—will not draw from Jewish sources alone. This is because relying solely on Jewish texts is apparently not sufficient to get his readers to where he wants to take them. That's an incredible admission from a guy who claims elsewhere (and implies across his other writing and activism) that "the argument that Jews are obligated to work towards a more just world . . . is dependent on a consistent and coherent reading of an unbroken tradition."[5] His reading of the tradition doesn't seem all that consistent and unbroken if it needs to be supplemented by other ethics and philosophies. He elaborates:

> I will be thinking through and with [Jewish] texts that have come through many centuries of study. I will not give them a veto . . . over other possibilities, but will rather start with a subtle and nuanced reading of certain texts in order to draw from them a conceptual vocabulary that I can employ to understand the issues we are discussing. This drawing out will not be a claim for a literalist reading of texts or an insinuation of (the discourse of) commandedness into the political and ethical vocabulary of justice. It will rather be a display of the textured use of the vocabulary that the Jewish

legal/textual tradition presents. This is itself a goal, since *the larger exercise . . . is staking a claim to a Judaism that privileges justice*, and in which justice is the warp and woof of its texture.[6]

In case you didn't understand what any of that meant, Cohen is trying to outline his interpretative procedure. He says he'll be lifting terminology from traditional Jewish sources out of their contexts and giving them new meanings. This is exactly what we've seen and bemoaned in our survey of biblical passages— context is ignored and novel meanings are attached to terms and stories that the texts never intended and that in some cases don't even make sense. And what, in the end, is the point of this oppressive process? For Cohen it's to create a "Judaism that privileges justice." That sounds awfully like a Judaism that says whatever Cohen wants it to say.

The truth is, you can probably go to the texts of any religious tradition or political ideology and make them say whatever you want, if you're unashamedly selective enough. We saw a bit of that in our study of the appropriation of the Prophets. You can make the prophets come off as opponents of ritual when the only passages you quote are ones where they criticize it. There are other examples too. Here's a more subtle one. Shmuly Yanklowitz, the Orthodox rabbi and Jewish social justice activist, struggles to find Jewish legal prohibitions on child labor. This shouldn't be all that surprising, since most rabbinic legislation originates in pre-modern times, when child labor was common. In a note on the subject, he therefore relies on American civil law to make his point, writing that the "prescription to obey the laws of the land should suffice as a [Jewish legal] imperative to ensure that we honor child labor laws."[7] That's fine. But at the

same time, the flagship campaign of his Uri L'Tzedek organization, the Tav HaYosher, a certificate of ethical practice awarded
to qualifying restaurants in recognition of the fulfilment of certain criteria, omits from these criteria any mention of the civil
illegality of hiring undocumented or illegal aliens. Evidently,
civil illegality is applicable only when it fits the social justice
agenda.

Among the advocates of Jewish social justice who are most
unashamed in their selectivity is Michael Lerner, who can always be relied upon to articulate what his peers are thinking
but do not dare to say. There are vast portions of the Bible that
do not conform to the agenda of Jewish social justice. Naturally,
most biblical ritual would fall into this category, including sacrifices and dietary laws. Indeed, much of Leviticus, the third
book of the Pentateuch (which is the holiest portion of the Hebrew Bible to Jews), is devoted to these topics, as are significant
portions of the rest of the Torah. We have already noted Lerner's distaste toward such practices—inherited from the Classical Reformers—in our examination of the Prophets. But what
exercises him the most is the violence of the Bible. Like it or not,
the Bible contains a good deal of violence and a not insignificant amount of that violence is not only rewarded by God but
sometimes even commanded by Him.

Lerner himself raises several examples, including Moses'
wars against the nations neighboring the Land of Israel and Joshua's military campaign upon entering the Promised Land. He
also laments the prophet Samuel's beheading of the king of the
Amalekites after Saul, the Israelite king, fails to do so in contra-
vention of God's command. These passages ought to force Jewish activists to confront the implications of Jewish power, a
prospect that makes them very uncomfortable—not least

because it might require them to reevaluate their negative feelings toward the State of Israel. (You might have noticed how little the Jewish social justice movement appeals to the books of Joshua, Judges, Samuel, or Kings, doubtless because these deal with Jewish sovereignty in the Land of Israel.) But rather than engage with these texts, Lerner lumps them all into a category he calls the "Joshua tradition" and declares that they are "not the voice of God."[8] (His sentiment echoes that of the twentieth-century Jewish philosopher Martin Buber, who, upon being asked about Saul and the Amalekite king, reportedly responded: "I do not believe Samuel understood the will of God."[9]) Predictably, Lerner strongly insinuates that this "voice of cruelty and fanaticism and intolerance and oppression," which is "masquerading as the voice of God," is to be associated with the political Right, while the opposing "voice of love, justice, and transcendence"—expressed in the texts he likes—is represented by the Left. How, then, is one to know which is the voice of God and which is the voice of, let us say, conservatism? Lerner helpfully advises:

> Whatever parts of the tradition help you to connect with the recognition of the other as created in the image of God, whatever tends to give you confidence and hopefulness about the possibility of joining as partners with God in the task of healing and repair of the universe, those are the parts of the tradition that have been revealed, that have the mark of God in them.

This is Lerner's flowery way of saying that whatever inspires you to be a better leftist and do tikkun olam is the true voice of God. Whether or not this "Lerner tradition" succeeds in differentiating itself from the imaginary "Joshua tradition," it is certainly distinct from the Jewish tradition.

You may find Lerner's overt selectivity amusing. As perhaps you should. The literature of the Jewish social justice movement is replete with comically desperate attempts to marshal biblical passages to further political ends. The mission statement of Arthur Waskow's Shalom Center, alluding to the Exodus story, is equally ludicrous.

> When The Shalom Center addresses a specific issue—like [the] climate crisis, or the Iraq war, or the systematic combination of disemployment [sic] and overwork, or spiritual emptiness—our approach is deep and systemic, looking beneath the specific issue to the power dynamics that have shaped it. Jewish tradition underlines this question through the archetypal story of Pharaoh: enslavement, xenophobia, and damage to the earth (the plagues) are rooted in Pharaoh's addiction to his own top-down, unaccountable power. For example, in our pre-Passover message in February, 2008, we invited members of the Jewish community to deepen their understanding of the holiday by considering "Who or what is Pharaoh in our world today, bringing eco-disastrous plagues upon our heads? Can we face the Pharaohs who are turning the great round earth itself into [Egypt]?"[10]

This practically parodic passage isn't peripheral—it's a mission statement. You'll notice some familiar themes: the favored approach is "deep and systemic" and the story of Pharaoh is "archetypal." The invitation to try to identify the "Pharaoh in our world today" speaks to the perennial search for oppression reminiscent of Michael Walzer's conclusion to his *Exodus and*

Revolution. But consider the reference to "Pharaoh's addiction to his own top-down, unaccountable power." The Shalom Center conveniently ignores the fact that the acquisition of that power by Pharaoh was facilitated originally by Joseph through policies designed to alleviate the famine—policies that are celebrated by the Jewish social justice movement. As we noted earlier, the easy corruption of such power is precisely one of the main concerns of those who oppose big government today. Most bizarre, however, is the mission statement's expressed regret that the plagues somehow caused "damage to the earth" and their rendering as "eco-disastrous." In this self-defeating portrayal, the instruments of redemption in the Bible have themselves become the very catastrophe that the Jews must reverse. One wonders if we're all even reading the same book anymore.

As it happens, some Jewish social justice activists don't appear to be reading at all. There are instances when they fabricate sources to support their argument where none exist. The website of the Schusterman Family Foundation, for example, explains the organization's "values" by referencing a Talmudic aphorism quoted as follows (with the words in brackets included):

> While no one person is obligated to complete the task [of *tikkun olam*], neither is anyone free to desist from it.[11]

In the authentic Hebrew text, the word "task" appears as "*melachah,*" a term of an entirely different order from tikkun olam. No reference is made to tikkun olam in the original statement whatsoever. (This surely ought to have been obvious, given the phrase appears in brackets.) The aphorism is totally made up. And, to reiterate, it's one of the "values" of this foundation—one of the most generous and well-known Jewish philanthropies in America.

What are we to make of all this? The Jewish social justice movement is trying to convince us that its activists can develop moral positions—unwaveringly liberal positions—independent of traditional Jewish sources, and then turn to those sources only to find them in unflinching agreement with their pre-existing beliefs. If this were actually the case, it would represent a prodigious coincidence. Hillel Halkin rightly challenges this improbability, writing in a censorious review of *Righteous Indignation*: "On everything Judaism has a position—and, wondrously, this position just happens to coincide with that of the American liberal Left."[12] But the truth is that they have not found the sources in agreement with their politics. Hence, in order to convince the American Jewish community that its politics is rooted in the Bible, they have resorted to eisegesis, gross selectivity, and even fabrication. Sadly, the biggest casualty of this routine is their own relationship to their faith. The late Reform rabbi and leading Jewish social justice activist in his time Arnold Jacob Wolf complained about this phenomenon from within the movement. He candidly observed that

> our Jewish program looks pretty much like that of the ACLU [American Civil Liberties Union] or the Democratic Party . . . God seems to require of us no more and no less than a vote for Al Gore or for saving the whale.[13]

He went to say that "our good faith is suspect when we demand so little of ourselves." Regrettably, such criticisms have fallen on deaf ears.

A SUSPECT FAITH

The biblical interpretations of the Jewish social justice movement can be comical, confusing, and crafty. They can also be dark. Consider the issue of immigration. Everybody has an opinion on whether America should be a country of open borders that welcomes economic migrants and political refugees without question, or whether doing so might impact the nation's security, undermine its laws, or threaten the economic and personal wellbeing of its citizens. Liberals might incline one way; conservatives another. Dara Silverman argues in *Righteous Indignation* that there is an authentically *Jewish* approach to the dilemmas of illegal immigration and refugees in the contemporary United States.[14]

Silverman is the national coordinator for a social justice group called Showing Up for Racial Justice. When she wrote her essay for *Righteous Indignation* in 2008, she was the executive director of the New York City–based Jewish social justice group Jews for Racial and Economic Justice, an organization that would later go on to support Occupy Wall Street and Black Lives Matter. In Silverman's view, Jews should push for a liberal immigration policy in the United States not merely due to the Jewish experience of migration over many centuries, but also because of what, apparently, the Bible says. Predictably, some of her argument is simply baffling. For example, she mentions Numbers 15:15, which commands that you should "have one law for the stranger and the citizen among you," and contends that the verse can be applied to immigrant "strangers" today whose migration to America the Jews—being "citizens" of the United States—should support. Omitted from this dubious analysis, however, is any attempt at reconciling the verse's reference to "law" with her support for *illegal* immigration. But then again this isn't actual Judaism—it's a Judaism that says whatever Silverman wants it to say.

Yet this reference to strangers and citizens is also revealing. Silverman underscores the point by recourse to Exodus 23:9, which requires a Jew to "welcome the stranger, because you were once a stranger in Egypt" (the verse actually talks about not *oppressing* a stranger and says nothing about *welcoming* them, but never mind). Silverman appeals to these verses in order to justify her insistence that "it is crucial to join with immigrants . . . to fight for comprehensive immigration reform . . . and for immigrant justice." Now, you might be thinking that maybe Silverman has a point. After all, this biblical injunction not to oppress the stranger, or *ger* in Hebrew (pl. *geirim*), is hardly obscure—it's repeated over and over again in the Pentateuch (for example, in Ex. 22:20, Lev. 19:33–34, Num. 9:14, and Deut. 24:20–22). But what's interesting about this citation—which features throughout Jewish social justice activism in the area of immigration and elsewhere—is not what it says about immigrants but what it implies about American Jews.

Silverman's purpose in bringing it up is, of course, to portray immigrants to the United States as geirim. The implication is that American Jews are the "citizens" that the Bible has in mind. Hence the Jews, along with their non-Jewish fellow Americans, are somehow obligated to legal and illegal immigrants (needless to say, for Silverman and her activist peers, this "obligation" requires opening borders and economically supporting migrants regardless of their circumstances, status, or intentions). But in traditional discourse, from the Jewish point of view who is a ger? It's complicated, but put simply, in the Bible the ger is a temporary sojourner in a land not his own. Hence the Jews, whose homeland is the Land of Israel, were strangers in the land of Egypt.[15] Therefore, notwithstanding the merits of treating gentile immigrants to America, who come to the country to settle permanently, with due sensitivity and compassion, from the perspective of the Bible and traditional Judaism the real geirim in the United States today are actually American Jews. Their true homeland is still the Land of Israel. In a nod to traditional Jewish theology, in Modern Hebrew the verb a Jew uses to refer to his or her living in the Diaspora is *gar* (the same root as that of ger). This is because the Jews—including American Jews—are ultimately strangers themselves whose sojourn in the Diaspora is, theologically speaking, only temporary.

Silverman's rendering of gentile immigrants as geirim—and she is hardly alone in this—inverts this traditional assumption. Instead of the Jews temporarily sojourning in a land not really their own, the Jews have become permanent residents. The effect of this reversal is to transform the United States (or any given Diaspora country) into the Jewish Promised Land—and the Jews from strangers to natives. (To be clear, we're not talking about the practical rights and obligations of American citizenship, to which an American Jew is as entitled and subject as any other American, but rather we're discussing the theological ramifications of substituting a Diaspora country for the Land of Israel in the overall worldview of Judaism.) A profound theological position is quietly being adopted here: the Diaspora is the ultimate home of the Jewish People. In effect, the Diaspora, rather than the Land of Israel and Jerusalem its capital, is Zion.

Similar efforts to abandon the idea that the actual Land of Israel is Zion are evident across Jewish social justice activism. Such efforts aren't new, of course—the Classical Reformers exorcised the Land of Israel from their religion too. And today, this sentiment is everywhere. In the Jewish social justice reading of the Exodus, the Promised Land is not an actual place but anywhere social justice reigns, and the movement's *Haggadahs* routinely substitute the traditional prayer "Next Year in Jerusalem" for "Next year in a world of peace and justice." The same attitude was apparent also in the 2011 Occupy Wall Street protests. Reacting to the eventual eviction of the protestors from New York City's Zuccotti Park, Daniel Sieradski likened the protest's demise to the ancient exile of the Jews from Jerusalem. This wasn't mere hyperbole—it was because, in being exiled from the prospect of achieving social justice, they were being exiled from Zion.[16] In reality, social justice does not yet prevail anywhere, and being a utopian ideology, never will ("wherever you live it is probably Egypt"). But everywhere is *potentially* Zion. The actual Zion of the Jewish tradition is no more significant than any other geographic location.

In a sense, this is a prerequisite for the very idea of Jewish social justice. Only if the whole world is potentially Zion can Jewish activists plausibly cite traditional Jewish laws intended for Jewish life in the Land of Israel to support contemporary political policies in the United States. The implication of Jewish social justice is that everywhere is potentially Zion and everyone is ultimately a citizen of Zion—and so they must abide by the (faux) "Jewish values" of social justice. (There is an irony in the fact that advocates of Jewish social justice in the United States, who wish to impose these pseudo-Jewish values upon all of America, are often the most vocal opponents, from a distance, of any moves toward the introduction of stricter traditional Jewish law in Israel.)

To take another example, consider that omnipresent verse in the Jewish social justice movement: "Justice, justice you shall pursue" (Deut. 16:20). This line is so fashionable that it even features in the slogans of several organizations devoted to tikkun olam. Its popularity is equaled, however, by its abuse. For one thing, the text offers no reason to interpret "justice" to mean the economic centralization or gender and cultural diversity of social justice. If anything, the context—a segment of the Bible dealing with the Israelite judiciary—points to a conventional understanding of "justice" as contractual right and criminal punishment upheld by judges and courts. (In fact, it's worthwhile noting also that the text goes on—in Deut. 17:3 and even 16:21—to condemn the Israelite who comes to worship aspects of the natural world instead of the God of Israel, a critique that should perhaps give pause to modern-day Jewish pantheists and their panentheist fellow travelers like Arthur Green.) Most pertinent, however, is the fact that Jewish activists are so obsessed with the verse's opening that they ignore its conclusion. In full, the verse reads: "Justice, justice you shall pursue, so *that you may live to inherit the Land which the Lord your God is giving you.*" For decades activists have used this verse in campaigning to establish a Kingdom of God—a liberal paradise—in America, yet the actual purpose of pursuing justice is that the Jews remain worthy of the Land of Israel!

In traditional Jewish thought there is an unbreakable bond between the Jewish People and the Land of Israel. This is especially true of Jerusalem, the ancient capital of Israel that is also known as Zion. The historical attachment of Jews to Israel dates back to God's original biblical call to Abraham to journey to the Land that will be shown him—and His promise to Abraham to give that Land to his descendants. But that attachment is also the requisite for many of the laws commanded at Sinai; it's fulfilled through the inheritance of the Land by the tribes of Israel under Joshua; it underlies the major Jewish festivals; it's consummated by the Davidic monarchy and the construction of the Temple; it's integral to the prophetic visions of redemption; it's ubiquitous in the biblical exegesis and legal codes of the rabbis; and it has found expression in Jewish prayer for over two millennia—prayer that is traditionally recited facing in the direction of Zion. Modern Zionism—the political and cultural effort to ingather the exiles and make the Land of Israel the center of Jewish life again—is simply the latest expression of this long-standing Jewish connection to the Land of Israel. The Land of Israel is not simply a concept or a condition or the designation of the fulfilment of social justice worldwide, but a real and fixed geographic place—a place where the Jews will eventually be ingathered and then, in the words of the Book of Isaiah (2:3), "out of Zion shall go forth the Torah and the word of the Lord from Jerusalem."

Clearly, there is a tension between the Jewish social justice view of Israel and that of traditional Judaism. That is not evident merely from the Jewish social justice movement's subtle misreading of biblical verses, but is also spelled out explicitly in its literature. Take Shmuly Yanklowitz, who is the founder and president of the Orthodox social justice organization Uri L'Tzedek. Although he identifies as a "religious Zionist," he is still first and foremost a Jewish social justice activist. Hence he asserts in his book *Jewish Ethics and Social Justice: A Guide for the 21st Century*, in a section titled "A Jewish Imperative to Live in the Diaspora?," that while residence in Israel should be encouraged, nevertheless "there is also a crucial duty to reside in the Diaspora."[17] This is because "the Torah demands that we, as a nation, commit to pursuing justice; to be warriors against injustice, it behooves us to be stationed everywhere around the globe." Thus even an advocate of Jewish social justice, who, being an Orthodox rabbi, cannot ignore the central role of the Land of Israel in Judaism, is unable to avoid the logic of social justice—which points back to the position of Classical Reform that dispenses with the Jewish attachment to the Land of Israel and declares that the rightful place of the Jews is in the Diaspora.

This logic is unavoidable because it is part of the theology of Jewish social justice. In his *Radical Judaism*, Arthur Green does not merely refuse to accord any messianic or proto-messianic meaning to the existence of a Jewish State, which would be one thing, but he declines to give it any religious meaning whatsoever. He sees it as no more than a regrettable historical necessity in the face of antisemitism—a special case that social justice may just have to suffer (although it doesn't seem like he's keen to tolerate it much longer). But as Daniel Landes, the director of a Jewish seminary in Israel, has remarked, it's incredible that Green doesn't see any religious meaning in Israel—because he sees it in absolutely everything else.[18] Landes notes Green's acknowledgment that Israel is necessary for Jewish survival—but it has no real place in Green's Judaism. "Green defines himself as a secular Zionist," Landes observes, "which is astonishing, because nothing else in his book is secular. Every mosquito, rock, indigenous religious practice, every person, place, or thing, is given a spiritual status." Remember that Green sees everything as interconnected—as part of the One. The One is in a process of ever revealing itself through the diversity of life. Every manifestation of that diversity is a part of divinity revealing itself—so every manifestation has religious significance. The obligation that Creation puts on all of us is to assist that process of revelation by facilitating and celebrating all this diversity. Except, that is, when it comes to the Jews and their state. Israel has no meaning—uniquely, there seems to be nothing divine in its revelation. This is rather curious. As Landes concludes, "the State of Israel is, for Green, something of a problem."

For Green, a state to protect the Jews need not even have arisen in the ancient Jewish homeland in particular—in actual Zion—except that that location "seemed natural." But instead of this geographical choice being something to welcome and affirm, it instead puts "our values" to the test. Israel has become "colonialist," and for the Jews not to share the Holy Land would constitute a failure by them and their tradition of "a vital test." For Israel to exist as a "garrison state" would be "a betrayal of the best of Jewish values." Those "Jewish values," it goes without saying, constitute social justice. And social justice, it seems, cannot tolerate a state like Israel that protects its citizens in their homeland from enemies all around who would kill them. Green is delivering a warning. His and his fellow activists' willingness to tolerate this special case is nearly spent.

So what is Israel to do? It's stuck in a catch-22. To be a truly Jewish State as far as social justice is concerned, Israel cannot be narrowly geared for the Jews—because that would be a betrayal of the universalism of social justice, which represents "the best of Jewish values." But if Israel is not geared for the Jews, then in reality it won't be a Jewish State at all—and any talk of "Jewish values," whatever they might be, will be irrelevant.

Israel may not have pride of place in Green's thinking—but the Diaspora does. If actual Zion is not at the center of this theology, then *potential Zion* must be—i.e. everywhere else. Echoing the Classical Reformers, Green believes the exile of the Jews is over. Those Jews still living in the Diaspora are doing so not because they must (as in exile) but out of choice. He insists, in a section of his book titled "A Diasporist Judaism," that the long wandering of the Jews is "an essential part of the experience and legacy of Israel." It's a positive thing. Isaac Mayer Wise made the same argument almost a century and a half ago. This wandering, Green claims, is preferable to living in the Land of Israel.

Green is not the only advocate of a "Diasporic Judaism." Aryeh Cohen, for example, equates Jewish participation in the democratic institutions of the Diaspora countries with Jewish sovereignty in Israel. The rise of democracy in the Diaspora is, in his view, a fine substitute for the Jewish return to the Land of Israel. Jewish participation in democratic institutions can be understood as a "Jewish return to sovereignty with others, in which the sovereignty of others is complementary to Jewish sovereignty."[19] In other words, return to Jewish sovereignty in the Land of Israel is unnecessary, because the Jews can be sovereign in the democratic countries of their dispersion. But whereas Cohen is interested in bringing Jewish sovereignty out from Israel into the Diaspora, there is a complementary and more sinister approach that involves bringing the non-sovereignty of the Jews into Israel. Its leading spokesperson is Judith Butler.

Butler is an academic at the University of California, Berkeley, who supports the boycott of Israel, is a member of the Academic Advisory Council of the anti-Zionist Jewish Voice for Peace, and has spoken approvingly of Hamas and Hezbollah— both proscribed terrorist groups sworn to Israel's destruction.[20] In her book *Parting Ways: Jewishness and the Critique of Zionism*, Butler asserts that "Diasporic Judaism" is a counter to Jewish sovereignty in the Land of Israel, and argues in favor of a "one-state solution" to the Arab-Israeli conflict—a solution in which Israel does not exist. Like Green, Butler believes that Israel is not

Jewish until it abandons its focus on the Jews—and it can learn how to do so from the Diaspora. The "Diasporic," she contends, doesn't function as a negative exile: the Jews are *meant* to be a wandering people, and they're meant to live with non-Jews. But whereas the Classical Reformers viewed the dispersion positively because of the benefit they imagined it could bring to the gentiles, Butler celebrates it because of what it can do for the Jews. The point and the glory of the Diaspora, she believes, are that it forces "cohabitation with the non-Jew and eschews the Zionist linkage of nation to land." The exile and dispersion of the Jews are good things because they undermine the national character of the Jewish People.

But Butler goes further. The dispersion, she elaborates, isn't simply a geographical situation; it's also an "ethical modality." What she means is that it's the very idea of cohabitation and the encounter with other (non-Jewish) values that are the essence of exile. Her argument is that exilic Judaism is about imbibing the idea of living with others and not being exclusively Jewish. In ancient Israel, the Jews existed apart from the rest of humanity in their own sovereign country, and that separateness was bad; now the Jews in the Diaspora live with the rest of humanity, and that coalescence—living with others and adopting their values—is good. Thus the teaching of "Diasporic Judaism" is that exclusive Jewish sovereignty—represented today by Zionism—is evil, whereas Jewish coexistence with others in gentile lands where the Jews are not sovereign should be encouraged. These "Jewish ethics," Butler writes, "not only demand a critique of Zionism, but must transcend its exclusive Jewishness in order to realize the ethical and political ideals of living together in radical democracy." Ethical Judaism, in other words, is anti-Zionist.

Butler's theory—that Judaism requires adherence to non-Judaism—is prima facie absurd. That her book provides no treatment of any traditional Jewish texts (with the exception of a passing and unfair reference to Lurianic Kabbalah) undermines the pretense that Butler has any interest in actual Judaism. Instead, to bolster her case she cites various twentieth-century Jewish and Arab thinkers, including Walter Benjamin, Hannah Arendt, and Edward Said—none of whom were mainstream Zionists (to say the least). It isn't Zionism that has departed from Jewishness, but Butler herself.

Butler's project has the dual purpose of ending what she foolishly believes to be the subjugation of the Arabs by Israel and of comforting those Jews who profess to feel alienated from Judaism due to the State of Israel. Her sophistry is presented in the name of social justice and tikkun olam. "The notion that to be a Jew is to be a Zionist [is] a historical equation that is to be countered if Jewishness is to remain linked with the struggle for social justice," Butler explains. Defending herself from critics, she claims there are Jewish traditions that value cohabitation and oppose all violence (although, whatever they are, as a supporter of Hamas it would appear that she herself does not subscribe to them). "It is most important that these traditions be valued and animated for our time," she counsels, because "they represent diasporic values, struggles for social justice, and the exceedingly important Jewish value of 'repairing the world' (*Tikkun*)."[21] Tikkun olam is a specifically "Diasporic value" that represents the "authentic Judaism" of the Diaspora. It's a value that the State of Israel—by its very existence—is alleged to be sabotaging. Tikkun olam and Israel have parted ways.

Social Justice vs. Israel

In 2003, a rabbinical student at the Conservative Jewish Theological Seminary made headlines when she wrote a short Torah commentary for the school newsletter that was allegedly critical enough of Israel to be denied publication (it is consequently not now publicly available). According to reportage of the incident, the supervising rabbi insisted that the religious bulletin was not a venue for political statements. The student subsequently distributed copies of the article to her peers on campus, but, according to a contemporary account, only after having changed references to criticism of "Israel" and the "Jewish State" to "the Israeli government."[1] This is a tried and tested tactic employed by those uncomfortable with or opposed to Jewish sovereignty in the Land of Israel but who wish to hide this sentiment from others in order to shield themselves from criticism and gain legitimacy. The student had her defenders, including Shaul Magid, a professor of Jewish philosophy then also at the Jewish Theological Seminary and now at Indiana University. He argued that "American Jewry need to get their head around what it means for a person to publicly support Israel and yet be critical of its government," a nuance undermined, it would seem, by the very episode on which he was commenting. (As it happens, Magid is a contributor to *Righteous Indignation*, where his essay appeals to "both progressive Zionists and . . . those who may not call themselves Zionists" in making the case for a binational Jewish/Arab state. One wonders if this is also an example of supposed public support for Israel tempered by mere "criticism of its government.") It is worth noting that this student's apparent need to lambast the Jewish State took place during the worst period of Arab terrorist attacks against civilians in Israel's history. The student was Jill Jacobs.

Jacobs is now a Conservative rabbi and prominent Jewish social justice campaigner, and we've encountered her several times in previous chapters. The author of multiple books and articles on Jewish social justice, since graduating from the Jewish Theological Seminary she has served as the director of education at the Jewish Council on Urban Affairs and the rabbi-in-residence at Jewish Funds for Justice, a Jewish social justice organization funded by George Soros (it has since merged with Progressive Jewish Alliance to form Bend the Arc, of which, you'll remember, Soros' son Alexander is chairman). Jacobs is now a board member of J Street, the liberal political lobby that supports congressional candidates who are least friendly to Israel, regularly endorses policies opposed by the government of Israel, and actively backed the Obama administration's contentious nuclear pact with the Islamic Republic of Iran, which has made no secret of its desire to wipe Israel off the map. Jacobs is also the executive director of T'ruah: The Rabbinic Call for Human Rights, which is geared toward rabbis and cantors in the Jewish social justice movement. Her husband, also a rabbi, is on the rabbinic council of Jews for Racial and Economic Justice, which you'll recall endorsed Occupy Wall Street and Black Lives Matter, the platform of which accuses Israel of committing genocide. Jacobs has been regularly listed as one of *Newsweek's* fifty most influential rabbis in America and one of the *Forward's* fifty most influential Jews.

Since 2003, the situation at rabbinical schools has worsened. In 2011, Daniel Gordis, an ordained Conservative rabbi, award-winning author, and senior vice president at Shalem College in Israel, wrote an essay about swelling anti-Zionism among young rabbis in America.[2] He listed a number of incidents that alerted him to this troubling development, including the addition by a group of rabbinical students of the establishment of the State of Israel to the historical events worthy of mourning on the solemn day of Tisha b'Av; a rabbinical student who chose to celebrate his birthday in Ramallah, the seat of the Palestinian Authority, in a bar adorned with Palestine Liberation Organization (PLO) posters advocating death to Jews; a rabbinical student who sought recommendations of where to buy a prayer shawl with the proviso that it could not originate in Israel; a synagogue that interviewed two rabbinical graduates for pulpit posts who expressed views hostile toward Israel; an Israel Defense Forces major who recounted that a rabbi of a major American synagogue refused to shake his hand; a dean who told his rabbinical students he would have voted against the creation of the State of Israel; and complaints by Zionist students of their loneliness on rabbinical campuses. Many of the Jewish social justice personalities we have come across teach at these seminaries, which are in any case organs of the various non-Orthodox denominations—Reform, Reconstructionist, Renewal, and Conservative—that are devoted to tikkun olam. The question therefore arises as to whether these two phenomena—social justice and anti-Zionism—are connected.

It should be obvious that there is a relation. For one thing, protests at college campuses across the nation are typically undertaken in the name of social justice, including demonstrations against Israel, and Jews exhibiting even the remotest sympathy for the Jewish State—indeed sometimes merely by virtue of being Jewish—are harassed and excluded from other social justice activism. Anyone with eyes to see can perceive that social justice has an Israel problem. Inevitably, therefore, ambivalence—even manifest antipathy—toward Israel arises within the Jewish social justice movement as well. Leading Jewish activists have made no secret of their sentiments. We already saw, for example, the insignificance Arthur Green accords to Israel. Meanwhile, Aryeh Cohen writes about "how I lost my Zionism," Leonard Fein about his "battered Zionism," Jay Michaelson about "losing love for Israel," and Michael Lerner describes himself as a "post-Zionist."[3] (It's also interesting that an anti-Zionist blogger, Richard Silverstein, maintains a blog on the topic of Israel called Tikun Olam.) Openness to or support for the boycott of Jews living in (at least certain portions of) the Land of Israel—or opposition to efforts to combat it—is common in the Jewish social justice movement, as is condemnation of policies instituted by the Israeli government (policies, in many cases, that would be adopted by any Israeli government, and historically have been, regardless of its partisan makeup). Liberal American rabbis and other Jewish activists are endlessly penning open letters to the Israeli consulate, or the Israeli embassy, or the Israeli government, conveying their displeasure with how Jews are exercising their hard-won sovereignty. (A recent missive, for example, came to the defense of an American rabbi barred from entry to Israel because she advocates for a boycott of the country, a campaign Israel sees as posing a strategic threat to its economic wellbeing and security. The letter described the matter of support for such boycotts of Jews in Talmudic terms as "a controversy for the sake of heaven" and invoked the needs "to create peace, justice, and equality" and "to see all people as created in the image of God" in declaring solidarity with the rabbi.)[4] Expressions of fraternal sympathy for or solidarity with Israel's Jews—even when Israel is at war— are all too rare.

Historically, versions of Judaism committed to social justice have always had an Israel problem. The Classical Reformers who bequeathed social justice to their descendants jettisoned the immemorial Jewish hope to return to Zion. Rather than long for the end of the exile, they sought to embrace it. Isaiah may have prophesied that out of Zion shall go forth the Torah, but why wait for the ingathering of the Jews to the Promised Land, they wondered, when the Torah of social justice could be administered directly in the lands of their dispersion right now? The relationship between Jewish social justice and Jewish attachment to Zion was therefore shaky from the start.

Much, of course, has happened since then. Classical Reform gave way to contemporary American Judaism, and American Jews did adopt the Zionist cause. Consequently, anti-Israel activism in the Jewish community emerged less from Classical Reform—although theological echoes remain—than from the milieu of 1960s anti-American radicalism. The United States had to be made to repent for its offenses at home and abroad, these radicals asserted, and among its foreign transgressions was its reciprocated support for the State of Israel. Obviously the Jewish radicals felt especially responsible for this particular sin, and they directed no small amount of energy in trying to extirpate it. These efforts, taking at first the form of several small anti-Israel groups, ultimately culminated in Breira: A Project of Concern in Diaspora-Israel Relations.

Breira operated through the mid-1970s, bringing together extreme liberal Zionists, non-Zionists, and anti-Zionists. It drew from the New Left, the Havurah movement, radical Jewish youth, Hillel foundations, socialist Zionists, and from the ranks of Reform and Conservative rabbis.[5] Its members included Arthur Waskow, a founder of Jewish Renewal and the author of *The Freedom Seder*; Michael Lerner, soon to launch *Tikkun*; the *Forward*'s Samuel Norich; Leonard Fein, who founded *Moment* magazine and the Jewish social justice organization Mazon; Michael Strassfeld, who co-edited the Jewish Catalogs of the Havurah movement; David Saperstein, formerly the long-serving executive director of the Religious Action Center of Reform Judaism; Lawrence Kushner, who writes books on Jewish social justice; Aviva Cantor, the founder of the Jewish feminist magazine *Lilith* and the Jewish Liberation Project; Gerry Serotta, who went on to help found New Jewish Agenda and chair T'ruah; and Ruth Messinger, the founder of the American Jewish World Service and former Democratic candidate for the New York City mayoralty. Another member was a young Thomas L. Friedman, now the foreign policy columnist for the *New York Times*. Breira's chairman was Arnold Jacob Wolf, the late Reform rabbi and renowned radical activist.

The group took its name from a contemporary Israeli adage.

"Ein breira," Israelis would say, meaning, "there is no alternative [but to prevail]." Israelis would use this phrase to remind
themselves of the existential war in which their country was
perpetually afflicted by neighboring Arab states—and to impel
themselves to victory. By worrying contrast, Breira was deliberately implying that there was in fact such an "alternative."
Judging by Breira's activities, this consisted of the attempted
legitimation of the Soviet-backed PLO, which was openly engaging in pioneering and unrepentant terrorism against Israel
and Jews worldwide at the time.

We have seen how these radicals began in that period to appropriate Scripture and the Jewish tradition to justify their politics, and their hostility toward Israel was no exception. Rael
Jean Isaac, in a devastating pamphlet on Breira, observed that
for these Jews, who were committed to a Judaism that equated
to radicalism, "there could actually be a religious basis for the
attack on Israel." If Judaism taught the Jews to "preach the destruction of America"—and they believed it did—then anything
that prevented them from doing that was tantamount to an
interference with the Jewish religion. Israel was just such an
interference. These radicals, Isaac explained, found that the
commitment of their fellow American Jews to the preservation
of Israel stood in the way of their willingness to embark upon
an attack on American foreign policy. Far from advancing the
distinctively Jewish mission, Israel actually impeded it."[6]

In view of this, Breira advocated the idea that the Jewish State
may itself be contrary to Judaism. One of its founding members,
meanwhile, asked whether the interests of the Jewish Diaspora
and those of Israel were not antithetical. Central to Breira's
mission was redirecting the energies of American Jewry away
from Israel. Those energies were better spent in the Diaspora,

where "authentic Judaism," which had no need for the actual Zion, could flourish. Back then, the mainstream American Jewish community considered Breira's positions anathema. Under communal pressure and suffering from internal wrangling, the group eventually disbanded.[7]

But Breira lived on in its members, who of course were the major promoters of tikkun olam in the 1980s and since. Successor organizations emerged, including New Jewish Agenda and *Tikkun* magazine, as well as Americans for Peace Now, Jewish Peace Lobby, and Jewish Peace Network.[8] New Jewish Agenda perpetuated Breira's stances on Israel—at a protest against the Jewish State at the Philadelphia Holocaust Memorial, for instance, the group called for a "Palestinian Holocaust Memorial"—and exploited emerging rifts within American Jewry over the 1982 Lebanon War.[9] However, Breira's downfall taught Jewish social justice activists to think twice about how to approach the matter of Zionism and Israel.

Whereas Breira focused exclusively on Israel, New Jewish Agenda tried to avoid sharing its predecessor's fate by taking a new approach. It would incorporate Israel into an expanded range of political issues that it would tackle, rather than emphasize its anti-Israel activity. New Jewish Agenda comprised essentially the same crowd as Breira, but its members hoped that this time, by mixing Israel in with other concerns—including labor, housing, education, healthcare, feminism, abortion, homosexuality, affirmative action, immigration, environmentalism, and nuclear weapons—they would draw less ire from the mainstream Jewish community. Nevertheless, this strategy too failed. New Jewish Agenda came under pressure and collapsed.

The downfalls of Breira and New Jewish Agenda presented the Jewish social justice movement with a problem. One organization dedicated absolute attention to Israel and foundered, and the other diluted its attention and also folded. In light of the legacies of these two groups, the challenge to Jewish social justice activists today is to identify the best way to proceed in trying to alienate Diaspora Jewry from the Jewish State and America from Israel. Jewish social justice organizations have therefore taken several different approaches to the Israel issue.

Most of the tikkun olam groups we've encountered in previous chapters have avoided adopting a specific position on Israel entirely, in favor of attending exclusively to domestic social justice topics. Having learned the lesson of Breira and New Jewish Agenda, they fear the reaction of mainstream American Jewry to the sort of anti-Israel views they would be taking. However, these activists' hesitation to publicize their opinions on Israel should not be mistaken for neutrality. "The Jewish social justice field is wrestling with Israel as an issue," wrote Shifra Bronznick and Didi Goldenhar in a 2008 study for the Nathan Cummings Foundation, observing that many of the main Jewish social justice groups "have been reluctant to take a position on Israel."[10] The report submits that this hesitation stems from an apprehension toward "the political consequences among their donors, constituents, and community-based partners." The implication is that, were these Jewish social justice groups in fact to articulate positions on Israel, those positions would be so extreme that they might alienate even those supporters who are otherwise sympathetic to the cause of social justice. After all, many of these groups are led by former members of Breira and their younger acolytes, so they remember well what happened the last time they made their opposition to Israel too prominent. These Jewish activists understand what social justice really means for Israel and American Zionism—even while the rest of American Jewry, which is otherwise supportive of social justice, does not. To the extent that there is an ideological rationale for this position, it is the one articulated by (among others) Arthur Green: Israel is a special case because of historic Jewish suffering, and notwithstanding its sinfulness and alliance with the United States, it can be tolerated, albeit temporarily.

It is not just that these groups do not opine on Israel, however; they are also disinclined to operate there. Dyonna Ginsburg, the executive director of the Israeli organization Bema'aglei Tzedek, has criticized this reluctance of American Jewish social justice groups to cooperate with their Israeli counterparts, blaming it on their fear of being seen to associate with the Jewish State.[11] This is not about financial prudence but ideological principle. Consider Avodah, a Jewish social justice group interested in poverty work. Avodah announced a program to send alumni to engage in social justice work in Israel, but following a petition from one hundred of them who complained that the program violated the organization's "own commitment to pluralism"—because it would "marginalize" the non-Zionists among them—the program was duly canceled.[12] As the Nathan Cummings report observes, "that the next generation expresses negativity or indifference to Israel, also puts Israel lower on [the] priority list" for Jewish social justice groups.

For some groups, merely dissociating themselves from Israel is not enough. Rejecting the division between Israel and the other elements of social justice, they insist on taking the approach of New Jewish Agenda, history notwithstanding, and include active opposition to Israel within their political agitation. One activist explained that the story of New Jewish Agenda shows that separating the matter of Zionism from the rest of an organization's politics and treating it as a "special case" "can undermine a group's ability to maintain the consistent commitment to justice that makes radical work coherent and effective."[13] This approach is not unrelated to the principle of intersectionality—the idea that all struggles for justice are interconnected and therefore alliances between victims are not only strategic but ideologically necessary. According to this logic, if you do not recognize that challenging "Zionist oppression" is part of social justice—if you try to pretend for pragmatic or ideological reasons that it is separate from social justice or a tolerable special case—then your social justice efforts are disingenuous and are not going to succeed.

One organization that takes this holistic approach is T'ruah. Jill Jacobs is T'ruah's executive director, Sidney Schwarz sits on its board of directors, and its advisory board includes Arthur Green and Elliot Dorff. Among its supporters are Ruth Messinger and Samuel Norich. Named for one of the blasts of the *shofar* (ram's horn), which is blown at certain times of the Jewish calendar, T'ruah adopted the name because the sound "calls us to take action to create a more just world and indicates our belief in the possibility of liberation." In particular, this blast, consisting of staccato notes, "reminds us of the brokenness of the world, while also calling us to be partners with God in healing this brokenness," familiar themes all.[14]

T'ruah began when the American branch of Rabbis for Human Rights, an organization based in Israel best known for taking participants on intentionally misleading tours of Arab neighborhoods to engender as unfavorable an impression as possible of the Jewish State, split with its Israeli counterpart. This was not because the Americans disagreed with the Israeli group's tactics or objectives—in fact, it has been suggested that the Americans are even more extreme in their views than the

Israeli branch—but because they wished to extend their purview to cover alleged abuses of human rights in America as well. Their American campaigns have included support for the closure of Guantanamo Bay prison, reform of the police and criminal justice systems, various labor issues, and the creation of "sanctuary synagogues" for undocumented immigrants. Several of its members have been arrested, for example in a protest of the immigration policies of the Trump administration, a demonstration T'ruah organized in conjunction with Jews for Racial and Economic Justice, Avodah, and the Union for Reform Judaism.

On Israel, T'ruah opposes efforts by the Israeli government and state governments in the United States to counter the antisemitic boycott of the Jewish State, and supports the removal of Jews from Judea and Samaria (the biblical heartland of Israel).[15] It also partners with the disgraced group Breaking the Silence, which levels anonymous and defamatory accusations against the Israel Defense Forces. A sense of T'ruah's agenda can also be drawn from the positions taken by its leading members. Mordechai Liebling, for example, is the director of the Social Justice Organizing Program at the Reconstructionist Rabbinical College and previously served as the executive vice president of Jewish Funds for Justice. He sits on T'ruah's executive committee. Liebling endorsed the libelous (and since retracted) Goldstone Report, which falsely accused Israel of war crimes; he participated in a fast for Gaza (which is ruled dictatorially by the genocidal terrorist group Hamas) in solidarity with opponents of Israel's blockade of the area; he supports corporate divestment from Israel; and he calls for sanctions on the Jewish State if it fails to advance certain policies.[16] Several of T'ruah's board members have supported engagement with Hamas, which is sworn to Israel's destruction.

You'll recall that Shaul Magid defended Jill Jacobs in her student days with recourse to that tired insistence that "American Jewry need to get their head around what it means for a person to publicly support Israel and yet be critical of its government." If such "support" consists of the defense of a boycott of Israeli Jews and approval of organizations that call for the Jewish State's annihilation (or, more indirectly, the backers of such terrorist organizations), then Magid's complaints about American Jewry appear considerably less justified. Not just American Jewry but anyone, surely, would struggle to "get their head around" such Orwellianism. Whereas yesterday Magid defended Jacobs herself, today he defends T'ruah, her organization. "Many Jewish groups such as T'ruah or the *Tikkun* [c]ommunity are at the forefront of the protest movement against the occupation," he writes, presumably referring to the Jewish presence in Judea and Samaria. Implicitly affirming the doctrine of intersectionality, he lauds this stance as "consistent with their larger commitments against injustice," and goes on to blast "many other Jewish leaders in America" who stand for social justice at home but are silent when it comes to Israel's supposed crimes.[17] T'ruah thus fits neatly into the tradition of New Jewish Agenda.

T'ruah is one organization that eschews the division between social justice and the problem of Zionism. Another, as Magid mentioned, is *Tikkun*, of which he is an editor. Michael Lerner, *Tikkun*'s founder and editor-in-chief, was involved in Breira and New Jewish Agenda, as were many of the magazine's contributors, and the political views of the publication reflect that. *Tikkun* is "post-Zionist" and promotes the view that the survival of the Jewish State is much less important than—indeed hinders—the advance of social justice. While the magazine's opinions on the other elements of social justice have not elicited much opprobrium, its positions on Israel—such as presenting an award to the author of the Goldstone Report—rapidly became unacceptable in the mainstream American Jewish community.[18] Alexander Schindler, the former president of the Reform movement's Union of American Hebrew Congregations, the late Nobel laureate Eli Wiesel, and the former publisher of the liberal *New Republic* Martin Peretz all resigned from *Tikkun's* editorial board in protest over its hostility to the Jewish State.[19] Meanwhile, the renowned law professor and political liberal Alan Dershowitz has written that "*Tikkun* is quickly becoming the most virulently anti-Israel screed ever published under Jewish auspices," adding that "support for *Tikkun* is support for the enemies of Israel."[20] However, unlike New Jewish Agenda, *Tikkun* survives, notwithstanding its take on Israel. Its longevity suggests that the Jewish social justice movement has had some success in making Israel a more contested issue in American Jewry and opening the door previously shut for the radical views of Breira.

Whereas T'ruah and *Tikkun* have adopted the approach of New Jewish Agenda—diluting anti-Israel sentiments among the other concerns of social justice—there is a final category of Jewish social justice groups, comprising those that have chosen to emulate Breira's antipathetic fixation on Israel. Some of these groups are small, such as the Committee for a Just Peace in Israel and Palestine, which is concerned with "social, economic, environmental, and political justice," and Ta'anit Tzedek: Fast for Gaza, which opposed Israel's 2012 campaign to pacify Hamas terrorists out of a concern for justice. But there are also larger and more influential groups. The New Israel Fund, for example, is a controversial grant-making organization whose three "ideals" include "social justice" (the organization's five "issue areas" also include "social and economic justice"). Its president believes Israel is evil and guilty of ethnic cleansing, and the organization advocates for the removal of Jews from Judea and Samaria. The New Israel Fund supports groups that promote a boycott of Israel, and numerous grantees also favor the Arab "right of return," which would result in the demographic destruction of the Jewish State. Indeed one of the New Israel Fund's leading officials has declared indifference to the prospect of Israel becoming a majority Arab state.[21]

Among the most virulent of all Jewish social justice groups focusing on Israel, however, is Jewish Voice for Peace. Founded in 1996 in Berkeley, California, its board includes Judith Butler, Noam Chomsky, and Tony Kushner, and among its members is Daniel Sieradski of Occupy Judaism.[22] Jewish Voice for Peace supports the cleansing of any Jewish presence in Judea and Samaria and East Jerusalem (which includes the Temple Mount, Judaism's holiest site, and Zion); the sharing of the rest of Jerusalem (denying any especial Jewish attachment to the city); the Arab "right of return" (universally recognized as code for the destruction of Israel as a Jewish State); the involvement of foreign powers other than the United States in peace talks (an invitation to powers traditionally hostile to Israel to increase their influence in the region); the deployment of international peacekeepers in the area (to counteract Israel's military superiority); the breach and removal of Israel's naval blockade of Hamas-ruled Gaza (which seeks to prevent the smuggling of armaments into that bellicose territory by terrorists); and a global boycott of Israel (boycott being a centuries-old antisemitic weapon used against the Jews. Yes, these are Jews advocating for the boycott of Jews.).[23] And these are just its stated positions. In reality, Jewish Voice for Peace opposes Israel's existence, views the founding of the Jewish State as an event of comparable iniquity to the Holocaust, maintains that Israel is guilty of genocide, and discourages young Jews from traveling there. It opposes Israeli efforts to prevent terrorism, such as the security barrier that has saved countless civilian lives, and it defends Hamas' use of terror tunnels and refuses to describe that genocidal militia as a "terrorist" group (preferring to apply that label to the U.S. government instead). Jewish Voice for Peace's members have been known to question the historical Jewish connection to the Land of Israel, the group regularly opposes efforts to combat antisemitism on campuses, and it has defended or invited to its events terrorists, white supremacists, and avowed antisemites. Appropriately, the Anti-Defamation League lists Jewish Voice for Peace as one of the ten most anti-Israel groups in the United States.[24]

What motivates Jewish Voice for Peace in its activism? According to its website, its members are "inspired by [the] Jewish tradition to work together . . . [for] social justice."[25] The group has utilized propagandistic methods by now familiar to us, such as a despicable Haggadah that portrays modern Israel as ancient Egypt and the Arabs as the biblical Israelites, condemns the ten "plagues" that Israel has supposedly wrought upon the Arabs, and devotes a redemptive cup of wine to the Boycott, Divestment and Sanctions (BDS) movement, which promotes a boycott of the Jewish State.[26] During Israel's military conflict with Hamas terrorists in Gaza in 2012, Jewish Voice for Peace sided with Hamas against Israel, tweeting: "Taking a stance against injustice in Palestine is part of fixing this broken world #TikkunOlam #gazaunderattack."[27] More recently, a co-chair of Jewish Voice for Peace's rabbinical council founded a synagogue that rejects

Zionism and declares that the modern State of Israel was born through injustice.[28]

Jewish Voice for Peace is at the fringe even of the Jewish social justice movement. But while some might balk at the notion that it could even be classed in the same category as a group like T'ruah, which is much more representative of the Jewish social justice movement's views on Israel, nevertheless, the two groups are not quite as distant from one another as is convenient to believe. After all, both receive grants from some of the same funders, such as the Rockefeller Brothers Fund, and the two groups have even co-sponsored events (along with the New Israel Fund).[29] Most revealingly—and a portent of where the Jewish social justice movement is heading on Israel—T'ruah's own founding executive director and a past honoree, Reform rabbi Brian Walt (who ministers to a synagogue called Tikkun v'Or), went on to join Jewish Voice for Peace's Rabbinical Council. Apparently not seeing significant conflict between the two groups, he remains a member of T'ruah, which is evidently happy to have him. You will recall the similarities in the dogmas of the respective theologians of the two organizations as well: T'ruah's Arthur Green and Judith Butler of Jewish Voice for Peace.

Breira and New Jewish Agenda found themselves at odds with the Jewish community in their time and did not survive. But their successors seem to be faring better. T'ruah counts hundreds of rabbis among its members and supporters and Jewish Voice for Peace is a growing presence on college campuses. Although not every Jewish group that exhibits hostility to Israel or espouses anti-Zionism cites social justice as an aspiration, as these two groups do, nevertheless all those groups that do reference social justice find themselves on that part of the political spectrum. For example, J Street, the liberal foreign policy lobby that bills itself as "pro-Israel, pro-Peace" but whose pro-Israel bona fides have been questioned even by the liberal Anti-Defamation League, does not cite social justice as a motivation for its activism.[30] However, its campus branch, J Street U, does. When J Street U emerged several years ago, one of its first measures was to drop the "pro-Israel" label because it made many participants uncomfortable.[31] (Its leadership now openly defends those who seek to end Israel's existence.[32]) Thus we return to the question: Is there a connection between social justice and anti-Zionism?

The answer usually trotted out is that young Jews who care about social justice are estranged from Israel because of the country's policies. For example, Peter Beinart, the liberal Jewish political commentator, former editor of the *New Republic*, and currently a columnist at the *Forward*, published a widely read essay in 2010 titled "The Failure of the American Jewish Establishment."[33] He argued that the hawkish policies of Israel's government were alienating young liberal American Jews from the Jewish State, and American Jewish leaders who were otherwise sympathetic to liberalism were making an exception for Israel. This thesis could be summed up in one sentence:

> For several decades, the Jewish establishment has asked American Jews to check their liberalism at Zionism's door, and now, to their horror, they are finding that many young Jews have checked their Zionism instead.

Israel was to blame for the distancing that everyone perceived was taking place between young American Jews and Israel. This claim was by no means novel, but Beinart's stature—and the appearance of the article in the prestigious *New York Review of Books*—made the community take notice. The piece was such a hit that Beinart was immediately commissioned to expand it into a book, *The Crisis of Zionism*. The politics espoused in the book were no different, but in the two years between the article and the book Beinart had made a subtle but profound tweak in his argument, observing now that it was not so much Israel's policies—much as he disagreed with them—that were pushing young Jews away from the Jewish State, but their own lack of Jewish engagement. "The harsh truth," he wrote, "is that for many young, non-Orthodox American Jews, Israel isn't that important because being Jewish isn't that important."[34] So much for blaming Israel for the feelings of liberal American Jews.

A better answer to the question of a connection between social justice and anti-Zionism is hinted at by Daniel Gordis.[35] When Gordis was confronted with anecdote after anecdote about how young American rabbis were turning on Israel, he postulated four reasons. The first was memory: whereas his generation grew up during the existential wars launched against Israel by the Arab world, the younger generation has come of age as Jordan made peace with Israel and during the terrorist campaign waged by Fatah, Hamas, and other Arab terrorist factions against Israeli civilians in the early 2000s (known as the Second Intifada). Earlier generations knew Israel as the weaker party, but now Israel is perceived as stronger and therefore, according to fallacious logic, necessarily the aggressor. Second, students today cannot imagine a world without a Jewish State. Consequently, they cannot conceive of the possibility that Israel is at risk, nor comprehend how different American Jewish life would be if Israel were not around. Third, these rabbinical students are uncomfortable with the concept of an "enemy," and foolishly imagine that peacemaking is premised on the idea that such things do not exist. These three factors all doubtless play a role in what we are witnessing in the younger generation, but Gordis considered the fourth reason to be the "most disturbing."

Gordis observed that the

> new tone in discussions about Israel is so "fair," so "balanced," so "even-handed" that what is entirely gone is an instinct of belonging—the visceral sense on the part of these students that they are part of a people, that the blood and the losses that were required to create the state of Israel is *their* blood and *their* loss . . . What is lacking in their view and their approach is the sense that no matter how devoted Jews may be to humanity at large, we owe our devotion first and foremost to one particular people—our own people . . . All this is simply a reflection of the decreased role of "peoplehood" in Judaism . . . Today's universalism leaves no room for the particularism that has long been at the core of Jewish life. And the evaporating devotion of some portion of today's rabbinical students to Israel is a direct result.

With objectivity inevitably comes diminishing attachment to one's own. In fact, to prove their impartiality when their Jewish identity might arouse suspicions of bias, students can even find themselves aligned with Israel's (yes) enemies. (Indeed in reality, these rabbis and activists are decidedly beyond "objectivity," but this just underscores Gordis' point.) This is not a formula for Jewish flourishing. As Gordis warns:

> When PLO posters advocating the death of Jews are no reason not to drink a beer and sing "Happy Birthday" in that

bar, we have produced a generation of future leaders whose instincts are simply not the instincts that have any chance of preserving Jewish life.

Gordis blamed this development on a "Protestantization" of American Judaism, analogizing the religious journeys of American rabbinical students to a Protestant religious awakening. They are both deeply individual affairs, not communal ones. Protestant worship is about reaching for the divine, he writes, whereas in the Jewish tradition it is just as much about creating a bond with other Jews. For Protestants, history and peoplehood are marginal (Is there such a thing as a Protestant people? he asks), whereas in Jewish liturgy they are omnipresent. He suggested that this substitution of communal faith with personal journey has detached young rabbis from their people.

Liberal Jews undertake political activism in the name of social justice. But those who grasp Jewish social justice better than anyone—young and older rabbis—seem to affiliate almost uniformly with groups that are hostile to Israel. The general rule appears to be that the stronger your commitment to tikkun olam, the weaker your Zionism and support for Israel. Among the Jewish social justice organizations, those that take a stance on Israel are invariably critical if not outright hostile, and the others hesitate to adopt a position on Israel at all for cunning pragmatic reasons. Borrowing Gordis' argument, we might conjecture that this trend of negativity toward Israel among Jews committed to social justice arises from an aversion to Jewish Peoplehood. In the next chapter, we shall see why the logic of Jewish social justice in fact makes this inevitable.

Should Judaism Survive?

On Rosh Hashanah 2016, Rabbi Joshua Stanton rose to the pulpit of his Reform synagogue in New Jersey to deliver his sermon. It was the first night of the Jewish New Year, and his congregants, barely filling half of the gargantuan sanctuary, waited to hear what Jewish wisdom their spiritual leader would impart on this awesome Day of Judgment. As might be expected on such an occasion, he enumerated a series of transgressions that demanded penitence. But these were not individual or communal sins. Instead, they were a "national and global list of transgressions and sources of suffering." They included the failure to welcome more Syrian refugees; the United Kingdom's democratic decision to withdraw from the European Union; laws discriminating against transgender individuals; legislative restrictions on abortion; the rise of white supremacy; mass incarceration and mandatory minimum sentencing; attacks on

African-Americans, Sikhs, and Muslims; gun violence; and "anti-intellectualism, attacks on science, and a head-in-the-sand approach to climate change." (And this was before the election of Donald Trump to the presidency!) Nothing about Rabbi Stanton's remarks, delivered at a temple committed to tikkun olam, was out of the ordinary. The preaching of liberalism in the name of Judaism from the pulpit is commonplace in American synagogues. And so is exploitation of Jewish festivals such as Rosh Hashanah as opportunities to push the political agenda of social justice.

The Jewish year is a calendar of Jewish social justice. On Rosh Hashanah, *Tikkun* magazine appeals for American and Israeli atonement for their myriad sins. On Yom Kippur, Jews do not attend synagogue to ask for forgiveness but descend to Occupy Wall Street to show solidarity with the 99 percent. Sukkot is not about commemorating the Israelite wanderings in the desert and the divine clouds of glory that escorted the Jews over those forty years, but, according to Arthur Waskow, is instead a time to promote nuclear disarmament. The month of Marcheshvan, which uniquely contains no holy days, is "Jewish Social Action Month." The organization Repair the World says Hanukkah, traditionally a celebration of ancient Jews successfully resisting assimilation, expelling invaders, and reestablishing their sovereignty in the Land of Israel, is in fact a time to think about humanity's impact on the environment. Purim is not the story of Jews overcoming attempted genocide against all odds or about the hidden hand of God in worldly affairs, but rather, according to Reform Judaism, about "turning injustice on its head" by highlighting persecution of ethnic minorities, discrimination toward women, and economic inequality. Passover and its Haggadahs are not celebrations of the

Israelite Exodus from Egypt but affirmations of every other type of "revolutionary liberation." Shavuot (the Festival of Weeks) is in traditional Judaism not only associated with the giving of the Torah but is also a harvest festival. The Religious Action Center says this holy day "calls to mind how we must ensure that the poorest and most vulnerable members of society have enough to eat," and that Shavuot is therefore best observed by lobbying against cuts to disability insurance and urging your congressman to oppose the Improving Child Nutrition and Education Act. Tisha b'Av, the most solemn day of the Jewish year, when no food or drink is consumed in mourning for the destruction of both ancient Temples in Jerusalem, is put to better use by Jews for Racial and Economic Justice to honor all African-Americans who have lost their lives to police violence. And the weekly Shabbat is not a reenactment of God's rest from His creative labors but an opportunity to run programs such as "Labor on the *Bimah*," which seeks to bring support for such matters as collective bargaining into the synagogue sanctuary. On and on it goes.[1] It is difficult to find this anything but depressing. Is this really to be the culmination of Judaism? The old joke that Reform Judaism is the Democratic Party platform with festivals thrown in is in fact an understatement. On the festivals, the American Jewish exaltation of social justice is not muted but amplified.

Tu b'Shvat is another example. In ancient times, this "new year for trees" was little more than an administrative fixture. Over the centuries it became an occasion to eat fruit—especially those fruits associated with the Land of Israel—and recite biblical verses relating to trees. In the nineteenth century, the Zionist movement encouraged the planting of trees in the Land of

Israel on this day. In the last few decades in America, however, Tu b'Shvat has become a veritable Jewish Earth Day—an excuse for Arthur Waskow to protest the felling of trees in redwood forests and for other Jewish social justice groups and synagogue committees to promote their opposition to fracking and their support for carbon taxes.[2] But, in an essay on the development of Tu b'Shvat, historian Tevi Troy observes that "all of the emphasis on ecological sustainability does not appear to be doing much to promote Jewish sustainability."

Troy is alluding to the breathtaking rates of assimilation among American Jews—the process by which Jews become less affiliated with Judaism and ultimately they or their children do not identify as Jews at all. Several major studies undertaken over the past two decades revealed an alarming state of affairs. The United Jewish Communities' National Jewish Population Survey (2000–1), the Pew Portrait of Jewish Americans (2013), and the Steinhardt Social Research Institute (Brandeis University) American Jewish Population Estimates (2013) all showed that the Jewish community is shrinking, aging, and marrying out. These trends are most pronounced among the non-Orthodox, where the rate of outmarriage is a whopping 71 percent. The non-Orthodox denominations evidently have much to answer for. The response of the Jewish social justice movement, of which these denominations are organs, has been more tikkun olam.

WHAT IT MEANS TO BE AN AMERICAN JEW

Jewish activists have proffered a number of reasons for why they pursue tikkun olam and encourage others to do so. One of them is, of course, that such activism is warranted by the Bible and traditional Jewish texts. As we have seen over the preceding chapters, it is not. Another reason is that the present emphasis on Jewish social justice is, in a sense, no novelty, as Jewish political activism in the United States has a long and impressive history. There were those Jews who agitated for better working conditions in New York City in the early decades of the twentieth century, those who supported Margaret Sanger and the fight for contraceptive liberties, those who struggled alongside African-Americans for civil rights, those who protested against the Vietnam War, and others. American history is crowded with Jewish figures pursuing liberalism, socialism, and radicalism, and today's advocates of Jewish social justice are the inheritors of this American Jewish activist tradition. Thus what is today called tikkun olam has always been at the heart of what it means to be an American Jew.

From a historical point of view, this assessment is not unreasonable, though it rather magnifies the activities of what was in every generation only a minority. But the mere observation that American Jews have always been political activists, however proud it might make some of their descendants, is not something that can sustain American Judaism. After all, if there is no substantive difference between tikkun olam and the ideology of social justice espoused by the broader political Left, there is nothing particularly Jewish about preaching tikkun olam. Tikkun olam is not what it means to be an American Jew; it is what it means to be an American liberal.

This may explain why so many prominent non-Jewish liberals—Bill Clinton, Mario Cuomo, Cornel West, and others— are so comfortable citing it. But nobody delighted more in tikkun olam than former president Barack Obama. He told the American Israel Public Affairs Committee in 2012 that tikkun olam "has enriched and guided my life," and an audience of Israeli students in Jerusalem in 2013 that he "has been inspired in my own life by that timeless calling within the Jewish experience—tikkun olam."[3] Given how important tikkun olam was to President Obama, it's hardly surprising that of all the Jewish rituals that Obama chose to introduce to the White House diary, it was that social justice blowout, the Seder night.

Obama's debt to tikkun olam owed much to the company he kept in earlier years. He spent much of his adult life in a staunchly liberal Jewish circle—a circle that included Breira chair Arnold Jacob Wolf—that saw social justice as the essence of Judaism, and he was also mentored by the late Democratic congressman Abner Mikva, who helped found J Street. Since, for these Jewish activists, tikkun olam pretty much captures what Judaism is all about, it made sense that Obama, well versed in tikkun olam as he was, believed himself to be the most Jewishly knowledgeable president in American history—and naturally Jewish liberals agreed.[4] In practice he was also the most liberal president in a generation, if not in American history, implementing piecemeal a program of social justice and demonstrating an unprecedented coldness toward Israel, a record that wholly justified his appellation as the "tikkun olam president."[5] And that was just another way of saying—as some did—that he was the "first Jewish president."[6]

The fact that American Jews have long engaged in political activism does not mean that that activism makes them Jewish. It just makes them more like everyone else undertaking that same activism.

TIKKUN OLAM AS ETHICS

Leonard Fein was a writer and founder of the Jewish social justice organization Mazon. He recognized that the Jewish community was facing a crisis of assimilation, and believed the answer was tikkun olam. In his book *Where Are We?: The Inner Life of America's Jews*, he argued that "Jewish continuity requires a . . . commitment to tikkun olam."[7] Why? According to Fein, many American Jews think ethics are the easiest part of Judaism to understand. Ethics are much easier to explain to their neighbors and children than Judaism's more esoteric rituals. Consequently, many Jews have come to see ethics as the essence of Judaism. This isn't a novel thought, of course—it goes back to Kant and the Classical Reformers. But Fein said that this Jewish ethical sensibility is represented by tikkun olam. That means that tikkun olam is the element of Judaism to which most American Jews can relate, and that it's viewed as the very essence of the Jewish religion. Fein went on to contend that if assimilation is due in part to Jews' feeling that they can't relate to Judaism and can't understand it, then logically the more significant tikkun olam becomes in American Judaism, the more likely estranged Jews are to understand their faith and even return to it. For "the sake of Jewish continuity we must be concerned with Jewish ethical values"—and that requires a commitment to tikkun olam. Tikkun olam is therefore the key to Jewish continuity.

Fein was mistaken. The popularity of ethics, which in his view are represented by tikkun olam, is not the answer to American Jewry's continuity problem—it is part of that problem. The Classical Reformers were drawn away from traditional Judaism and toward ethics because ethics made them less traditionally Jewish and more like everyone else. The same trend underlies much of American Jewish assimilation today. If tikkun olam has become an expression of that triumph of ethics over Judaism, then tikkun olam can hardly also be the answer to that assimilation.

Ethics, simply put, are a branch of moral philosophy and an ever-developing system of right conduct that is universally applicable—to all people at all times. It's religiously agnostic, and it's a product of reason that any human being is in principle capable of apprehending. But there's no way that ethics is the entirety of Judaism as traditionally understood: everything from sacrifices to Sabbaths would not fall under the rubric of ethics.[8] That leaves two possibilities.

One possibility is that ethics constitute merely one element of Judaism. Ritual would be the other main element. If this is the case, then to focus entirely on ethics and to treat it as the essence of Judaism is to ignore and distort the remainder of the faith's teachings. We saw this in action in the Jewish social justice interpretation of the Prophets. Due to misreading, the Prophets are popular texts for those who prize the ethical above all else. Maybe ethics are a part of Judaism, but in that case they're still not the whole story, and in any event, as we've seen, ethics in the Prophets are not as universal as many make out.

The other possibility is a little more controversial. This is the view that ethics are a philosophy that is at odds with Judaism. That means that ethics and Jewish faith, on a technical level, are incompatible. The rationale for this position is that ethics are about seeing and treating everyone the same, whereas Judaism is about Jews seeing themselves as distinct and having a closer relation to other Jews. The essayist Hillel Halkin has commented that "if ethics are what make a Jew like anyone else, they cannot also be what make him a Jew."[9] (Some people try to avoid this conclusion by promoting the idea of a particularly "Jewish ethics," but this is nonsense.)

Whether ethics are part of Judaism or at odds with Judaism, they certainly aren't the essence of Judaism as traditionally understood. The truth is actually that they're the opposite. The triumph of ethics over Judaism is ultimately the triumph of philosophical morality out of the sources of reason over religious law out of the sources of Revelation. This sentiment was expressed by former chief rabbi of the United Kingdom Lord Immanuel Jakobovits, who, playing off Micah 6:8, wrote: "*He* hath told thee, O man, what is good—He, and not reason."[10]

If ethics were sufficient, then there'd be no need for a religious legal code—especially a particularistic code like Judaism with so many seemingly antiquated assumptions and obligations. If you can work ethics out just by thinking about morality, then you don't need a prophet to reveal God's word to you—yet that's what Judaism (and other Abrahamic religions) is about. Ethics are therefore part of American Judaism's assimilation problem because ethical Jews don't need Judaism. Daniel Bell, the eminent sociologist, already observed this half a century ago when he wrote that the ethical "takes away from individuals that need for the particular identification which singles them out and shapes their community in distinctive terms."[11] If you're an ethical person, you don't also need to be Jewish.

It's more than that, however. Not only do ethical Jews not need Judaism—they *don't want* Judaism. The reason ethics are appealing is precisely because they don't differentiate between Jew and gentile—the same rights and obligations accrue to both alike. That was why the Classical Reformers liked ethics so much. So actually ethics directly equate to assimilation. Ethics treat a Jew not as a Jew but simply as a human being—which is the very meaning and purpose of assimilation.

The role of ethics—conceived as tikkun olam—in the process of American Jewish assimilation has even been recognized from within liberal Jewish circles. The late Reform theologian Eugene Borowitz observed that "not a few liberal Jews wanted ethics to be the essence of Jewish responsibility for that freed them from having to do acts which might openly identify them as Jews." The idea that social justice is the essence of Judaism, he concluded, "is thus often an apparently noble rationale for Jewish assimilation."[12] From a different perspective, the late Orthodox theologian Michael Wyschogrod astutely described ethics as "the Judaism of the assimilated."[13] (He goes on to say that "it cannot be denied that the ethical has been by far the most popular route for abandoning Judaism . . . The [Classical German] Reformers, whose primary interest was to integrate their Judaism with German culture, understood that *the* element in Judaism that more readily lent itself to that integration was the ethical.") If tikkun olam is ethics, then tikkun olam is far from the solution to American Jewish assimilation—it's part of the problem.

JEWISH OUTREACH

The idea that tikkun olam and Jewish continuity don't go together is not merely theoretical but is also borne out empirically. Consider the view of Sidney Schwarz. Whereas Fein made an abstract argument that tikkun olam is necessary for Jewish continuity, Schwarz claims that tikkun olam can be a very direct form of outreach as well. It's a practical way, he insists, to encourage assimilated, estranged, or otherwise distanced or indifferent Jews back to the Jewish tradition. In an essay titled "Can Social Justice Save the American Jewish Soul?," Schwarz asks: "What . . . might draw marginal Jews closer to the Jewish community?" Schwarz suggests: "I believe that social justice is one of the most compelling answers to that question."[14]

Schwarz's contention is that many assimilated Jews are engaging in social justice work anyway. They're effectively doing Judaism without knowing it, and if you tell them they're actually doing Judaism, they'll come back to the fold. He writes:

> Take the hypothetical American Jew who is an active member of a human rights organization, or who is active in local politics. Assume that this individual is not a member of any Jewish organization and gives no money to any Jewish causes. Engage this person in a conversation about what drives his or her volunteer and philanthropic activity, and in many cases we will find that it traces back to that person's Jewish roots, be it a grandparent role model, identification with one or more aspects of the Jewish historical narrative, or the reading of a book of Jewish fiction. Expose that person to a Jewish institution that speaks to his or her values, to a Jewish teacher who frames those values in the words of classical Jewish texts, to a social justice initiative sponsored by a Jewish organization, and there is a very good chance that such a person can be drawn closer to the Jewish community. I know. I have been part of such education and outreach for three decades.

Schwarz says he's seen "evidence of an unselfconscious Jewish identity among younger Jews." These young Jews, he advises, are eager to combine their passion for justice with their identi-

fication with "the texts and values of the Jewish tradition."
Schwarz is confident that Jews engaging in social justice more
generally can be enticed to continue their work through engagement with the Jewish community.[15]

Schwarz's rationale is dubious. If Jewish social justice is not
essentially Jewish, as we've shown, then its advancement is
hardly likely to be a profitable form of outreach. But let's say,
for argument's sake, that we'll accept the idea that social justice
does constitute a Jewish teaching. In that case, what would Jewish social justice look like as outreach? It would basically con-
sist in the (false) revelation to estranged liberal Jews already
engaging in social justice work that they're doing Judaism without realizing it. Okay. And then you entice them back to a Judaism whose essence is social justice. So then what? They just carry
on doing the same social justice work! So what exactly have you
achieved? If Judaism is just Jews doing social justice, then why
is outreach to a Jew who is doing social justice somewhere else
even necessary? If these Jews are believing and doing what Judaism teaches even without knowing it, and their encounter
with Judaism is neither likely nor supposed to alter those beliefs
or activities, then why bother reaching out at all?

If we try to answer this question, we find ourselves returning to the tension between particularism and universalism. If
you use tikkun olam as Jewish outreach then you're presuming
that particularism—Jewishness—makes some beneficial contribution to social justice work. But there's no explanation for this.
After all, social justice is fiercely universalistic and the Jewish
social justice movement finds particularism disturbing—even
chauvinistic. So it's not just that tikkun olam as outreach might
not work very well. It's that social justice itself implies that doing

Jewish social justice—i.e. social justice with some nominal vestige of particularism—is inferior to doing social justice with no Jewish attachment at all.

This is validated empirically. Two important studies—one in 2001 and the other in 2011—found that most liberal Jews involved in general social justice activism are either indifferent to pursuing their agenda within a Jewish context or positively opposed to doing so.[16] These findings suggest that any tikkun olam outreach over the first decade of this century has been unsuccessful. But the reports also seem to confirm that such outreach is inherently futile—since apparently those involved in social justice prefer to do their work without any Jewish connection. That's because social justice and Judaism are fundamentally at odds with one another. Both theoretically and in reality, promoting social justice with some kind of Jewish attachment is neither coherent nor appealing.

Maybe, though, there's a silver lining. Let's look at the matter from the perspective of a traditionalist Jew. For this Jew, the more Jews who engage with other Jews and build communities together, the better—even if they're doing social justice work which isn't in itself especially Jewish. Alas, even this hope is empirically unfounded. To use Jewish social justice as a means of outreach aiming at greater Jewish affiliation is, it transpires, to reverse cause and effect. The 2001 report concluded that Jewish religious involvement is the strongest predictor of volunteering through a Jewish organization—and not the other way around. Jews might get involved in Jewish-related activism if they're connected to Judaism, but they don't seem to get connected to Judaism by doing that activism.

These studies show that Jews are more likely to volunteer under Jewish auspices the more the emphasis is on particularism rather than the universalism of social justice.[17] Why is this? As the academic Yehudah Mirsky answers:

> It is unclear that tikkun olam can serve as a meaningful, long-term basis for Jewish identity in the absence of some other commitments, to Jewish peoplehood and civilization, to distinctively Jewish forms of spiritual life, the Jewish textual tradition, and so on. Simply encouraging young people who are otherwise indifferent to or estranged from Jewish life to engage in humanitarian work with no distinctive—let alone transformative—Jewish dimensions other than the label "Tikkun Olam" will strengthen neither Jewish identities nor Jewish life. Humanitarianism, social justice, and ecological advocacy are not distinctively "Jewish" as such, and while this makes for very meaningful points of contact with people of goodwill outside the Jewish community it also suggests that in and of themselves they will not reinforce stable Jewish identities over time, no matter how they are labeled.[18]

This isn't surprising. To the extent that Jewish social justice activists believe the Jews have a mission (and some of them like Arthur Green do not), then it's to get everyone to help repair the world together. The only beneficial contribution that Jewish particularism might make to social justice work inheres in the Jewish tradition's universalistic teachings about responsibility toward all human beings and to the entire world.[19] But this is also a catch-22! Jewish particularism is beneficial because it points toward universalism—but at the same time such universalism sabotages Jewish particularism.

The appeal of social justice is that it promotes universalistic morals. But that appeal is understandably strongest to those who find activities emphasizing specifically Jewish commitment and identity to be narrow and chauvinistic.[20] Such Jews cannot be won over to a Judaism whose primary teaching is social justice. And by this logic there's little reason why they need to be. This inescapable paradox renders tikkun olam not a means of outreach but yet again an affirmation of assimilation.

NO JEWISH FUTURE

Social justice is a route not to Jewish continuity but to alienation and assimilation. There's a fundamental divergence between Jewish social justice and traditional Judaism. That divergence is most evident in theology. Unlike Judaism, which is built upon a personal God, Revelation, the particularistic covenant, and the commandments, Jewish social justice holds a preference for man, Creation, universalistic morality, and reason. Unlike Judaism, which offers a particularistic path to universal redemption, Jewish social justice is universally incumbent and universally applicable. Jew and gentile alike must work toward social justice to benefit Jew and gentile alike: Jewish social justice makes no differentiation.

The consequence of this is that Jewish social justice effectively has no need for Jews qua Jews. Indeed, the very existence of Jews as a distinct people ultimately conflicts with Jewish social justice's universalistic aspirations. If the role of the Jews is to help repair the world, that role will end once the world is repaired, and in a repaired world there will be no Jews. There will be only human beings created in God's image.

What is interesting, however, is that this extreme universalism seems to apply, among minorities, only to the Jews. Jewish social justice encourages and celebrates communal difference and pride in every other ethnic and religious community except the Jewish community. Their generosity to others is not extended to Judaism except insofar as Judaism can be refashioned to teach universalistic social justice, which is for Jewish activists the only credible justification for Judaism's persistence. And so, what makes Judaism stand out is its universalism—its ambition not to stand out. As the novelist Cynthia Ozick remarked, universalism is the parochialism of the Jews. (The famed rabbi and musician of the last century, Shlomo Carlebach, observed the same sentiment when he visited college campuses. He would relate that when a student told him, "I'm Catholic," he knew the student was Catholic, and when a student told him, "I'm Protestant," he knew the student was Protestant. But when a student told him, "I'm a human being," he knew that student was a Jew.)

Whereas the Jews are subject to extreme universalism, the particularism of other communities is, apparently, to be protected at all costs. It is, for example, inconceivable that advocates of Jewish social justice would tell African-Americans or Muslims that ultimately they should abandon their particular cultures, practices, or beliefs. And yet when it comes to the Jewish community, it might eke out some temporary purpose in proselytizing social justice, but this ideology envisions the eventual end of the Jewish People. In fact, so uncomfortable are Jewish activists with Jewish particularism that even this pitiful purpose is too chauvinistic for some of them, like Arthur Green. What they celebrate in others they dismiss as chauvinistic in themselves.

The Kingdom of God—the world of social justice—will exalt all the diversity of life, including all the other faiths and cultures, except Judaism. The Jewish People alone must become obsolete. (These Jewish liberals would not dare to tender such an offensive assessment to other minority communities; it is a sign of their pathology that they do so to their own.) But why wait? If even the mission to teach social justice is too chauvinistic and can in any case be pursued outside of a Jewish context, then why should Jews perpetuate themselves even before bringing about the Kingdom of God? Surely the most immediate way to repair the world—the most straightforward contribution to this noble endeavor—is to stop being Jewish now? Not only is Jewish social justice a route to assimilation—the logic of tikkun olam endorses assimilation.

This is the final and most profound divergence of Jewish social justice from traditional Judaism. It is simply not plausible that a major teaching of Judaism could be the belief in its own abnegation, yet this is precisely the implication of tikkun olam, which undermines Jewish Peoplehood and forecasts the redundancy of the Jews. Social justice has no need for Jews: by its logic they need not concern themselves with perpetuating their people, need not limit themselves to Jewish partners, and need not raise their children to be Jewish. They need only work to repair the world—a pursuit that eventually involves their very dissolution into the rest of humanity. This is because ultimately there are no Jews. There are only human beings created in the image of God, and they are all One.

12

The Way Forward

Tikkun olam is an unreasonable answer to a reasonable theological question—what is the Jewish obligation to the wider
world? It is the favorite answer of the American Jewish
community—the Jews must engage in social justice work and
encourage others to do so too. This answer is espoused by myriad organizations, from countless synagogue pulpits, and in
numberless books and articles. It has guided the rabbinical and
lay leaders of the American Jewish community, has inspired
masses of American Jews, and animates liberal and radical
American Jewish political activism. American Jews are so enam-
ored of tikkun olam that they have come to believe that social
justice—which is nothing more than liberal politics—is the very
essence and indeed entirety of Judaism itself. Dyonna Ginsburg,
the executive director of the Israeli organization Bema'aglei

Tzedek, has lamented that there is a "growing sense that tik-kun olam has emerged as an alternative, rather than as a comple-mentary, form of Jewish identity."[1] And Jonathan Sacks, the former chief rabbi of the United Kingdom, has also observed that "there are [some] for whom social justice has become a sub-stitute for religious observance or God."[2] If social justice is the essence of Judaism, then Judaism's message to humanity is liber-alism, and the sole purpose of the Jewish People is to preach this politics to America. This, as we have observed, is the thrust of the Jewish social justice movement.

The belief in tikkun olam has inspired Jewish activists to self-righteous indignation, convinced as they are that their per-sonal political opinion is not only right and moral, but that it is also God's opinion. For all their condescension toward the Christian Right, in their own way liberal Jews affirm no less strongly the principle that voting for certain politicians can seal your place in Heaven or Hell. But at least the evangelicals are open about their wish to reintroduce religion to the public square. Jewish social justice activists campaign for a strict sepa-ration of Church and State—but do so as part of an enterprise whose stated goal is to utilize (faux) Jewish wisdom to craft do-mestic and foreign policies for the United States. Consider the *Religious* Action Center, which is the *political advocacy* arm of the Union of Reform Judaism. For such an organization to claim to root its political aspirations in religious theology and texts and lobby in Washington, DC, to realize those aspirations, while si-multaneously professing that it advocates for the "protection of government from religion," is staggering.[3] The laughable oppo-sition by the Jewish social justice movement to recent moves to repeal the "Johnson Amendment," which bars tax-exempt faith organizations from endorsing candidates for office, is of a piece.

The organizations and activists who constitute the Jewish social justice movement came to their support for liberal policies and radicalism independently of Judaism. They had their revolutionary politics long before they consulted the Bible or opened the Talmud. Only subsequently did they approach the Jewish canon to select and misread sources to their partisan advantage—sources that don't in fact endorse their political opinions. After all, if Jewish social justice were actually commanded by the Jewish tradition, surely more traditionalist Jews would be engaging in it. And yet when the Orthodox scholar Jacob J. Schacter, for example, kindly tried to rescue Jewish social justice by seeking to identify "sources from the Jewish tradition that we can draw upon to serve as the foundation for a commitment to tikkun olam or social justice as we now understand it," he was unable to find any that endorse political activism or structural overhaul of the economy.[4] Since their own faith tradition does not actually commend their politics, these liberal activists have fabricated some *fakakta* theology of universalism that erodes Jewish fraternity and distances its adherents from Israel, and whose logic culminates in the eradication of the Jewish People and its religion.

It is not credible that the Jewish mission in the world—the purpose of a people whose history goes back to antiquity—could so completely coincide with the agenda of the liberal wing of the Democratic Party of the twenty-first-century United States. It is not plausible that the ultimate objective of the Jewish People is its own abnegation. And it is not compelling to suggest that Judaism encourages the descendants of Abraham to cultivate an unpleasant and divisive indignation as their defining quality— for the real ways of the Torah are ways of pleasantness and all her paths are peace. We asked what is the Jewish obligation to the wider world? Tikkun olam is the wrong answer to that question.

So what, then, is the answer? "A wise question," said the medieval Jewish poet Solomon Ibn Gabirol, "already contains half the answer." So let's probe the question itself. Its terms already point to an answer other than tikkun olam. First, the question implies Jewish distinction: there is a separate Jewish body that has a relationship with the rest of the world. Immediately, the radical universalistic aspirations of the Jewish social justice movement are denied. Judaism teaches that there is a Jewish People that stands apart from the rest of humanity.

Second, according to the Bible that apartness is the result of a divine election of the Jewish People. That stature brings blessing to all of humanity (Gen. 12:3, 18:18, 22:18) and entails greater responsibility in the form of commandments—even if that responsibility is mainly toward fellow Jews. There is therefore a sense in which the relationship of the Jews toward the gentiles is characterized by obligation—albeit a rather indirect one. The Jews, it might be said, are a "holy nation" by virtue of being a "kingdom of priests" (Ex. 19:6).

Obligation is connected to election, and it's in the other aspects of this chosenness that that obligation is elucidated. In the same breath that God chose Abraham, He told him to go to the "land that I will show you" (Gen. 12:1). The Land of Israel is therefore fundamental to Israel's election—a particular people is chosen in the Bible, and that people is attached to a particular land. Much of the Torah (the Five Books of Moses) is dedicated to the preparation of the People of Israel to enter the Land of Israel. Most of the rest of the Hebrew Bible is about the Israelite nation's residence in, exile from, and return to that land. Plainly, the Bible and the Jewish tradition teach that the Jewish People—

the Children of Israel—best serve the God of Israel in the Land of Israel. That service takes the form of performance of the commandments of the covenant. That covenant expresses the relationship between Israel and its God, and between all Israelites under God. It's through this particularistic formula that universalistic results are achieved—through that service in that location benefits are prophesied to accrue to all peoples. Isaiah bears re-quoting:

> And it shall come to pass in the last days, that the mountain of the Lord's house shall be established at the top of the mountains, and shall be exalted above the hills; and all nations shall flow to it. And many people shall go and say, Come, and let us go up to the mountain of the Lord, to the house of the God of Jacob; and He will teach us of His ways; and we will walk in His paths: for out of Zion shall go forth the law, and the word of the Lord from Jerusalem. And He shall judge among the nations, and shall rebuke many people: and they shall beat their swords into plowshares, and their spears into pruning-hooks: nation shall not lift up sword against nation, neither shall they learn war any more. O house of Jacob, come, and let us walk in the light of the Lord (Isaiah 2:2–5).

The point about the Land of Israel is worth elaborating—not least because of the emphasis made by Jewish social justice radicals on the importance of the Diaspora. There is some ground in the Jewish tradition for the idea that the Jews' residence in the Diaspora has an eschatological benefit—that it serves some purpose in bringing about redemption in the end of days. But even for those traditional commentaries that bestow upon the Jewish dispersion an eschatological role—such as Lurianic

Kabbalah—the ultimate goal always remains a Jewish return to the Land of Israel. The notion that the messianic age itself somehow requires a perpetual Jewish presence in the Diaspora—that a "Diasporic Judaism" might be on a par with (or a substitute for) the Jewish restoration to the Land of Israel—is anathema to traditional Jewish thought. And certainly any notion that the Jewish People will dissipate into the rest of humanity is antithetical to traditional Judaism.[5]

The obligation of the Jewish People to the wider world is indirect—it's to live in the Land of Israel and to live out the covenant between Israel and God through the performance of those commandments that pertain to a Jew's relationship to God and those that pertain to relations between Jews. In that scenario, the greatest benefits will accrue to all mankind. As far as traditional Judaism is concerned, this is the mission of the Jewish People. This mission is hampered by exile. For all the many Jewish achievements—from religious learning to the arts and sciences—that the dispersion may have facilitated, the exile is an inherently adverse condition. To suggest the opposite is an inversion of millennia of Jewish practice, prayer, thought, and belief.

At the present time, however, not all Jews live in the Land of Israel. In fact, around half of the worldwide Jewish population lives beyond its boundaries. From the theological point of view, the home of the Jewish People is the Land of Israel. But in practice it has been many centuries since a majority of Jews has lived there—and all things being equal many Jews will continue to live in the Diaspora for the foreseeable future. (Although the home of the Jewish People is the Land of Israel, whether individual Jews living in the Diaspora have an immediate religious Jewish legal obligation to "make *aliyah*," i.e. to move to Israel, is beyond our scope.) It is one thing for the Jews of the Land of Israel to have an indirect obligation to the wider world—whether now or in the messianic era—whereby obedience to the commandments brings benefit to all mankind. But do the Jews of the Diaspora today, given their more direct encounter with the gentile world, have a more direct obligation to that world? If tikkun olam is not the answer to this question, then what is?

TOWARD A JEWISH POLITICS

There is an idea with a long pedigree in moral thought that holds that concentric circles of love and obligation are the basis of a healthy society. The innermost circle is you, yourself. The biblical imperative to love your neighbor as yourself presumes that in the first place you will love yourself above all—and this is only natural. You are after all obligated to yourself—to safeguard your physical, mental, and moral health; your prosperity; and your reputation. Then you love those who are extensions of yourself—those closest to you. That love is expressed through fulfilment of obligations, such as devotion to your spouse, provision for your children, and respect and care for your parents. Then comes your community, and your nation, and eventually all of humanity and the natural world.[6] The great eighteenth-century philosopher Edmund Burke articulated this idea:

> To be attached to the subdivision, to love the little platoon we belong to in society, is the first principle (the germ as it were) of public affections. It is the first link in the series by which we proceed towards a love to our country and to mankind.[7]

Traditional Judaism presents a similar pattern. The particularistic covenant that forms the basis of Judaism also creates concentric circles of obligation, prioritizing the Jew himself or herself, followed by the Jew's family, community, and fellow Jews.[8] (It goes without saying that Jews are required by Jewish law to obey the laws of their countries of residence.) The question is what happens after that.

It is certainly incumbent upon Jews to provide assistance to individual non-Jewish neighbors: the gentile hungry should be fed, the gentile naked should be clothed, and the gentile homeless should be sheltered. Such charitable assistance is encouraged in the Jewish tradition—and nothing in this book should be taken as suggesting otherwise. As we noted at the start, social justice and tikkun olam are not about charity but about politics, and the examination in the preceding chapters has considered whether political activism in pursuit of the liberal agenda of social justice is referred to in the traditional texts as "tikkun olam" (it isn't), whether that agenda is endorsed by those texts (it isn't), and whether such activism is good for the Jewish community and humanity (it isn't). We haven't talked about interpersonal charitable activity because we haven't needed to—it is laudable, and those who engage in it are praiseworthy.

But beyond such charity and volunteerism, is there a direct obligation toward the gentile world? According to Jacob J. Schacter, traditionally speaking the answer is: no. "The fact is," he writes,

> that such an obligation is absent from the vast majority of Jewish primary sources from the post-biblical to the pre-modern period. The authoritative texts of the Jewish tradition—the

Talmud and its commentators, [legal] response literature and codes—are almost silent on the obligation.[9]

We've seen why this may be the case from the theological point of view—because ultimately the Jews are supposed to live not around the world but in the Land of Israel. But given also the circumstances of Jewish history, Schacter's assessment is less remarkable than it may at first seem.

The biblical era was focused on Jewish life in the Land of Israel—hence the Jewish encounter with the gentiles was then not particularly pertinent. Thereafter, in the post-biblical era, the Jesus era, the Jews were scattered across the gentile world, but this period was characterized by Jewish confinement to ghettos, as well as by persecutions, pogroms, inquisitions, expulsions, and genocide. Although individual Jews interacted with their gentile neighbors, for the Jewish community as a whole mere survival was the priority. Only in the modern period, after the Jews were emancipated from their ghettos, might other considerations in their relationship with the gentiles have become relevant. But emancipation carried its own drawbacks: the Jews were welcome in society as individual citizens, but Judaism, like other faiths, had no place in the public square. The Jews were emancipated as human beings—not as Jews. Any notion of a Jewish obligation to gentiles was therefore subordinated to ethics, which govern the relations between all men. Moreover, the invitation to Jews to join mainstream society was more theoretical than real: in many places Jews were still expected to assimilate or convert, and antisemitism by no means disappeared—as twentieth-century history can attest. In any event, emancipation only pertained to Western European

Jewry—its effect in Eastern Europe and Russia was more limited and it had no impact on Middle Eastern and North African Jewry. Thus even in the modern period, world Jewry was still in no position to reflect seriously on its possible direct obligations to the wider world.

Theologically and historically, there is little precedent for a direct Jewish obligation to wider society. However, in today's Western world Jews are (exceptions notwithstanding) not only freer than they were for centuries, but are also enfranchised. Consequently, they have a role to play in both civil society and in the governance of the democratic polity. Although traditional Judaism would certainly not go as far as Aryeh Cohen in suggesting that Western democracy is a substitute for Jewish sovereignty in the Land of Israel, nevertheless Jews are more empowered today than they ever have been. Accordingly, Jews are all but forced to engage politically with wider society in the Diaspora—and thus the question arises as to how they should do so.

The first priority of the Jews in exile must be concern with the security, welfare, and ultimately the survival of the Jewish community. This approach emerges from the theological presumption that the exile is negative and temporary and that the dispersion of the Jewish People across the world is unlikely to yield universal good. It is the survivalist mentality—and it has brought the Jews this far. If the best the Jews can do for the gentiles is to earn a restoration to the Land of Israel and keep the covenant there, then their exilic focus must be on their survival and return. The injunction in Jeremiah 29:7, which we quoted earlier, speaks to this point: "Seek the peace of the city to which I have exiled you, and pray to the Lord on its behalf, for in its peace you will have peace." Jeremiah was advising the people to uphold local political stability not so much for its own sake but because that was the best hope for Jewish preservation for the duration of the exile, at the end of which they could return home to Israel. The Talmud provides a related rationale for decent relations between Jews and gentiles—"for the sake of ways of peace."[10] This rationale appears in the Mishnah almost immediately following those laws instituted "for the sake of *tikkun ha'olam*." The two justifications are both used sparingly in the Talmud, and they have sometimes been conflated by Jewish social justice activists—but they are different.[11] For one thing, this phrase actually does refer to relations between Jews and gentiles. This rationale is pragmatic and its reasoning is straightforward: Jews should treat gentiles decently in large part because those gentiles might then reciprocate.[12] This can build trust between neighboring communities, leading to further mutual cooperation and peace. While peace may be pleasant in itself, it also contributes to the security and welfare of the Jewish community in exile.

But in addition to prayer and good communal relations, what does this first approach mean politically? After all, it is one thing to get along with fellow citizens—but what might this approach mean at the ballot box? Well, it might mean that where a political issue impacts the Jewish community directly, the Jews support that side of the debate that most greatly benefits the community. The sorts of relevant issues would include American-Israeli relations and connected foreign policy areas, campaigns against antisemitism, and the promotion of tax incentives for Jewish and religious education. As for issues that don't have a direct bearing on the Jewish community, individual Jews could decide for themselves independently of any religious mandate. Really, this ought not to be so outlandish: for some reason it has become controversial to posit that perhaps the God of Israel is not particularly bothered about marginal tax rates in America.

This outlined approach may appear uncomfortably parochial at first blush. But in fact it's neither extraordinary nor at all demeaning to the public good—it just mirrors the behavior of all other political communities in the United States. Think, for instance, of Cuban-American opposition to the Castro regime, or African-American protests against discrimination, or evangelical support for school prayer. Each of these is an ostensibly parochial interest—yet each is part of the fabric of American politics and enjoys the support of millions of fellow citizens outside of those communities. For Jews to advocate on behalf of the issues that mean the most to their community is no less American than the advocacy of any of these other communities.

Interestingly, Jewish social justice activists are mindful of the appeal of this approach. So they often try to insist that the policies they support not only have the common good in mind but also directly benefit the Jewish community. In other words, social justice covers this concern for Jewish survival. For example, Ruth Messinger, the activist and former Democratic politician, has suggested that if gentiles see Jews pursuing social justice, they might be less inclined to expressions of antisemitism.[13] That is to say, if the haters see the Jews doing universalistic work instead of being concerned only with themselves, they might hate the Jews a little less. Ignoring the idea—shamefully popular among Jews so desperate to win the adoration of their detractors—that Jews' behavior can reduce antisemitism (or, conversely, can cause it), the logic underlying Messinger's argument is specious. As we have seen, Jewish social justice undermines the very idea of a Jewish People and accelerates assimilation into the rest of society. It is absurd, therefore, to believe that in order to discourage antisemitism, Jews should engage in activity that will lead to their own disappearance. Indeed, this is the opposite of the right response to antisemitism; as Harvard scholar Ruth Wisse has argued, the way to overcome antisemitism is to resist the temptations of the universalistic illusion—to be more Jewish, not less.[14]

Another argument from the Jewish social justice movement making the case that their work directly helps the Jews comes from Aryeh Cohen. In his reading of Jeremiah, he implies that if the welfare of the city is enhanced through social justice and the Jews gain peace from the welfare of the city, then the Jews have also gained from social justice.[15] (This is similar to—but not quite the same as—the activists' truism that Jews are human beings and all human beings gain from social justice.) Cohen's proposition is also dubious, however, and not just because the assimilation to which social justice leads is decidedly not good for the Jews. More than that, the agenda of social justice is uniformly left-wing, and whereas the Jews may once have benefitted from liberalism, the growing illiberalism of the American Left and its hostility toward the Jews hardly corroborate Cohen's contention.

Furthermore, not only does social justice not help the Jews directly, but it actually makes things harder for them. For example, the high price of Jewish education in the United States does nothing to alleviate the high rates of Jewish assimilation. But since the agenda of social justice insists on the strictest separation of Church and State in American education, in line with liberal sensibilities, Jewish social justice activists object to tax incentives or other policies that might make the cost of Jewish schools more affordable. This tension has been noted by Peter Beinart, who, though himself politically liberal, is nonetheless alive to the adverse impact of Jewish social justice in the realm of education on Jewish welfare.[16]

Beyond parochial Jewish interests, some Jews may wish to promote an agenda of right conduct to which their fellow Americans should subscribe. This agenda comprises the seven commandments that, according to the Talmud, were given to the "sons of Noah," i.e. all humankind. These commandments are to establish a judicial system and to refrain from blasphemy, idolatry, sexual impropriety, bloodshed, theft, and the consumption of the limbs of a living animal.[17] Whereas Judaism is historically (and many would claim deliberately) not a proselyting faith, there is still a sense in which the gentiles should conduct themselves in a certain manner. This Noahide code, as these seven precepts are known, constitutes that manner. (The relevance of the Noahide code is, however, unclear, as there's little consensus over the basis of these laws, their application outside of the Land of Israel or prior to the messianic age, whether Jews need actively to teach them to gentiles, whether gentiles are obligated to obey accompanying rabbinic legislation, and so on.)[18]

American Jews using their vote to promote a certain conception of morality in the United States is certainly a possibility— and it's likely that many traditionalist Jews do consider rabbinic views on moral questions when they place their vote. This, too, is not unique to Jews—other religious communities already organize politically to promote their opinion of right conduct, such as the Christian Right and, for that matter, the Christian Left. Both of these groups seek to enact legislation and secure judicial judgments that regulate behavior in accordance with their religious views. And, by the way, American liberal secularists do this as well—they too seek to impose their moral visions of society upon the electorate. Just because those visions happen to arise from non-religious philosophies and assumptions doesn't place them outside of this category. The political activism of the Jewish social justice movement also falls into this bracket.

A CHOICE

American Jewry is faced with a choice. It can follow the lead of the Jewish social justice movement, whose indignation is fueled by the self-righteous belief that any opposition to its politics is an affront to justice and to God—a movement that is prostituting Jewish civilization for petty partisan profit. But this path leads only to more American Jewish estrangement from the Jewish People, to distance from Israel, and ultimately to assimilation.

Alternatively, American Jews can reimagine the possibility that their ancient heritage has something unique to say—something greater than a mere echo of the political and cultural fads of our time. This doesn't necessarily mean jettisoning liberal politics. Rather, it means approaching the classical Jewish texts with honesty and curiosity and without prejudice and preconception. It means opening oneself to the practices and beliefs of one's forebears and to the proposition that their wisdom should be learned, their contributions celebrated, their sacrifices mourned, and their dedication emulated. It means deciding that what they preserved for this generation should be handed down unspoiled to the next. A Jewish community that chooses this alternative will be revitalized—and, if it so chooses, can also resuscitate liberalism in America.

Notwithstanding what we've noted in the preceding

chapters, it remains the case that the many ordinary Jews who have been sold the fiction that tikkun olam is Judaism's primary teaching and who act on it are motivated by noble intentions. They wish to help others and make the world a better place—objectives, however vague, with which nobody would quibble. Given how that sentiment pervades their beliefs, religious practices, and political activism, their commitment to doing good as they see it is admirable. But noble intentions alone do not a holy people make. However noble the motive of American Jews, their pursuit of tikkun olam is a betrayal of the traditional faith of their people. That faith holds that through Abraham's Jewish progeny all the peoples of the earth will be blessed (Gen. 22:18).[19] Jews and non-Jews alike should be alarmed by the prospect of tikkun olam succeeding in assimilating the Jewish People into all of humanity, for then that blessing will be no more.

ACKNOWLEDGMENTS

The matter of my authoring a book against *tikkun olam* has often come up in conversation, and I am grateful not only for the entertainment value of people's reactions, but also for the many opinions and anecdotes they have shared, the traditional sources and contemporary articles they have highlighted, and the encouragement they have offered.

My heartfelt thanks go as well to my religious teachers and learning partners over the years, without whose patience and diligence my understanding of and connection to the heritage of the Jewish People would be greatly diminished.

I should also like to take the opportunity to acknowledge my significant debt to my nurturing mentors and sensitive editors through the years for their guidance and support; the time and attention I have received from them has been well beyond anything I merited.

In particular, I wish to thank Elliot Balaban, Suzanne Balaban, Adam Bellow, Eric Cohen, Ben Elton, Phil Getz, Chaya Glasner, Simon Gordon, Roger Hertog, Daniel Johnson, Anthony Knopf, Neal Kozodoy, Bill Kristol, Margot Lurie, John Podhoretz, Kevin Reilly, Meir Soloveichik, Ken Weinstein, two anonymous reviewers, and the congregants of Hampstead Garden Suburb Synagogue. I would also like to express my gratitude to Devora Steinmetz, David Silber, and their family for their warm friendship and boundless hospitality; to the editorial staff at *Commentary*; to the superb production team at St. Martin's Press; and to my former colleagues, friends, and "fellow fellows" at the Tikvah Fund, which also provided a generous grant that made this work possible.

With the help of Heaven, this book is dedicated to my parents. I love them dearly.

NOTES

INTRODUCTION

1. Jane Kanarek, "What Does Tikkun Olam Actually Mean," in *Righteous Indignation*, Or N. Rose, Jo Ellen Green Kaiser, Margie Klein, eds., Jewish Lights Publishing, 2008, p. 15. See also Eugene B. Borowitz, "A Jewish Theology of Social Action," *CCAR Journal: A Reform Jewish Quarterly*, Spring 2008; and Erin M. McClanahan, "The Contextualization of *Tikkun Olam* in American Reform Judaism," Religious Studies theses paper, 2010, p. 29.
2. David Saperstein, "Religious Leadership and Politics," in *Righteous Indignation*, p. 45.
3. For example, the 2016 platform of the Democratic Party contained references to "racial justice," "environmental justice," "climate justice," and "reproductive justice." See 2016 Democratic Party Platform July 21, 2016, http://www.presidency.ucsb.edu/papers_pdf/117717.pdf (accessed Jan. 6, 2018). Meanwhile, "social justice" was one of the four planks of the Green Party in its 2016 party platform. See Green Party Platform 2016, http://www.gp.org/platform, August 2016 (accessed Jan. 6, 2018).

4. Or N. Rose, Jo Ellen Green Kaiser, and Margie Klein, "Introduction," in *Righteous Indignation*, p. xvii.

5. Jonah Dov Pesner, "Redemption for Radicals," in *Righteous Indignation*, p. 89.

6. More than seven in ten American Jews say tikkun olam is an important Jewish tenet that informs their beliefs and activity, and over eight in ten American Jews consider "pursuing justice" (they mean social justice) to be an important Jewish tenet that informs their beliefs and activity. See Robert P. Jones and Daniel Cox, *Chosen for What? Jewish Values in 2012*, Public Religion Research Institute, 2012, p. 2. Tikkun olam has been described as a "hallmark of Reform Judaism" ("What Is Reform Judaism?," http://reformjudaism .org/whatisrj.shtml [accessed Jan. 11, 2018]), the movement of over a third of American Jews, and it features in the most recent Statement of Principles of Conservative Judaism—with which another quarter of American Jews affiliate. The tiny Reconstructionist and Renewal dominations also strongly emphasize tikkun olam, and it has even begun quietly appearing in the small Orthodox community as well—for example, at Yeshiva University's Center for the Jewish Future, which "promotes and nurtures the enduring Jewish value of *tikkun olam*" ("YU Center for the Jewish Future," Yeshiva University, http://www.ejewisheducation.com/about-us/yu-center -for-the-jewish-future/ [accessed Jan. 11, 2018]). Organizations include Jewish Community Action, which lists "our fundamental responsibility to repair the broken world" as the first of its "core values" ("Anachnu Ma'aminim (We Believe)—Our Core Values" http://jewishcommunityaction.org/about/core-values [accessed Jan. 11, 2018]); the Jewish Council on Public Affairs, whose work, "especially in matters relating to democratic pluralism and social justice, reflects the profound Jewish commitment to tikkun olam, the repair of the world" ("About Us," JCPA, www.jewishpublicaffairs .org/about-jcpa/ [accessed Jan. 11, 2018]); the Coalition on the Environment and Jewish Life, which seeks "to expand the contemporary understanding of such Jewish values as tikkun olam" to incorporate ecological concerns ("About Us," COEJL, http://coejl .org/aboutus/ [accessed Jan. 11, 2018]); the Jewish Council on Urban Affairs, which works to ensure our children are not "burdened with a broken world" ("What Is Jewish about JCUA," JCUA,

https://jcua.org/about-us/jewish-values/ [accessed Jan. 11, 2018]); and Jews United for Justice, which "is a grassroots community that seeks to repair the world" ("About Us," Jewish United for Justice, http://www.jufj.org/content/about-us [accessed Jan. 11, 2018]). There are plenty of other organizations, including some that incorporate tikkun olam into their names, such as Tikkun Olam Women's Foundation and Repair the World. In addition to those groups that reference tikkun olam expressly, there are more still that are devoted to "social justice."

7. Those topics include "the economy, the deficit, or the upcoming election." See "Election Day and Tikkun Olam," PJ Library, November 2012, http://pjlibrary.org/pj-blog/index.php/archives/3863/election-day-and-tikkun-olam/ (accessed Jan. 14, 2013); and "PJ Library Books," PJ Library, https://pjlibrary.org/Books-and-Music/Books (accessed Sept. 6, 2016).

8. For example, Brandeis Hillel Day School http://www.bhds.org/marin/Parent-association/tikkun-olam-repairing-the-world/index.aspx; Brawerman Elementary School http://www.brawerman.org/pages/tikkun_olam; Golda Och Academy; Heschel Day School http://www.heschel.org/page.cfm?p=505; Madison Jewish Day School http://www.madisonjewishdayschool.com/; Ronald C. Wornick Jewish Day School http://www.wornickjds.org/middleschool/; Valley Beth Shalom Day School http://www.vbsds.org/podium/default.aspx?t=123175; and The Weber School http://www.weberschool.org/student-life/tikkun-olam/index.aspx accessed Jan. 14, 2013. In addition, note the curricula provided by external educational organizations and consultancies, for instance, Areyvut, which "enables Jewish youth to infuse their lives with the core Jewish values of . . . *tikkun olam*" http://www.areyvut.org/about_us/ (accessed Jan. 14, 2013); JESNA's "Incorporating Social Justice into Jewish Education" project, at http://www.jesna.org/sosland/resources/tikkun-olamsocial-justice-/incorperating-social-justice-into-jewish-education; and the Jewish Women's Archive's "Living the Legacy: A Jewish Social Justice Education Project," at http://jwa.org/teach/livingthelegacy (accessed Jan. 1, 2013). There are isolated other educational materials and classes offered on *tikkun olam:* for instance, Columbus Museum of Art's "Judaism and Social Justice: Making the World a Better Place," at http://artand

socialissues.cmaohio.org/pdf/judaism_and_social_justice.pdf accessed 1.15.13.

9. Including Reform Judaism's North American Federation of Temple Youth http://www.nfty.org/about/13principles/; Conservative Judaism's United Synagogue Youth http://www.usy.org/yourusy /sato/; NCSY http://bbyo.org/about/mission/; Camp Ramah http://www.ramahberkshires.org/node/228; and BBYO http:// bbyo.org/about/mission/ (accessed Jan. 14, 2013).

10. "L'Taken Social Justice Seminars," Religious Action Center, http:// rac.org/confprog/ltaken/ (accessed Jan. 14, 2013).

11. For Panim, see http://panim.bbyo.org/ and http://panim.bbyo .org/teens/programs/panim_el_panim/ (accessed Jan. 14, 2013). For Or Tzedek, see http://www.ortzedek.org/ (accessed Jan. 14, 2013).

12. http://www.jewishfed.org/dillerteenaward (accessed Jan. 14, 2013).

13. http://www.hillel.org/about/default (accessed Jan. 14, 2013).

14. Regarding the Jeremiah Fellowship, see http://bendthearc.us /jeremiah-fellowship and http://www.jufj.org/jeremiah; regarding the Jewish Organizing Fellowship, see http://www.joinforjustice .org/programs-projects/jewish-organizing-fellowship/; regarding the Amos Fellowship, see http://www.utzedek.org/takeaction/on -campus/amos-fellowship.html; and for Avodah Corps, see http:// www.avodah.net/where-will-i-work/ (accessed Jan. 14, 2013).

15. http://www.moishehouse.org/about.asp (accessed Jan. 14, 2013).

16. See, for example, http://rac.org/social/worship/ (accessed Aug. 28, 2013).

17. http://www.juf.org/tov/default.aspx (accessed Jan. 14, 2013).

18. http://tivnu.org/community-programs/ (accessed Sept. 6, 2016).

19. http://www.covenantfn.org/awards/awards-program (accessed Aug. 25, 2013).

20. For the Jewish Federations, see https://jewishfederations.org/about -jfna (accessed Jan. 6, 2018); for the Schusterman Foundation, see http://www.schusterman.org/about-us/mission-values (accessed Jan. 14, 2013); for the Blaustein Foundation, see http://www .blaufund.org/foundations/jacobandhilda_f.html (accessed Jan. 14, 2013); for the Rose Youth Foundation, see http://www.rcfdenver .org/RYF/ (accessed Jan. 14, 2013); for the Tikkun Olam Women's Foundation, see http://www.shalomdc.org/page.aspx?id=128070

(accessed Jan. 14, 2013); for Jewish Helping Hands, see http://jewishhelpinghands.org/about/ (accessed Jan. 14, 2013); and for the Jewish Funders Network, see http://www.jfunders.org/mission and http://www.jfunders.org/jfn_by_the_numbers (both accessed May 1, 2017). For more Jewish foundations supporting social justice, see Shifra Bronznick and Didi Goldenhar, "Visioning Justice and the American Jewish Community," Nathan Cummings Foundation, 2008, pp. 34–35.

CHAPTER 1

1. John J. Appel, "The Trefa Banquet," *Commentary*, February 1, 1966.
2. Byron Sherwin, "Tikkun Olam: A Case of Semantic Displacement," *Jerusalem Center for Public Affairs*, November 1, 2014.
3. This description of the story of Isaac Mayer Wise, the birth of American Reform Judaism, and the establishment of American Jewish lay leadership relies on Howard M. Sachar, *A History of the Jews in America*, Vintage, 1993; and Michael N. Barnett, *The Star and the Stripes: A History of the Foreign Policies of American Jews*, Princeton University Press, 2016. For a fuller discussion of the development of the Reform movement's gradual calls for political measures in the name of social justice, see Leonard J. Mirvis, "The Social Justice Movement and the American Reform Rabbi," American Jewish Archives, June 1955.
4. Quoted in Mirvis, "The Social Justice Movement and the American Reform Rabbi."
5. Richard T. Ely, *Social Aspects of Christianity, and Other Essays*, Thomas Y. Crowell and Company, 1889, p. 92.
6. Quoted in Murray N. Rothbard, "Richard T. Ely: Paladin of the Welfare-Warfare State," *The Independent Review*, vol. IV, no. 4, Spring 2002.
7. Quoted in in Clifford F. Thies and Ryan Daza, "Richard T. Ely: The Confederate Flag of the AEA?," *Econ Journal Watch*, vol. 8, no. 2, May 2011, pp. 147–56.
8. Samuel Zane Batten, *The Social Task of Christianity: A Summons to the New Crusade*, Fleming H. Revell Company, 1911, p. 113.
9. Washington Gladden, *The Church and Modern Life*, Houghton, Mifflin and Company, 1908, p. 201.

10. Walter Rauschenbusch, *A Theology for the Social Gospel*, The Macmillan Company, 1922, pp. 135–36 (emphasis added).

11. Gladden, *The Church and Modern Life*; George D. Herron, *The Christian Society*, Fleming H. Revell Company, 1894, p. 127; Rauschenbusch, *A Theology for the Social Gospel*, p. 228.

12. In addition to its socialistic message, other darker elements of social justice became clear in the ensuing years, including the antisemitism of Father Coughlin.

13. David Saperstein, "Religious Leadership and Politics," in *Righteous Indignation*, Or N. Rose, Jo Ellen Green Kaiser, Margie Klein, eds., Jewish Lights Publishing, 2008, pp. 45–52, esp. pp. 45–46.

14. Riv-Ellen Prell, *Prayer and Community: The Havurah in American Judaism*, Wayne State University Press, 1989, pp. 69–111. For a contemporary discussion of the origins of the Havurah movement, see Bill Novak, "The Making of a Jewish Counter Culture," *Response*, vol. 4, no. 1–2, 1970, pp. 5–10.

15. Quoted in Stephen J. Whitfield, "Famished for Justice: The Jew as Radical," in L. Sandy Maisel, ed., *Jews in American Politics*, Rowman and Littlefield Publishers Inc., 2001, p. 215.

16. Quoted in Norman Podhoretz, *Why Are Jews Liberals?*, Doubleday, 2009, pp. 127–28.

17. The following brief biography of Michael Lerner is taken from Jonah Goldberg, *Liberal Fascism*, Doubleday, 2007, pp. 330ff.

CHAPTER 2

1. Thomas Friedman, "Repairing the World," *New York Times*, March 16, 2003.

2. Philologos, "The Politics of Repair," *Forward*, March 28, 2003.

3. The following brief survey of *tikkun olam* in American Judaism borrows from Jonathan Krasner, "The Place of Tikkun Olam in American Jewish Life," The Jerusalem Center, November 1, 2014, http://jcpa.org/article/place-tikkun-olam-american-jewish-life1/ (accessed Dec. 31, 2014); and Lawrence Fine, "*Tikkun*: A Lurianic Motif in Contemporary Jewish Thought," in *From Ancient Israel to Modern Judaism: Intellect in Quest of Understanding—Essays in Honor of Marvin Fox*, vol. 4, Jacob Neusner et al., eds., Scholars Press,

1989, pp. 35–53. The interested reader is directed to these more extensive histories.

4. Mordecai M. Kaplan, *The Meaning of God in Modern Jewish Religion*, Wayne University Press, 1995 (1937), pp. 23–24.

5. Although the popular contemporary understanding of *tikkun*, or repair, has been in connection with social justice, there has been an important auxiliary use of the idea in postwar American Jewish thought, namely in post-Holocaust theology. This theology has embraced *tikkun* as capturing the sense of brokenness that the Holocaust left behind, and gave expression to the possibility of mending. For a survey of this use of *tikkun*, see Jonathan Krasner, "The Place of Tikkun Olam in American Jewish Life," The Jerusalem Center, November 1, 2014, http://jcpa.org/article/place-tikkun-olam-american-jewish-life1/ (accessed Dec. 31, 2014). For the most developed and well-known articulation of this theology, see Emil Fackenheim, *To Mend the World: Foundations of Post-Holocaust Jewish Thought*, Indiana University Press, 1982. This use of *tikkun olam* has not proved popular outside of academic circles, and, tending as it does to reflect the particularistic impulse of Jewish thought, is largely irrelevant to Jewish social justice activism.

6. See Deborah Dash Moore, "Inventing Jewish Identity in California: Shlomo Bardin, Zionism, and the Brandeis Camp Institute," in *National Variations in Jewish Identity: Implication for Jewish Education*, Steven M. Cohen and Gabriel Horenczyk, eds., SUNY Press 1999, pp. 201–23.

7. "Brandeis-Bardin Campus: History," American Jewish University, http://confbbc.aju.edu/AJU_History.html (accessed Jan. 6, 2018).

8. http://usy.org/teens/usy/social-actiontikun-olam/ (accessed Jan. 6, 2018); Fine, "Tikkun"; Jill Jacobs, "The History of 'Tikkun Olam,'" *Zeek*, June 2007.

9. Ruth Wisse, "Anti-semitism and *Tikkun Olam*: How Jews Can Best Repair a World in Crisis," The 28th annual Harold E. Hoffman Memorial Lecture, October 4, 2012.

10. Richard Siegel, Michael Strassfeld, and Sharon Strassfeld, eds., *The First Jewish Catalog: A Do-It-Yourself Kit*, Jewish Publications Society, 1965, p. 8.

11. Quoted in Jonathan Krasner, "The Place of *Tikkun Olam* in American Jewish Life," The Jerusalem Center, November 1, 2014, http://jcpa.org/article/place-tikkun-olam-american-jewish-life1/ (accessed Dec. 31, 2014).

12. *The First Jewish Catalog*, p. 251.

13. Sharon Strassfeld and Michael Strassfeld, eds., *The Third Jewish Catalog: Creating Community*, Jewish Publications Society, 1980, p. 47.

14. The discussion of New Jewish Agenda is indebted to Ezra Berkley Nepon, *A History of New Jewish Agenda*, Thread Makes Blanket Press, 2012.

15. "Statement of the Jewish Liberation Project," *Response*, vol. 3, issue 1, Spring 1969, pp. 26–27.

16. Nepon, *A History of New Jewish Agenda*, pp. 63–67; Ethan D. Bloch, "One Voice Less for the Jewish Left: New Jewish Agenda, 1981–1993," http://newjewishagenda.files.wordpress.com/2012/01/ethan-bloch.pdf (accessed Oct. 22, 2012).

17. "*Tikkun*'s Core Vision," *Tikkun*, http://www.tikkun.org/nextgen/tikkuns-core-vision (accessed Oct. 29, 2012).

18. The Miami Platform of 1997, which specified the relationship between Reform Judaism and Zionism, did mention Reform Judaism's "historic commitment to *tikkun olam*," but did not elucidate the idea.

19. Hillel Halkin has made a similar observation in Hillel Halkin, "How Not to Repair the World," *Commentary*, July 2008.

20. Although in practice *tikkun olam* overlaps completely with liberal politics, some political conservatives have attempted—unsuccessfully—to appropriate the phrase for their own political ends. See, for example, Michael Spiro, "Being a Politically Conservative Reconstructionist," *Reconstructionism Today*, vol. 11, no. 3, Spring–Summer 2004; Steven Bayne, "A Torah of Justice—A View from the Right?," Walking With Justice series, Bradley Shavit Artson and Deborah Silver, eds., The Ziegler School of Rabbinic Studies, http://www.aju.edu/Media/PDF/Walking_With_Justice-A_Torah_of_Justice_-_A_View_from_the_Right.pdf (accessed Jan. 6, 2018); Noam Neusner, "Mitt Romney Is Real *Tikkun Olam* Candidate," *Forward*, August 29, 2012; Ari Fleischer quoted in Nathan Guttman, "Jewish Republicans Dragged into GOP Battle Between Tea Party and Moderates," *Forward*, April 8, 2013; and, more

generally, Joel Alperson, "Abusing *Tikkun Olam*," *Forward*, March 19, 2012.

21. Michael Lerner, *Jewish Renewal: A Path to Healing and Transformation*, Harper Perennial, 1995, p. 329.

CHAPTER 3

1. Arthur Waskow, "Rabbis Against Climate Change," *Forward*, June 6, 2015, http://forward.com/opinion/national/309548/rabbis-against-climate-change/ (accessed Sept. 17, 2017).

2. Arthur Waskow, "Rabbinic Letter on Climate," Shalom Center, October 29, 2015, https://theshalomcenter.org/RabbinicLetterClimate (accessed Sept. 17, 2017).

3. Ellen Bernstein, "Rereading Genesis: Human Stewardship of the Earth," in *Righteous Indignation*, Or N. Rose, Jo Ellen Green Kaiser, Margie Klein, eds., Jewish Lights Publishing, 2008, pp. 55–59.

4. Michael Lerner, *Jewish Renewal: A Path to Healing and Transformation*, Harper Perennial, 1995, p. 338.

5. "Jewish Views on LGBT Equality," Reform Judaism, https://reformjudaism.org/jewish-views-lgbt-equality (accessed Sept. 17, 2017).

6. "Inclusion," Reconstructionist Judaism, https://www.jewishrecon.org/act/inclusion (accessed Sept. 17, 2017).

7. "Statement Responding to Same-Sex Marriage Ruling," Reconstructionist Judaism, June 30, 2015, https://www.jewishrecon.org/news/statement-responding-same-sex-marriage-ruling (accessed Sept. 17, 2017).

8. Lawrence Kushner, *Repairing the World: Introducing Jewish Spirituality*, Jewish Lights Publishing, 2001, p. 34.

9. Arthur Green, *Radical Judaism: Rethinking God and Tradition*, Yale University Press, 2010. All quotations from Green in this chapter are from this volume. Another example of this sort of theology is Jay Michaelson, *Everything Is God: The Radical Path of Nondual Judaism*, Trumpeter Books, 2009. The following analysis also draws from Daniel Landes, "Hidden Master," Review of Arthur Green, *Radical Judaism: Rethinking God and Tradition* (Yale, 2010), *Jewish Review of Books*, Fall 2010, pp. 20–22.

10. The reading of the verse as commanding a Jew to love his/her

fellow Jew as him/herself is the Jewish legal reading of the verse (Maimonides, Hilchot De'ot 6:3). The interested reader is also referred to the famous Talmudic dispute between Rabbi Akiva and Ben Azzai over the most important verse in the Torah (Jerusalem Talmud Nedarim 9:4; Bereishit Rabbat 24:7; Sifra/Torat Kohanim). Green struggles with this dispute (see Arthur Green, *Seek My Face: A Jewish Mystical Theology*, Jewish Lights Publishing, 2003, p. 78), while Leonard Fein collapsed it (see Leonard Fein, *Where Are We?: The Inner Life of America's Jews*, Harper and Row, 1988, p. 220), but ultimately, in *Radical Judaism* (p. 143 and p. 155), Green accepts the traditional terms of the debate but predictably takes the untraditional position that Ben Azzai is correct.

11. See Jonathan Sacks, "*Tikkun Olam*: Orthodoxy's Responsibility to Perfect God's World," speech delivered to the Orthodox Union West Coast Convention, December 1997.

CHAPTER 4

1. Panim, "Rabbi Sid Schwarz," http://www.rabbisid.org/success-stories/panim/ (accessed Jan. 6, 2018).
2. Sidney Schwarz, *Judaism and Justice: The Jewish Passion to Repair the World*, Jewish Lights Publishing, 2006 (2008), pp. 34–35. Other citations from Schwarz in this chapter are from this volume unless otherwise stated.
3. Aryeh Cohen, "The Jewish Vote," Justice in the City blog, May 23, 2012, http://www.justice-in-the-city.com/?p=311 (accessed Sept. 28, 2017).
4. Shmuly Yanklowitz, *Jewish Ethics and Social Justice: A Guide for the 21st Century*, Derusha Publishing, 2012, pp. 25–26.
5. Unlike Abraham, Noah was himself affected by the judgment of the world, while Abraham was merely an observer to Sodom's fate. God also gave Abraham an opening to pray—but did not give one to Noah. The divine judgment in the case of Sodom still appears to have been open to revision—God, you'll notice in the text, still intends to see for Himself what is happening in Sodom. In Noah's case, God's judgment of the world has already been made. And, finally, Abraham had the opportunity to learn from Noah, who lived ten generations before him.

6. Jill Jacobs, *There Shall Be No Needy: Pursuing Social Justice through Jewish Law and Tradition*, Jewish Lights Publishing, 2009, p. 10.

7. Joshua Stanton, "On Living Faith: Abraham and a Jewish Theology of Protest," *Tikkun*, February 20, 2012, http://www.tikkun.org /tikkundaily/2012/02/20/on-living-faith-abraham-and-a-jewish -theology-of-protest/ (accessed Sept. 20, 2012).

8. Midrash Tanchuma, Vayeira 5.

9. Elliot N. Dorff, *The Way into Tikkun Olam*, Jewish Lights Publishing, 2007, p. 52.

10. Michael Lerner, *Jewish Renewal: A Path to Healing and Transformation*, Harper Perennial, 1995, p. 44 (emphasis added).

11. Mishnah Avot 5:4.

12. Abraham's appeal for Sodom is absent from the lists presented by the Book of Jubilees; Pirkei d'Rabbi Eliezer; Avot de Rabbi Natan; Midrash Tehillim 18; Rashi; Ramban; Rabbeinu Yonah; Meiri; Bartenura; Me'am Lo'ez; Gra; and Tiferet Yisrael.

13. In fact, to view the covenant as contingent on Abraham's reaction to God's preliminary verdict may well be to confuse cause and effect. Genesis 18:19 actually makes more sense if you think that God only initiates this conversation with Abraham because of the covenant He has already established with him and the progeny He's just promised him.

CHAPTER 5

1. Ron Kampeas, "Jewish Groups Still Angling for Health Care Bill Fixes," Jewish Telegraphic Agency (JTA), December 30, 2009, http:// www.jta.org/2009/12/30/news-opinion/politics/jewish-groups -still-angling-for-health-care-bill-fixes (accessed Sept. 14, 2017).

2. Sandra M. Fox and Martin I. Seltman, "The Blood of Our Neighbors: American Health-Care Reform," in *Righteous Indignation*, Or N. Rose, Jo Ellen Green Kaiser, Margie Klein, eds., Jewish Lights Publishing, 2008, pp. 94–101. All quotations from Fox and Seltman in this chapter are taken from this essay.

3. Jill Jacobs, *There Shall Be No Needy: Pursuing Social Justice through Jewish Law and Tradition*, Jewish Lights Publishing, 2009, p. 178.

4. "Reform of the Health Care System," Union of Reform Judaism Resolution, 1993.

5. Jacobs, *There Shall Be No Needy*, p. 10.

6. See also Yoram Hazony, *The Philosophy of Hebrew Scripture*, Cambridge University Press, 2012, p. 70ff, from which this chapter draws.

7. It has been suggested that the famine is, in fact, *caused* by Joseph's policy of seizing and hoarding grain. See Daniel Kaganovich and Jeremy England, "The Road to Egypt: Job Creators in the Ancient World," *Times of Israel*, October 18, 2012. For an extended discussion of the economic aspects of Joseph's activities in Egypt, see Moses L. Pava, *Business Ethics: A Jewish Perspective*, Ktav, 1997, pp. 159–77. However, as against the view that Joseph did not tell the Egyptian people of the impending famine, and therefore did not in fact monopolize the storage of grain, see Bereishit Rabbah 91:5.

8. See Rashi on Genesis 47:21. In an attempt to mitigate Joseph's role in this endeavor, the nineteenth-century German rabbi Samson Raphael Hirsch, commenting on the same verse, holds that Joseph refused the Egyptians' offer to sell themselves into servitude, though he did accept the sale of their land and proceeded to transfer the population.

9. For an illustration of Pharaoh's reluctance to grant Joseph's request to bury his father in Canaan, see Talmud Sotah 36b. For more in this vein, see Hazony's discussion of Joseph in Hazony, *The Philosophy of Hebrew Scripture*, pp. 120–29.

10. It is possible that Joseph's reassurance to his brothers that God will remember them to bring them out of Egypt, along with his request to be buried in the Land of Canaan and insistence that his bones not be removed from Egypt until his brethren are, indicates his recognition of the ramifications of his and Pharaoh's policies. See Genesis 50:24, Exodus 13:19, and also Robert Klapper, "Yosef ha-Tzaddik," Center for Modern Torah Leadership, http://www.torahleadership .org/categories/joseph_mai2_1.pdf (accessed Jan. 19, 2013).

11. The description of Joseph as a *tzaddik* is predominantly rooted in Kabbalistic commentary, for instance Zohar 194b. For references to Joseph as a tzaddik in the Midrashim, see Bereishit Rabbah 86:6, 87:2, 88:1, 88:3, 95:4. See also Rashi on Genesis 40:1; Ramban on Genesis 37:24; and Pirkei d'Rabbi Eliezer ch. 38, where Amos 2:6 is taken as an allusion to the sale of Joseph.

12. Micha Odenheimer, "A Jewish Response to Globalization," in *Righteous Indignation*, Rose, Kaiser, Klein, eds., pp. 293–302.

CHAPTER 6

1. Ezra Berkley Nepon, *A History of New Jewish Agenda*, Thread Makes Blanket Press, 2012, p. 25 and 39.
2. Arthur Waskow, "Violence and Nonviolence in Jewish Thought and Practice," in Stefan Merken and Murray Polner, eds., *Peace, Justice, and Jews: Reclaiming Our Tradition*, Bunim & Bannigan Ltd., 2007, pp. 117–32, esp. p. 124.
3. Robert Alter, "Revolutionism and the Jews 2: Appropriating the Religious Tradition," *Commentary*, February 1971.
4. Nepon, *A History of New Jewish Agenda*, p. 38.
5. "Passover Social Justice Resources," Jewish Social Justice Network, 2003, http://www.jewdas.org/wp-content/uploads/2011/04/jsjn2003haggadah.pdf (accessed Jan. 29, 2013).
6. "Next Year in a Just World," American Jewish World Service, 2017, https://ajws-americanjewishwo.netdna-ssl.com/wp-content/uploads/2017/03/haggadah_2017.pdf (accessed Jan. 6, 2018). See also Renee Ghert-Zand, "Passover Guides Serve Up a Side of Social Justice for the Seder Table," *Times of Israel*, March 31, 2017, http://www.timesofisrael.com/passover-guides-serve-up-a-side-of-social-justice-for-the-seder-table/ (accessed April 2, 2017).
7. Michael Medved, "The Preposterous Politics of Passover," *Commentary*, April 2011.
8. Alter, "Revolutionism and the Jews 2."
9. Jill Jacobs, *There Shall Be No Needy: Pursuing Social Justice through Jewish Law and Tradition*, Jewish Lights Publishing, 2009, p. 4 and p. 10. See also Gerald Cromer, "Tikkun Olam: Engaged Spirituality and Jewish Identity," The Rappaport Center for Assimilation Research and Strengthening Jewish Vitality, 2007, pp. 25–26.
10. Michael Walzer, *Exodus and Revolution*, Basic Books, 1985.
11. Elliot N. Dorff, *The Way into Tikkun Olam*, Jewish Lights Publishing, 2007, p. 55.
12. Michael Lerner, "The Founding Editorial Statement, *Tikkun*: To Heal, Repair and Transform the World," *Tikkun*, Fall 1986.
13. Jon D. Levenson, *The Death and Resurrection of the Beloved Son*, Yale University Press, 1993, pp. 37–38.
14. Andrea Peyser, "Colleges Aren't Just Politically Correct—They're Anti-semitic," *New York Post*, December 5, 2016, http://nypost.com

/2016/12/05/colleges-arent-just-politically-correct-theyre-anti
-semitic/ (accessed Jan. 2, 2017).

15. Walzer, *Exodus and Revolution*, pp. 12–13.

CHAPTER 7

1. Jonathan Neumann, "Occupy Wall Street and the Jews," *Commentary*, January 2012. This chapter draws further on this essay.

2. Ibid.

3. Sam Kestenbaum, "'Antifa's Most Prominent Jew' Booted from Twitter," *Forward*, June 9, 2017, http://forward.com/fast-forward/374276/antifas-most-prominent-jew-booted-from-twitter/ (accessed Oct. 10, 2017).

4. Sarah Posner, "Yom Kippur Prayers for Corporate Atonement at Occupy Wall St.: Rewriting Kol Nidrei," *Religion Dispatches*, October 6, 2011, http://www.religiondispatches.org/archive/atheologies/5222/yom_kippur_prayers_for_corporate_atonement_at_occupy_wall_st._/ (accessed Feb. 25, 2013). See also Marc Tracy, "How Jewish Is Occupy Wall Street: Commenting on Commentary," *Tablet*'s The Scroll, December 29, 2011, http://www.tabletmag.com/scroll/87123/how-jewish-is-occupy-wall-street (accessed April 7, 2013).

5. The Amos Fellowship is a program of Uri L'Tzedek. See http://www.utzedek.org/takeaction/on-campus/amos-fellowship.html (accessed Feb. 25, 2013). The Jeremiah Fellowship is a program of Bend the Arc, in collaboration with other Jewish social justice organizations such as Jews United for Justice. See "Jeremiah Fellowship," Bend the Arc, http://bendthearc.us/jeremiah-fellowship (accessed Feb. 25, 2013). There was also the short-lived Amos: The National Jewish Partnership for Social Justice. See "Amos: The National Jewish Partnership for Social Justice," American Jewish Archives, http://americanjewisharchives.org/collections/ms0701/ (accessed Feb. 25, 2013).

6. Michael Lerner, *Jewish Renewal: A Path to Healing and Transformation*, Harper Perennial, 1995, p. 131. Further citations from Lerner in this chapter will be from this book unless otherwise stated.

7. Sidney Schwarz, *Judaism and Justice: The Jewish Passion to Repair the World*, Jewish Lights Publishing, 2006 (2008), p. 47. Further citations

from Schwarz in this chapter will be from this book unless otherwise stated.

8. Sidney Schwarz, "Can Social Justice Save the American Jewish Soul?," in *Righteous Indignation*, Or N. Rose, Jo Ellen Green Kaiser, Margie Klein, eds., Jewish Lights Publishing, 2008, pp. 3–14.

9. Schwarz, *Judaism and Justice*, p. 50.

10. Lerner, *Jewish Renewal*, p. 131.

11. Ibid., p. 18. See also Michael Lerner, "The Founding Editorial Statement, *Tikkun*: To Heal, Repair and Transform the World," *Tikkun*, Fall 1986.

12. Lerner, *Jewish Renewal*, p. 133 (emphasis added).

13. Jill Jacobs, *There Shall Be No Needy: Pursuing Social Justice through Jewish Law and Tradition*, Jewish Lights Publishing, 2009, pp. 47–48.

14. *Tikkun* magazine has been hailed by the influential late liberal rabbi and a founder of the Havurah movement, Zalman Schachter-Shalomi, as a prophetic voice in our age. See Zalman Schachter-Shalomi, "An Age in Need of Prophets," *Tikkun*, Winter 2011.

15. Norman Podhoretz, *The Prophets: Who They Were, What They Are*, The Free Press, 2002, p. 315.

16. Ibid., pp. 187–89.

17. See also Isaiah 56:1–2, where ethics and ritual are also brought together.

18. Michael Walzer, *In God's Shadow: Politics in the Hebrew Bible*, Yale University Press, 2012, p. 209.

19. See also Podhoretz, *The Prophets*, pp. 265–87.

20. Walzer, *In God's Shadow*, p. 210.

21. Aryeh Cohen, "The 'Jewish' Vote," *Justice in the City*, May 23, 2012, http://www.justice-in-the-city.com/?p=311 (accessed Aug. 21, 2013). See also Mordecai M. Kaplan, *Judaism as a Civilization: Toward a Reconstruction of American-Jewish Life* (1934), Jewish Publication Society, 2010, p. 478.

22. Avot 3:2.

23. See Jacob J. Schacter, "*Tikkun Olam*: Defining the Jewish Obligation," in *Rav Chesed: Essays in Honor of Rabbi Dr. Haskel Lookstein*, vol. 2, Rafael Medoff, ed., Ktav, 2009, pp. 183–204; and also Jack Bieler, "A Religious Context for Jewish Political Activity," in *Tikkun Olam: Social Responsibility in Jewish Thought and Law*, David

Shatz, Chaim I. Waxman, and Nathan J. Diament, eds., Jason Aronson Inc., 1997, pp. 145–58.

24. Robert Alter, "Revolutionism and the Jews 2: Appropriating the Religious Tradition," *Commentary*, February 1971.

25. Ibid.

CHAPTER 8

1. "Bold Judaism Is," Beth Adam, https://bethadam.org/about/bold-judaism-is/ (accessed Oct. 28, 2017).

2. Nathan Guttman, "Ohio Democrat Wants to Be First Rabbi in Congress," *Forward*, October 18, 2017.

3. Mark Oppenheimer, "Could This Rabbi Be a First in Congress?" *Washington Post*, October 17, 2017.

4. See also Paul David Kerbel, "The *Tikkun Olam* Generation," *Conservative Judaism* 61, Number 3, Spring 2010, pp. 88–91, where a leading Jewish congressman tells the author: "I am in the Congress to do *tikkun olam*."

5. For some examples, see the entries in *The Tikkun Olam Project: An Initiative for International Development Cooperation and Humanitarian Assistance Exploratory Workshop*, The Harold Hartog School of Government and Policy, Tel Aviv University, June 11, 2006. See also Jill Jacobs, *There Shall Be No Needy: Pursuing Social Justice through Jewish Law and Tradition*, Jewish Lights Publishing, 2009, p. 38; and Eugene Korn, "The Mitzvah of *Tikun Olam*," Learning to Give, http://www.learningtogive.org/religiousinstructors/voices/mitzvah_tikkun_olam.asp (accessed March 25, 2013).

6. Jonathan Sacks, *To Heal a Fractured World: The Ethics of Responsibility*, Schocken Books, 2005, p. 9.

7. Jane Kanarek, "What Does *Tikkun Olam* Actually Mean?" in *Righteous Indignation*, Or N. Rose, Jo Ellen Green Kaiser, Margie Klein, eds., Jewish Lights Publishing, 2008, pp. 15–22. All references to Kanarek in this chapter will be from this essay.

8. Gilbert S. Rosenthal, "*Tikkun ha-Olam*: The Metamorphosis of a Concept," *Journal of Religion*, vol. 85, no. 2, 2005, from which this discussion borrows.

9. See Rosenthal, "*Tikkun ha-Olam*." See also Genesis Rabbah 11:6, 95:3, 84:7, 87:3, and 98:2.

10. Jill Jacobs, "The History of 'Tikkun Olam,'" *Zeek*, June 2007. Further references to Jacobs in this chapter are from this essay unless otherwise stated.

11. Mitchell First, "*Aleinu*: Obligation to Fix the World or the Text?" *Hakirah*, vol. 11, Spring 2011.

12. See, for example, I Samuel 20:31 and I Kings 2:12, where t-kh-n (and not t-k-n) is used in connection with the establishment of Jonathan's and Solomon's kingdoms, respectively. Psalms 9:8 too uses the same verb to describe the establishment of God's throne for judgment. And so does the blessing over Jerusalem in the Amidah prayer, recited three times daily, in reference to the establishment of the throne of David.

13. Gerald J. Blidstein, "*Tikkun Olam*," in *Tikkun Olam: Social Responsibility in Jewish Thought and Law*, D. Shatz, C. I. Waxman, and N. J. Diament, eds. (Northvale, NJ, 1997), pp. 17–59, esp. p. 26.

14. Jeffrey H. Ballabon, "A View of *Tikkun Olam* from Capitol Hill," in *Tikkun Olam*, pp. 223–37, esp. pp. 224–25.

15. These translations are taken from Philip Blackman, ed., *Mishnayoth* (London: Mishna Press, 1951); M. Simon, The Soncino Talmud (Hindhead 1935–48); and the Artscroll Schottenstein Edition of the Talmud (New York 1990–2004). C.f. Bava Metzia 14b, however, where ArtScroll veers from its usual translation of "for the benefit of society" in favor of "for the common good." Eugene Lipman cites yet more translations: Danby's "precautions for the general good," Strack's "for good order," and Zeitlin's "amendment," and suggests his own: "for the proper order of the Jewish community." Whatever the right rendering, Lipman rightly concludes, "it is a long way from that definition to 'build a better world.'" Eugene J. Lipman, "*Mipnei Tikkun Ha'Olam* in the Talmud: A Preliminary Exploration," in *The Life of Covenant: The Challenge of Contemporary Judaism—Essays in Honor of Herman E. Schaalman*, Joseph A. Edelheit, ed., Spertus College of Judaica Press, 1986, p. 108.

16. Gittin 4:3.

17. See Gittin 33a, 45a-b; and Pesakhim 88b. See also Hagigah 2b and Arakhin 2b.

18. Jacobs, "The History of 'Tikkun Olam.'"

19. Even Gerry Serotta, a founder of New Jewish Agenda, a former chair of Rabbis for Human Rights, North America (now T'ruah),

and one of the popularizers of the term *tikkun olam* in modern American Jewish discourse, acknowledges that the relevance of Talmudic *tikkun olam* is limited to Jews. See Jonathan Krasner, "The Place of *Tikkun Olam* in American Jewish Life," The Jerusalem Center, November 1, 2014, http://jcpa.org/article/place-tikkun-olam-american-jewish-life1/ (accessed Dec. 31, 2014).

20. Hillel Halkin, "How Not to Repair the World," *Commentary*, July/August 2008.

21. Sagit Mor, "*Tikkun Olam* in Early Rabbinic Literature," cited in Byron Sherwin, "*Tikkun Olam*: A Case of Semantic Displacement," Jerusalem Center for Public Affairs, November 1, 2014.

22. Lipman, "*Mipnei Tikkun Ha'Olam* in the Talmud," p. 108. Levi Cooper, "The Assimilation of *Tikkun Olam*," *Jewish Political Studies Review* 25, no. 3–4, Fall 2014. See also Vernon Kurtz, "*Tikkun Olam*: Particular or Universal?," in *Tikkun Olam*, David Birnbaum and Martin S. Cohen, eds., New Paradigm Matrix Publishing, 2015.

23. Rosenthal, "*Tikkun ha-Olam*."

24. Lipman, "*Mipnei Tikkun Ha'Olam* in the Talmud," p. 109.

25. http://www.on1foot.org/text/rav-kook-tzvi-yaron-mishnato-shel-harav-kook (accessed Mar. 13, 2013); and Arieh Lebowitz, "Why a Labor Movement Matters," in *Righteous Indignation*, p. 158. This source is also mentioned in Jacobs, *There Shall Be No Needy*, pp. 125–30.

26. J. David Bleich, *Contemporary Halakhic Problems*, vol. I. Ktav Publishing House, Yeshiva University Press, 1977, pp. 186–89.

27. The full text of the ruling is available in Tzvi Yaron, *Mishnato Shel HaRav Kook*, Ha-Mahlakah le-hinukh ule-tarbut Toraniyim bagolah, ha-Histadrut ha-Tsiyonit ha-'olamit (Hebrew), Jerusalem, 1974, p. 164.

28. Bleich, *Contemporary Halakhic Problems*, pp. 186–89. Other traditionalist rabbinic authorities, such as the Tzitz Eliezer, take a more lenient view, but they do not mention *tikkun olam*.

29. Jacobs, *There Shall Be No Needy*, p. 128.

30. Levi Cooper, "The Assimilation of *Tikkun Olam*," *Jewish Political Studies Review* 25, no. 3–4, Fall 2014.

31. Another commentary cited by Jacobs has similarly narrow relevance. Genesis Rabbah 13:13 is an abstruse passage with a decidedly mystical bent. "I [the Lord] have created it [the rain] *l'tikkuno shel olam v'yishuvo* [for the *tikkun* of the *olam* and its cultivation],"

in connection to Isaiah 45:8 ("Let the sky pour down righteousness; let the earth open"), making references to the masculine upper waters being received by the feminine lower waters. Again, this *tikkun* is more about stability than repair, the agent of the *tikkun* is God, and there is no normative implication or endorsement of liberal ecological activism.

32. "About Us," The Coalition on the Environment and Jewish Life, http://coejl.org/aboutus/ (accessed Jan. 7, 2013).

33. Coalition on the Environment and Jewish Life, "Wonder and Restraint: A Rabbinical Call to Environmental Action," in *Righteous Indignation*, pp. 67–75.

34. http://multi.jewishpublicaffairs.org/coejl/resources/jewish -energy-covenant-campaign-declaration/ (accessed Jan.13, 2018). See also Midrash Zuta and Torah Temimah. Some other commentaries take different approaches.

35. http://multi.jewishpublicaffairs.org/coejl/resources/jewish -energy-covenant-campaign-declaration/ (accessed Jan. 7, 2018).

36. "Social Action: *Tikkun Olam*: The Backstory, an RJ conversation with Howard Schwartz," *Reform Judaism Online*, Winter 2009.

37. For a more detailed discussion of Lurianic Kabbalah, see G. Scholem, *Major Trends in Jewish Mysticism* revised edition, Shocken, 1995 [1941], pp. 244–86, particularly p. 273ff; and Lawrence Fine, *Physician of the Soul, Healer of the Cosmos: Isaac Luria and His Kabbalistic Fellowship*, Stanford University Press, 2003, esp. pp. 124–49, from which this summary draws.

38. Byron L. Sherwin also points out that "For the Kabbalists, *tikkun olam* is a theocentric concern, not an anthropocentric, political, or social one." Byron L. Sherwin, *Faith Finding Meaning*, Oxford University Press, 2009, pp. 33–35.

39. Yitzchok Adlerstein, "The Highjacking of *Tikkun Olam*," Cross-Currents Blog, May 4, 2007, https://cross-currents.com/2007/05 /04/the-hijacking-of-tikkun-olam/ (accessed Oct. 17, 2017).

40. Cf. Howard Schwartz, "How the Ari Created a Myth and Transformed Judaism," *Tikkun*, March 28, 2011.

41. Michael J. Broyde, "Jewish Law and American Public Policy: A Principled Jewish View and Some Practical Jewish Observations," in *Formulating Responses in an Egalitarian Age*, Marc D. Stern, ed., Rowman and Littlefield Publishers, 2005, pp. 109–29, esp. pp. 115–17.

42. Leonard Fein, *Where Are We?: The Inner Life of America's Jews*, Harper and Row, 1988, pp. 128–29 (emphasis added).

43. Arthur Green, *These Are the Words: A Vocabulary of Jewish Spiritual Life*, Jewish Lights Publishing, 2012 (Second edition), pp. 185–86 (emphasis added).

44. Eugene Borowitz, *Renewing the Covenant: A Theology for the Postmodern Jew*, Jewish Publications Society, 1996 [1991], p. 51 (emphasis added).

45. Reported in Austin Greenberg, "Righteous Vigor: Social Activist Calls for Change," *The Wisconsin Jewish Chronicle*, March 7, 2008.

46. Aryeh Cohen, "Should We Be Saying Kaddish for the Jewish Left?" Justice in the City blog, June 12, 2012, http://bendthearc.us/news /should-we-be-saying-kaddish-jewish-left (accessed Mar. 25, 2013).

47. A. J. Wolf, "Repairing *Tikkun Olam*—Current Theological Writing," *Judaism*, Fall 2001.

48. Aryeh Cohen, "Does *Tikkun Olam* Mean Anything Anymore?" June 11, 2013, *Daily Beast*, https://www.thedailybeast.com/does -tikkun-olam-mean-anything-anymore (accessed Oct. 16, 2017).

CHAPTER 9

1. Margie Klein, "Why Liberal Jews Should Read an Orthodox Social Justice Book," *Zeek*, March 22, 2012.

2. Jill Jacobs, *There Shall Be No Needy: Pursuing Social Justice through Jewish Law and Tradition*, Jewish Lights Publishing, 2009, pp. 4–5. See also Jill Jacobs, "Why Are Orthodox Organizations Embracing Christian Values?" *Forward*, November 16, 2017.

3. Hillel Halkin, "How Not to Repair the World," *Commentary*, July/ August 2008.

4. Aryeh Cohen, *Justice in the City: An Argument from the Sources of Rabbinic Judaism*, Academic Studies Press, 2012, p. 9.

5. Aryeh Cohen, "Does *Tikkun Olam* Mean Anything Anymore?" *Daily Beast*, June 11, 2013, https://www.thedailybeast.com/does -tikkun-olam-mean-anything-anymore (accessed Oct. 16, 2017).

6. Aryeh Cohen, "Hearing the Voice of the Poor," in *Righteous Indignation*, Or N. Rose, Jo Ellen Green Kaiser, Margie Klein, eds., Jewish Lights Publishing, 2008, pp. 135–46, esp. pp. 138–39 (emphasis added). See also Cohen, *Justice in the City*, p. 11.

7. Shmuly Yanklowitz, *Jewish Ethics and Social Justice: A Guide for the 21st Century*, Derusha Publishing, 2012, p. 194.

8. Michael Lerner, *Jewish Renewal: A Path to Healing and Transformation*, Harper Perennial, 1995, p. 91ff. Shmuly Yanklowitz, an Orthodox advocate of Jewish social justice, tries, with questionable success, to find a middle ground: Shmuly Yanklowitz, "How Do We Relate to Morally Difficult Texts in Jewish Tradition?" *Jewish Week*, February 27, 2013.

9. Cited in Michael Robinson, "Living Nonviolently," in *Peace, Justice, and Jews: Reclaiming Our Tradition*, Stefan Merken and Murray Polner, eds., Bunim & Bannigan Ltd., 2007, pp. 63–69, esp. p. 66.

10. "About The Shalom Center," Shalom Center, http://theshalomcenter .org/content/about-shalom-center-mission-more (accessed Jan. 28, 2012).

11. Avot 2:16, quoted in "Mission & Values," Charles and Lynn Schusterman Family Foundation, http://www.schusterman.org/about -us/mission-values (accessed March 25, 2013). See also Bennett Murashkin, "Jewish Secularism," in *Peace, Justice, and Jews*, pp. 54–62, esp. p. 58.

12. Halkin, "How Not to Repair the World."

13. A. J. Wolf, "Repairing *Tikkun Olam*—Current Theological Writing," *Judaism*, Fall 2001.

14. Dara Silverman, "And If Not Together, How?: Jews and Immigration in the United States," in *Righteous Indignation*, pp. 163–68.

15. Rabbinic thought interprets the *ger* as a proselyte to Judaism, which is even more irrelevant to immigration to the United States.

16. Daniel Sieradski, "After Raid, Occupy's Ideas Live On," *Forward*, November 16, 2011.

17. Yanklowitz, *Jewish Ethics and Social Justice*, pp. 87–88.

18. Daniel Landes, "Hidden Master," Review of Arthur Green, *Radical Judaism: Rethinking God and Tradition* (Yale, 2010), *Jewish Review of Books*, Fall 2010, pp. 20–22.

19. Aryeh Cohen, "Two Types of Sovereignty: Zionism and Diaspora," Justice in the City blog, August 20, 2012, http://www.justice-in-the -city.com/?p=344 (accessed Jul. 31, 2013). A former managing editor of *Tikkun*, Joel Schalit, also celebrates the rise of a Diaspora "competitive" with Israel. See Joel Schalit, "Everything Falls Apart," in *Righteous Indignation*, pp. 270–74.

20. Richard Landes and Benjamin Weinthal, "The Post-Self-Destructivism of Judith Butler," *Wall Street Journal*, September 9, 2012.

21. Judith Butler, "Judith Butler Responds to Attack: 'I Affirm a Judaism That Is Not Associated with State Violence,'" *Mondoweiss*, August 27, 2012, http://mondoweiss.net/2012/08/judith-butler-responds-to-attack-i-affirm-a-judaism-that-is-not-associated-with-state-violence.html (accessed Jul. 31, 2013). The justification of anti-Israel sentiment on the basis of a Jewish charge to pursue justice is very common. Another example is the United Nation Special Rapporteur on the "situation of human rights in the Palestinian territories occupied since 1967," Richard Falk, who explores this understanding of Judaism: Richard Falk, "On Jewish Identity," Global Justice in the 21st Century blog, January 15, 2011, http://richardfalk.wordpress.com/2011/01/15/on-jewish-identity/ (accessed Jul. 31, 2013).

CHAPTER 10

1. Tara Bahrampour, "Neighborhood Report: Morningside Heights; A Rift at Jewish Theological over an Article about Israel," *New York Times*, March 9, 2003.

2. Daniel Gordis, "Are Young Rabbis Turning on Israel?" *Commentary*, June 2011. See also Daniel Gordis, "Of Sermons and Strategies," *Jerusalem Post*, April 1, 2011.

3. Aryeh Cohen, "How I Lost My Zionism," Open Zion, *Daily Beast*, March 15, 2012, http://www.thedailybeast.com/articles/2012/03/15/how-i-lost-my-zionism.html (accessed Jul. 31, 2013); Leonard Fein, "My Battered Zionism: Liberal Zionists Speak Out," *Huffington Post*, April 26, 2012, http://www.huffingtonpost.com/leonard-fein/liberal-zionists-speak-out-the-many-faces-of-zionism_b_1454082.html (accessed Jul. 31, 2013); Jay Michaelson, "How I'm Losing My Love for Israel," *Forward*, September 16, 2009; Michael Lerner, *Jewish Renewal: Path to Healing and Transformation*, Harper Perennial, 1994, pp. 219–64, esp. p. 264.

4. "More Than 200 Liberal US Rabbis Want Israel to Lift Travel Ban on BDS Leaders," *JTA*, August 9, 2017, https://www.jta.org/2017/08/09/news-opinion/united-states/more-than-200-liberal-us-rabbis-sign-letter-against-israel-bds-travel-ban (accessed Oct. 11, 2017).

5. Michael E. Staub, "If We Really Care about Israel: Breira and the Limits of Dissent," in *Wrestling with Zion: Progressive Jewish-American Responses to the Israeli-Palestinian Conflict*, Tony Kushner and Alisa Solomon, eds., Grove Press, 2003, pp. 89–105.

6. Rael Jean Isaac, "Breira: Counsel for Judaism," *Americans for a Safe Israel*, 1977.

7. Isaac, "Breira"; Joseph Shattan, "Why Breira?" *Commentary*, April 1977; Staub, "If We Really Care about Israel," pp. 89–105.

8. Staub, "If We Really Care about Israel," pp. 89–105.

9. Tevi Troy, "I Think That I Shall Never See a Jew as Lovely as a Tree," *Commentary*, February 2015.

10. Shifra Bronznick and Didi Goldenhar, "Visioning Justice and the American Jewish Community," Nathan Cummings Foundation, 2008, pp. 59–60.

11. Dyonna Ginsburg, "Re-anchoring Universalism to Particularism: The Potential Contribution of Orthodoxy to the Pursuit of *Tikkun Olam*," in *The Next Generation of Modern Orthodoxy*, Shmuel Hain, ed., Yeshiva University Press, 2012, pp. 3–23.

12. Jack Wertheimer, "The Ten Commandments of America's Jews," *Commentary*, June 2012.

13. Daniel Rosza Lang/Levitsky, "Hidden Agenda: Lessons from NJA, Lost and Learned," in *A History of New Jewish Agenda*, Ezra Berkley Nepon, ed., Thread Makes Blanket Press, 2012, pp. 93–107, esp. pp. 105–6.

14. "Our Name and History," T'ruah, http://www.truah.org/about /our-name-and-history/ (accessed Oct. 22, 2017).

15. "More Than 200 Liberal Rabbis Want Israel to Lift Travel Ban on BDS Leaders," *JTA*, August 10, 2017, http://jewishweek.timesofisrael .com/more-than-200-liberal-us-rabbis-want-israel-to-lift-travel -ban-on-bds-leaders/ (accessed Nov. 1, 2017); "Local Governments Must Not Abandon Free Speech to Shield Israel from Criticism," T'ruah, http://www.truah.org/press/speech/ (accessed Nov. 4, 2017); Jill Jacobs, "Anti-BDS Law Can't Be 'Pro-Israel' If It Tramples on Free Speech," *JTA*, June 14, 2016, https://www.jta.org/2016/06 /14/news-opinion/opinion/anti-bds-law-cant-be-pro-israel-if-it -tramples-on-free-speech (accessed Nov. 4, 2017).

16. Daniel Greenfield, "Obama's Favorite New Anti-Israel BDS Group Joins Him for Chanukah," *Frontpage*, December 14, 2015, http://

www.frontpagemag.com/fpm/261115/obamas-favorite-new-anti
-israel-bds-group-joins-daniel-greenfield (accessed Nov. 4, 2017);
Richard Silverstein, "Rabbis Chide South African Jewish Leadership,
Wish Goldstone Mazel Tov on Grandson's Bar Mitzvah," Tikun
Olam blog, April 21, 2010, https://www.richardsilverstein.com
/2010/04/21/rabbis-chide-south-african-jews-wish-judge-goldstone
-mazel-tov-on-grandsons-bar-mitzvah/ (accessed Nov. 4, 2017);
Stephen Leavitt, "To the Chagrin of Some Jews, Presbyterians Denounce Divestment—#BDSFail," Jewish Press, July 6, 2012, http://
www.jewishpress.com/news/eye-on-palestine/to-the-chagrin-of
-some-jews-presbyterians-denounce-divestment-bdsfail/2012/07/06
/0/?print (accessed Nov. 4, 2017); "Cease Fire Now in Gaza," paid
advertisement by Tikkun Community, https://www.vosizneias
.com/files/ceasefiregaza.pdf (accessed Nov. 4, 2017).

17. Shaul Magid, "Is It Right to Compare Ferguson to Gaza? Reflec-
    tions from a Jewish Protester," Tikkun, December 11, 2014.

18. Dan Pine, "The Progressive Prophet: Michael Lerner Reflects on
    25 Years of Tikkun Magazine," J Weekly, March 4, 2011, https://www
    .jweekly.com/2011/03/04/the-progressive-prophet-michael-lerner
    -reflects-on-25-years-of-tikkun-magaz/ (accessed Nov. 5, 2017).

19. Michael Lerner, ed., Tikkun Reader: Twentieth Anniversary, Rowman
    and Littlefield, 2007, p. 6.

20. Alan Dershowitz, "The Accusation: 'Moral Pervert' Hit Piece
    Shouldn't Have Been Spread," J Weekly, Oct. 20, 2006.

21. "Values," New Israel Fund, http://www.nif.org/about/values/ (ac-
    cessed Jan. 11, 2017); "Advocacy," New Israel Fund, http://www
    .nif.org/what-we-do/advocacy/ (accessed Jan. 11, 2017); "President
    of New Israel Fund Says Israel Is Evil," Elder of Ziyon, September 12,
    2017, http://elderofziyon.blogspot.com/2017/09/president-of-new
    -israel-fund-says.html (accessed Nov. 1, 2017); "New Israel Fund,"
    NGO Monitor, http://www.ngo-monitor.org/article/new_israel
    _fund (accessed Jun. 24, 2013); Noah Pollak, "Wikileaks Bombshell:
    New Israel Fund Official Endorses End of Jewish State," Commen-
    tary, September 6, 2011, http://www.commentarymagazine.com
    /2011/09/06/wikileaks-new-israel-fund-endorses-end-of-jewish
    -state/ (accessed Jun. 24, 2013). The New Israel Fund denies that
    this view represents that of the organization.

22. "Jewish Voice for Peace Seeks Social Justice, Equality, Human

Rights (Your Letters)," Syracuse *Post-Standard*, December 9, 2016, http://www.syracuse.com/opinion/index.ssf/2016/12/jewish _voice_for_peace_seeks_social_justice_equality_human_rights _your_letters.html (accessed Nov. 5, 2017).

23. "Mission," Jewish Voice for Peace, http://jewishvoiceforpeace.org /content/jvp-mission-statement (accessed Jun. 21, 2013); and Zach Novetsky, "Another Response to Peter Beinart on Israel-Agnosticism," Open Zion, *Daily Beast*, August 31, 2012, http://www.thedailybeast .com/articles/2012/08/31/another-response-to-peter-beinart-on -israel-agnosticism.html (accessed Jun. 21, 2013).

24. "ADL Identifies Top 10 Anti-Israel Groups in America," Anti-Defamation League, October 14, 2010, http://www.adl.org/press -center/press-releases/israel-middle-east/adl-identifies-top-10-anti -israel-groups-in-america.html (accessed Jun. 23, 2013).

25. "Mission," Jewish Voice for Peace.

26. Jewish Voice for Peace Passover Haggadah 2012/5772, http:// ijvcanada.org/wp-content/uploads/2014/04/hagadah_jvp_final _2012.pdf (accessed Jan. 7, 2017).

27. JewishVoiceForPeace, "Taking a Stance . . ." Twitter, November 21, 2012, https://twitter.com/jvplive/status/271311605059440640 (accessed Jun. 23, 2013).

28. Jonathan Paul Katz, "Can a Non-Zionist Synagogue Survive—and Spread?" *Forward*, July 13, 2015, http://forward.com/opinion/311886 /are-non-zionist-synagogues-like-tzedek-chicago-the-way-of-the -future/ (accessed Jul. 20, 2015).

29. "Rockefeller Brothers Fund," NGO Monitor, http://www.ngo -monitor.org/funder/rockefeller_brothers_fund; "Jewish Funds for Justice," Rockefeller Brothers Fund (accessed Jan. 11, 2018); https:// www.rbf.org/grantees/jewish-funds-justice-inc; Ziva Dahl, "The Rockefeller Brothers Fund Is Bankrolling Israel's Destruction," *Algemeiner*, March 28, 2016, https://www.algemeiner.com/2016/03/28 /the-rockefeller-brothers-fund-is-bankrolling-israels-destruction/; "International Activities by Israeli NGOs," NGO Monitor, https:// www.ngo-monitor.org/reports/international_activities_by _israeli_ngos0/ (accessed Nov. 1, 2017).

30. Eric Fingerhut, "Foxman Blasts J Street on Palin, Questions Its 'Pro-Israel' Slogan," *JTA*, November 20, 2009.

31. "Who We Are," J Street U, http://www.jstreetu.org/about/who-we

-are (accessed Jun. 24, 2013); Hilary Leila Krieger, "J Street's Campus Branch Drops Pro-Israel Slogan," *Jerusalem Post*, October 27, 2009.

32. Shiri Moshe, "J Street U: Calling for Israel's Destruction Isn't Always Antisemitic," *Algemeiner*, November 14, 2017, https://www.algemeiner.com/2017/11/14/j-street-u-calling-for-israels-destruction-isnt-always-antisemitic/ (accessed Nov. 26, 2017).

33. Peter Beinart, "The Failure of the American Jewish Establishment," *New York Review of Books*, June 10, 2010.

34. See also Jordan Chandler Hirsch, "Diaspora Divided," *Jewish Review of Books*, Spring 2012; and Matthew Ackerman, "Who Cares about Peter Beinart," *Times of Israel*, April 2, 2012, http://blogs.timesofisrael.com/who-cares-about-peter-beinart/ (accessed Aug. 31, 2012).

35. Daniel Gordis, "Are Young Rabbis Turning on Israel?" *Commentary*, June 2011.

CHAPTER 11

1. "High Holiday Workbook," *Tikkun*, September 21, 2011, http://www.tikkun.org/nextgen/high-holiday-workbook-2 (accessed Oct. 12, 2017); "8 Nights of Sandy Service: Support 350.org's Climate Change Work," Repair the World, December 16, 2012, http://werepair.org/blog/8-nights-of-sandy-service-support-350-orgs-climate-change-work/17213 (accessed Jan. 7, 2013); "Economic Justice," Religious Action Center, https://rac.org/economic-justice (accessed Oct. 12, 2017); "Oppose Cuts to Disability Insurance," Religious Action Center, http://action.rac.org/p/dia/action3/common/public/?action_KEY=19597 (accessed Oct. 12, 2017); "Urge Congress to Increase Access to Child Nutrition Programs," Religious Action Center, http://action.rac.org/p/dia/action3/common/public/?action_KEY=18440 (accessed Oct. 12, 2017); "Largest Ever Mobilization of Jews for Black Lives Matter," Jews for Racial and Economic Justice, August 12, 2016, http://jfrej.org/largest-ever-mobilization-of-jews-for-black-lives-matter/ (accessed Jan.8, 2017); "Labor on the Bimah Packet," Jews United for Justice, http://www.jufj.org/content/labor-bimah-packet (accessed Jan. 11, 2018).

2. Tevi Troy, "I Think That I Shall Never See a Jew as Lovely as a Tree," *Commentary*, February 2015.

3. For further examples, see President Obama's speech to the Union for Reform Judaism's Biennial: Barack Obama, "Keynote Address," December 16, 2011; his interview with Jeffrey Goldberg in May 2015: Jeffrey Goldberg, "'Look, It's My Name on This': Obama Defends the Iran Nuclear Deal," *The Atlantic*, May 21, 2015, http:// www.theatlantic.com/international/archive/2015/05/obama-inter view-iran-isis-israel/393782/ (accessed Jul. 20, 2015); and his speech to the Adas Israel Congregation: Barack Obama, speech, Adas Israel Congregation, Washington, DC, May 22, 2015. See also Levi Cooper, "The Assimilation of *Tikkun Olam*," *Jewish Political Studies Review* 25, no. 3–4, Fall 2014, which lists more examples of Obama citing tikkun olam as well as members of his administration doing so.

4. Natasha Mozgovaya, "Obama Awards Rock Icon Bob Dylan Highest Presidential Honor," *Haaretz*, May 30, 2012; Peter Beinart, "What Obama Understands About Jews," Open Zion, *Daily Beast*, May 31, 2012, http://www.thedailybeast.com/articles/2012/05 /31/what-obama-understands-about-jews.html (accessed Jun. 27, 2013). In a similar vein, the *Forward* ranked Barack Obama as "plus one" on its 2011 "Forward Fifty." See "Forward50," *Forward*, http:// forward.com/specials/forward-50-2011/barack-obama/ (accessed Jun. 27, 2013).

5. Steven M. Bob, "The '*Tikkun Olam*' President," *Jerusalem Post*, December 31, 2011.

6. Peter Beinart, *The Crisis of Zionism*, Times Books, 2012, pp. 79–99; Joshua Keating, "Does Obama Actually Have to BE Jewish?," *Foreign Policy*, September 4, 2012, http://blog.foreignpolicy.com/posts /2012/09/04/does_obama_actually_have_to_be_jewish (accessed Feb. 27, 2013). In addition to Obama's commitment to social justice rendering him a Jewish president, one also cannot help but recall the messianic imagery and enthusiasm that accompanied his presidential campaign and election in 2008. In fact, President Obama reportedly described himself as the "closest thing to a Jew" to have served in the Oval Office. See Times of Israel Staff, "White House Steps Carefully Around Obama's Reported 'Closest Thing to a Jew' Comment," *Times of Israel*, June 4, 2015, http://www.timesofisrael .com/white-house-stands-by-obamas-common-bonds-with-jews/ (accessed Jul. 30, 2015).

7. Leonard Fein, *Where Are We?: The Inner Life of America's Jews*, Harper and Row, 1988. All Fein citations will be from this book unless otherwise stated.

8. Even the somewhat anomalous Orthodox school of Samson Raphael Hirsch, which tried to harmonize Jewish beliefs and practices—including ritual—with Kantian ethics, nevertheless did not disregard those particularistic elements of Judaism, but, to the contrary, tried to highlight their ethical value in order to defend their continued relevance.

9. Hillel Halkin, *Letters to an American Jewish Friend: A Zionist's Polemic*, Jewish Publication Society, 1977, pp. 96–97.

10. Immanuel Jakobovits in *The Condition of Jewish Belief: A Symposium Compiled by the Editors of* Commentary *Magazine*, Jason Aronson, 1995, pp. 109–17. For a construal of ethics as part of Judaism, see Michael Wyschogrod, *The Body of Faith: God in the People Israel*, Jason Aronson, 1996 [1983], pp. 173–222. For a rejection of ethics as part of Judaism, see "Religious Praxis: The Meaning of Halakha," (1953), in Yeshayahu Leibowitz, *Judaism, Human Values, and the Jewish State*, Harvard University Press, 1992, pp. 3–29.

11. Daniel Bell, "Reflections on Jewish Identity," *Commentary*, June 1961.

12. Eugene B. Borowitz, "Rethinking the Reform Jewish Theory of Social Action," *CCAR*, Fall 1980.

13. Wyschogrod, *The Body of Faith*, p. 181, p. 190ff.

14. Sidney Schwarz, "Can Social Justice Save the American Jewish Soul?" in *Righteous Indignation*, Or N. Rose, Jo Ellen Green Kaiser, Margie Klein, eds., Jewish Lights Publishing, 2008, pp. 3–14. References here are to this essay unless stated otherwise.

15. This sentiment has also been expressed by Ruth Messinger and Daniel Almagor; see Ruth Messinger, "Foreword," in Sidney Schwarz, *Judaism and Justice: The Jewish Passion to Repair the World*, Jewish Lights Publishing, 2006; and *The Tikkun Olam Project: An Initiative for International Development Cooperation and Humanitarian Assistance Exploratory Workshop*, The Harold Hartog School of Government and Policy, Tel Aviv University, June 11, 2006, p. 25. See also Gerald Cromer, "*Tikkun Olam*: Engaged Spirituality and Jewish Identity," The Rappaport Center for Assimilation Research and Strengthening Jewish Vitality, 2007, pp. 42–45. Rick Jacobs, the president of the Union of Reform Judaism, has also suggested that

"tikkun olam is the gateway for most young Jews to live a life of Jewish commitment," in Rick Jacobs, "Don't Give Up on Jews Who Care about Being Jewish," *Haaretz*, October 10, 2013, http://www.haaretz.com/opinion/.premium-1.551719 (accessed Jan. 8, 2017).

16. Steven M. Cohen and Leonard Fein, "American Jews and Their Social Justice Involvement: Evidence from a National Survey," Amos: The National Jewish Partnership for Social Justice, November 21, 2001, p. 4, and p. 24; F. Chertok, J. Gerstein, J. Tobias, S. Rosin, and M. Boxer, "Volunteering + Values: A Repair the World Report on Jewish Young Adults," Repair the World, 2011, pp. 30–38. Elsewhere, the use of social justice as "the handmaiden of [Jewish] continuity" has been criticized on the basis that "social justice should be an end in itself." See Sigal Samuel, "*Tikkun Olam* Is Trending," Open Zion, *Daily Beast*, November 11, 2012, http://www.thedailybeast.com/articles/2012/11/11/tikkun-olam-is-trending0.html (accessed May 13, 2013).

17. Chertok, Gerstein, Tobias, Rosin, and Boxer, "Volunteering + Values," p. 31ff.

18. Yehudah Mirsky, "*Tikkun Olam*: Basic Questions and Policy Directions," Jewish People Policy Institute (JPPI), 2008.

19. Schwarz, "Can Social Justice Save the American Jewish Soul?" pp. 3–14.

20. Mirsky, "*Tikkun Olam*."

CHAPTER 12

1. Dyonna Ginsburg, "Re-anchoring Universalism to Particularism: The Potential Contribution of Orthodoxy to the Pursuit of *Tikkun Olam*," in *The Next Generation of Modern Orthodoxy*, Shmuel Hain, ed., Yeshiva University Press, 2012, pp. 3–23.

2. Jonathan Sacks, *To Heal a Fractured World: The Ethics of Responsibility*, Schocken Books, 2005, p. 9.

3. "Church/State Issues and the Reform of the Jewish Movement," Religious Action Center, http://rac.org/Articles/index.cfm?id=3321&pge_prg_id=11285&pge_id=2391 (accessed Jan. 17, 2013).

4. Even the undated letter that he quotes from a leading Orthodox rabbi of the last century, Ahron Soloveichik, to the social justice organization Jewish Funds for Justice, is limited to grassroots assistance

and generosity. Jacob J. Schacter, "*Tikkun Olam*: Defining the Jewish Obligation," in *Rav Chesed: Essays in Honor of Rabbi Dr. Haskel Lookstein*, vol. 2, Rafael Medoff, ed., Ktav, 2009, pp. 183–204. For the beginnings of a more reasonable attempt to draw from traditional Judaism a very narrow element of social justice (though emphatically not the statism of today's social justice), see Sacks, *To Heal a Fractured World*, pp. 30–43.

5. There are a number of medieval rabbinic authorities who appear to suggest that all gentiles will convert to Judaism (or at least come to observe the Noahide code—on which see later in chapter 12) in anticipation of or during the messianic period. But the expectation that the gentiles will all become Jewish is quite different from the notion that the Jews will all become gentiles.

6. It might be argued that the commandment to love your (Jewish) neighbor as yourself in fact militates against a theory of hierarchical or concentric relationships, by equalizing one's love for oneself with that for one's neighbor. But even this interpretation accepts the premise that it is through preferential love (in this case for oneself) that one comes to love others. Regardless, this commandment—the most important verse in the Torah according to Rabi Akiva of the Talmud—still affirms the distinction between your neighbor, i.e. fellow Jews, and the world beyond.

7. Edmund Burke, *Reflections on the Revolution in France*, L. G. Mitchell, ed., Oxford World's Classics, 1993 [1790], p. 47.

8. See Meir Y. Soloveichik, "The Universalism of Particularity," in *The Next Generation of Modern Orthodoxy*, Shmuel Hain, ed., Yeshiva University Press, 2012, pp. 36–50.

9. Schacter, "*Tikkun Olam*," pp. 183–204. As Schacter points out, even Elliot N. Dorff's *The Way into Tikkun Olam (Repairing the World)*, Jewish Lights Publishing, 2005, which, like much of Dorff's writing, is of more scholarly quality than other works in the Jewish social justice literature, deals, despite its name, all but exclusively with Jewish obligations to fellow Jews rather than gentiles. Like Schacter, Gerald Blidstein concludes: "I think we can safely say that 'responsibility for the welfare of general society' is not the highest priority in our scheme of things, at least on the day-to-day level. The people Israel seems called upon primarily to keep its house in order and to care for its own, to serve God and to witness to Him.

At the same time this exemplary life ought to have an overall incremental impact on mankind as a whole." See Gerald J. Blidstein, *"Tikkun Olam,"* in *Tikkun Olam: Social Responsibility in Jewish Thought and Law,* D. Shatz, C. I. Waxman, and N. J. Diament, eds., Jason Aronson, 1997, pp. 17–59, esp. p. 55.

10. In particular Gittin 61a. This rationale is not limited to Jewish-gentile relations, however, and is also applied to intra-Jewish affairs.

11. See, for example, Albert Vorspan and David Saperstein, *Jewish Dimensions of Social Justice: Tough Moral Choices in Our Time,* UAHC Press, 1998, p. 6, where "ways of peace" is understood as involvement in the work of social justice.

12. Levi Cooper, "The Assimilation of Tikkun Olam," *Jewish Political Studies Review* 25, no. 3–4, Fall 2014.

13. See, for example, Susan Freudenheim, "Ruth Messinger: Social Justice with a Smile," *Jewish Journal,* March 23, 2016, http://www.jewishjournal.com/los_angeles/article/ruth_messinger_social_justice_with_a_smile (accessed Jul. 19, 2016).

14. Ruth Wisse, *If I Am Not for Myself: The Liberal Betrayal of the Jews,* Simon & Schuster,1992, p. 69.

15. See also David Saperstein, "Religious Leadership and Politics," in *Righteous Indignation,* Or N. Rose, Jo Ellen Green Kaiser, Margie Klein, eds., Jewish Lights Publishing, 2008, pp. 45–52.

16. Peter Beinart, *The Crisis of Zionism,* Times Books, 2012, pp. 184–88.

17. Talmud Sanhedrin 56a-b. The rabbis suggest other commandments as well (indeed these are categories of commandments, and include within them many more). Commentators disagree as to whether these laws were taught to Adam or Noah.

18. See J. David Bleich, *"Tikkun Olam:* Jewish Obligations to Non-Jewish Society," in *Tikkun Olam,* pp. 61–102; and Michael J. Broyde, "The Obligation of Jews to Seek Observance of Noahide Law by Gentiles: A Theoretical Review," in *Tikkun Olam,* pp. 103–43.

19. God's blessing to Abraham was sealed by the patriarch's preparedness to sacrifice his son Isaac—a feat, incidentally, to which Immanuel Kant took great exception.

INDEX